Stitches, Patterns and Projects for Crocheting

Also by Wanda Bonando

Stitches, Patterns and Projects for Knitting

Stitches, Patterns and Projects for Needlecraft (with
Marinella Nava)

STITCHES, PATTERNS AND PROJECTS FOR
CROCHETING

Originally published in Italian in 1978 by Arnoldo
Mondadori Editore S.p.A., Milan under the title *Guida
all' Uncinetto*

Copyright © 1978 Arnoldo Mondadori Editore S.p.A., Milan
English translation copyright © 1984 Arnoldo Mondadori
Editore S.p.A., Milan

Translated by Sylvia Mulcahy

Charts on pages 116, 125, 126, 136, 147, 151, 154, 156, 160,
198, 202-3, 204, 210 and the key on page 113 by Barbara
Clarkson

FIRST U.S. EDITION

Library of Congress Cataloging in Publication Data

Bonando, Wanda.
    Stitches, patterns and projects for crocheting.
    (Harper colophon books; CN 1095)
    Translation of: Guida all' uncinetto.
    Includes index.
    1. Crocheting. I. Title.
TT820.B6813 1984   746.43′4   83-48327
ISBN 0-06-091095-X (pbk.)

84 85 86 10 9 8 7 6 5 4 3 2 1

Printed in Italy by Arnoldo Mondadori Editore, Verona

WANDA BONANDO

Stitches, Patterns and Projects for Crocheting

HARPER COLOPHON BOOKS
HARPER & ROW, PUBLISHERS
NEW YORK. CAMBRIDGE. PHILADELPHIA. SAN FRANCISCO
LONDON. MEXICO CITY. SAO PAULO. SYDNEY

Contents

Chart of corresponding crochet hook sizes

English	1	2	3	4	5	6	7
American		K/10¼	J/10	I/9	H/8	H/8	G/6
European	7.50	7	6.50	6	5.50	5	4.50
English	8	9	10	11	12	13	14
American	F/5	E/4	D/3	C/2	B/1		
European	4	3.50	3.25	3	2.50	2.25	2

The author wishes to thank:
Signora Graziella Mentasti, Mrs. Ruth Olson and the
Ghelfi brothers, "Casa della Lana", Como, Italy, for
their kind collaboration; and
The Vergottini Tricot Boutique, Milan, for the Lurex cap
described on page 180.

* * *

The usual sign * (asterisk) is used to indicate a group of
stitches to be repeated throughout all the instructions
for stitches, motifs and patterns. Groups contained
between two asterisks are to be repeated as many
times as indicated or for the whole row or round.

Brackets are also used, especially where groups are
to be repeated within other groups.

INTRODUCTION

The art of crochet and its antecedents

The history of the crochet hook is closely linked to its more illustrious ancestors, the embroidery needle and the lace bobbin. Needlepoint lace and bobbin lace are so often depicted in paintings of the elegant ladies and gentlemen of the Renaissance that we almost take them for granted. Delicate edgings, frills and furbelows decorate the garments of royalty and of the aristocracy and one is made aware that the artist felt himself challenged to reproduce faithfully the fragile and intricate work which had been so patiently and skillfully executed by the lacemakers. One has only to recall the famous painting by Jan Vermeer, *The Lacemaker,* in the Louvre, which clearly demonstrates the regard Vermeer had for this craft of the people, so much appreciated by kings and queens, gentlemen and gentlewomen.

Needlepoint lace and bobbin lace, like all work whose origins are uncertain, have their own legends. One of the oldest and most evocative tells of a young Venetian sailor who, on the day of his marriage, gave his bride a piece of rare seaweed he had found on the seashore. Its delicate tracery and frills were so beautiful that when the bridegroom was obliged to return to his ship soon after the wedding, his young wife, seeking to record his symbolic gift for ever, tried to imitate the intricate forms, using the finest of thread and her sewing needle; she thus became the legendary inventor of needlepoint lace.

The demand for lace in Venice became so great that the governors of this small but glorious Republic, then at its height, had to issue laws prohibiting its immoderate use. However, lacemaking developed into one of the most prosperous cottage industries in the islands of the lagoon and the work was highly prized. Only the reputation of the beautiful glass produced on Murano rivaled that of Italian lace in France, Britain and Flanders. A history of the Sforza family expressly mentions the making of lace from 1493 and, about two hundred years later, ladies of all the great families were adorning themselves with the most beautiful and valuable examples of the craft. Lace collars, cuffs and shawls enhanced the beauty of their wearers both in public and in private, while the long hair of the young girls was interwoven with gold and silver lace ribbons.

In France, embroidery in the Italian style had been learned by French women and girls from the entourage of Catherine de' Medici, Dowager Queen of France on the death of her husband, Henry II. The Sun King, Louis XIV, adored the lavish use of lace and saw to it that Italian workers were encouraged to start production in his country.

French women soon became so proficient that French lace threatened to rival the Venetian products and the government of "La Serenissima" stepped in once more.

Lacemakers were forbidden to work outside the boundaries of the Republic, under pain of imprisonment of their whole family and, should this not prove a sufficient deterrent, the death penalty was invoked. However, French competition quickly overtook the Italian industry with the development of bobbin lace which was later to reach its peak of perfection in Belgium.

Exactly when this variation started is not known although there are, as usual, some delightful legends about it, one of which is rather similar to the story of needlepoint lace in Venice. It is said that the Prince of Bruges had decided to hold an embroidery competition in which all the most skillful workers in the district were to participate. Many pieces of linen were embroidered with costly threads in complicated patterns and more expensive designs were rejected than were ultimately used. One young girl, who had no money to buy linen or to pay an artist to draw a design for her, was desperately unhappy at not being able to enter the competition, for she was one of the cleverest lacemakers in the area. Gazing sadly at her modest equipment, a needle, pins, wooden bobbins and a ball of thread, she was suddenly inspired. The frost had made a delicate tracery of ice on her windowpanes; the lines were fine and the design was enchanting. The little lacemaker worked night and day, trying to reproduce the pattern of the ice. Needless to say, when she presented her work to the judges, the decision was unanimous. She was awarded the prize and bobbin lace had arrived.

Within a short time, this craft became part of the normal education for Flemish girls in all the schools and convents, by order of Charles V. In the next three centuries, the lacemaking industry was to reach new heights of perfection. In Belgium, Holland, Britain and France, women worked far into the night by candlelight, and neighbors would gather together in the house of one of the women to sing songs and ballads to the rhythm of their work.

In the outskirts of Courtrai, a special flax was grown which was suitable only for lacemaking. It was so fine and delicate that it had to be worked in a damp atmosphere, as dry air would have caused it to break. The lacemakers, therefore, had to work in cellars, barely able to see in the semi-darkness, their sense of touch enabling them to avoid making mistakes. This demanding work was very ill-paid, although it took ten months to make a pair of cuffs for a gentleman and, to do this, the women had to work fifteen hours a day. Needless to say, the price for such adornment was high.

As the fortunes of Venice declined in the seventeenth century, the lace industry had almost completely given way to that of France. However, as Napoleon strode through Europe, the French method of bobbin lace was brought to the islands of the lagoon and the women were quick to realize its timesaving advantages over the old-fashioned needle technique.

In 1872, a winter that was harder than usual hit the inhabitants of Venice. They were icebound and their fishermen were unable to work. These resourceful people decided, therefore, to bring back the craft of .needlepoint lacemaking in the belief that their traditional skill would support them in this time of want. Only one woman could be found who could remember the way to do it, Cencia Scarpaiola, and she was traced by one of the ladies of the court of Queen Margaret, the

Countess Adriana Marcello. Thanks to La Scarpaiola, the craft was restored. Thus was founded the School of Burano and the tradition continues to this day.

There are two or three other crafts whose influence must also have contributed to the emergence of crochet. One of these was macramé. Precise details are not known but it would seem to have originated and been developed in France and Italy, where evidence is found dating from the sixteenth century. It was certainly a very popular pastime among British and American sailors who, in their leisure hours, would demonstrate their skill at making knots by producing all kinds of useful objects. Among these were such things as covers for the ship's bell, cases for their own pipes, articles of clothing, belts, etc. The knotting of various thicknesses of ropes, of differing lengths, to form squared fabrics and patterns slightly similar to those of needlepoint and bobbin lace, was widely practiced in North, Central and South America, Spain and Portugal. Although the results were very much cruder and more rustic than lace, any material could be used such as strips of leather, straw, wool and cotton.

Knitting, too, is related to crochet although it is not known which craft was the first to emerge as examples of both have been traced to ancient China and, particularly, to Egypt and Arabia.

So it can be said that crochet is linked to all the popular crafts so far mentioned and probably to others, as well, which may have emerged briefly and then disappeared.

During the Renaissance, many designs that had been worked in lace for altar cloths in the churches and the lace trimmings on the garments of the aristocracy were being

Lace ruff – featured in a portrait by Rubens

imitated in crochet, for lace was far too costly for the ordinary people to buy. Richelieu, Guipure and Honiton (*filet*) styles of crochet are almost identical to the needlepoint and bobbin laces of the same names.

The word "crochet" almost certainly stems from "croc", the French term for "hook", but its popularity in Britain from the beginning of the nineteenth century can largely be accounted for by the onset of the Industrial Revolution when cotton mills, established in the damp atmosphere of the north of England, began to produce fine cotton thread which was cheaper than linen.

The greatest exponents of all were probably the Irish, who introduced crochet into their country around 1820. At that time, although crochet was widely used, it had little artistic merit as it was limited to a few basic stitches. Just as in Burano during the notorious winter of 1872, the women of Ireland sought to balance their domestic budgets by perfecting a craft with which they were already familiar. As a result, they became highly proficient and developed skills which were to make Irish crochet renowned throughout the world.

Using a very delicate, fine thread, they created designs with shamrock leaves, the symbol of Ireland, raised rosettes and rings on a background of chain stitch lace and small "picots".

The rosettes of Ireland became famous for their whiteness, the delicacy of their design and for the refined taste of the final result when combined with the beautiful linen fabric for which the country has long been known. Even nowadays, "Irish point" crochet is among the most highly valued work in this type of craft, although we are fortunate today in being able to obtain crochet cottons in many thicknesses and colors. Work can now be as austere or as colorful as the crocheter wishes and possibly one of the most striking effects is achieved by working simple designs in black and mounting them on white fabric or vice versa.

The earliest known formal school of crochet was started in 1847 by a Mrs. Susannah Meredith but the first books of instruction date from 1820.

It is almost certain that the more refined skills of crocheting were brought to Ireland from France in the second half of the nineteenth century when a young Irish woman called Honoria Nagle, who had been sent by her family to complete her education in Paris, became aware of the dire poverty in her own country. She realized that high society was outrageously wasteful and extravagant while the poor lived in unspeakable squalor. She recruited a few of her friends and took them with her to some Carmelite nuns in France to learn the intricacies of the craft of crochet. When they felt sufficiently competent, these self-appointed teachers returned home and began teaching anyone who wished to learn. Naturally, they began in their own home districts and thus Cork in southern Ireland and Monaghan in the north became the main centers. By about 1870 there were between 12,000 and 20,000 women engaged in the work, adapting patterns from as far afield as Italy and Greece. As the skill was perfected, the demand grew because ladies' fashions were becoming more and more smothered in expensive lace frills; jabots, collars and cuffs and similar trimmings in crochet, were less costly.

Queen Victoria's beloved Consort, Prince Albert, was also indirectly responsible for the growth in demand for the work as, at the Great Exhibition of 1851 which was largely his brainchild, this cottage industry was well represented and manufacturers and designers from all parts of the world became aware of its potential.

With the expansion of colonialism and the enthusiasm of the missionaries in the nineteenth and early twentieth centuries, crochet was taught in the most out-of-the-way places in the world. In the heart of Africa, in the islands of the Azores and of the West Indies, in tiny villages in the vast expanses of China, the influence of the industrious religious sisters can still be seen. A little touch of shamrock in Jamaica, an imitation of Flemish lace in the Azores, a piece of German "filet" in South America and so on. But what makes this aspect particularly relevant is that, crochet being such a flexible medium, local influences have crept in. Local flowers and fruits are reproduced such as poinsettias, hibiscus and pineapples in the West Indies, exotic butterflies seem to land on delicate openwork table centerpieces, and even appliqué work by the Seminole Indians of America, is reproduced in crochet.

"Filet" patterns representing the wonderfully asymmetrical shapes of coral, found in the Pacific Islands, are particularly exciting and palm trees, of course, lend themselves very well to this treatment. The fauna, too, can be beautifully mirrored with birds, deer, rabbits and fish being worked into curtains, bedspreads and table linen.

Nearer home, forget-me-nots, violets, daisies and orchids are often seen decorating placemats and other household articles, for these three-dimensional decorations are a challenge to the skillful crocheter's own powers of invention, as she tries to reproduce the beauty of nature around her.

Crochet work continued to be extremely popular until the outbreak of the First World War when fashion took a more practical turn. Also with the development of the sewing machine, dresses could be made and trimmed so quickly and prettily that hand-crocheted trimmings seemed outmoded.

Now, however new possibilities are being discovered to utilize crochet, and, as always happens when an old art or craft form re-emerges, the only limiting factor is individual imagination.

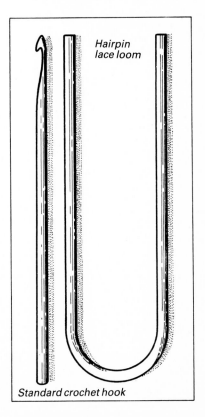

Hairpin lace loom

Standard crochet hook

Double-headed
crochet hook

Long crochet
hook
for Afghan stitch

Variations of basic crochet

All types of crochet are based on the chain stitch. However, there are slightly differing techniques which are divided into two main groups: Common or German crochet and afghan stitch, also known as Tunisian crochet.

Common crochet is also divided into more than one type, according to the working technique: "filet" or openwork crochet, Irish crochet, Friulian and Hairpin crochet are the main variations.

In German or Common crochet, the hook is usually about five inches long but the size of the hook itself may be very tiny, if a fine cotton (No 60) is to be used, or very thick if a bulky 3-ply knitting wool is employed. The finer hooks are generally made of stainless steel while the thicker ones are usually in coated aluminum, plastic, wood or, in the case of very old hooks, ivory or bone.

The distinguishing feature of Common crochet is that the basic stitches are linked into a ring and the subsequent rows built up on this in increasingly large rounds, either going continuously round and round or back and forth. This system does not necessarily mean that the finished article will be circular (it may be square, triangular, etc.) but it does mean that each "round" will start and finish at the same point, corners being adjusted to lie flat as the instructions will show.

"Filet" or trellis stitch is usually worked back and forth in rows, the open mesh acting as a background for the pattern which is worked in blocks.

Irish crochet consists of a simple background consisting of chain lace with raised flowers and shapes of various kinds forming a three-dimensional design. In this type of work, the raised decorations are sometimes made first and then linked into the work gradually as the pattern is built up.

Friulian crochet is similar to Irish but less delicate, with a rather rustic appearance.

Hairpin lace crochet involves the use of a U-shaped tool rather like a hairpin, from which it derives its name. As it is not possible to increase or decrease in hairpin crochet, it is usual to make strips of different lengths and then join them together or they can be used individually as decorative edgings or insertions.

Afghan stitch is also called Tunisian crochet or "tricot" crochet ("tricot" is the French word for knit) because all the stitches remain on the hook during the first stage of each row, just as with knitting, while in the second stage they are worked off until only the last stitch remains. An afghan hook is therefore of the same thickness for its full length and is usually between 12–16 inches (30–40 cm) long, with a knob at one end to prevent the stitches from falling off. Sometimes, however, there is a hook at both ends which allows for two threads to be worked simultaneously.

Crochet is easy

What advice should be given to a beginner embarking upon crochet? Perhaps the first thing is to be comfortable and relaxed. If a slow, rhythmical movement is aimed at rather than jerky, aggressive jabs, speed will come after a little while.

Once you have mastered the wayward hook, there are only a few basic stitches to be learned. They are all that are needed to be able to make the most delightful articles for the home, fashion garments, children's and babies' clothes, men's and boys' ties, pullovers, soft toys, rugs, etc.

All the more apparently complicated stitches are merely combinations of two or more of the basic stitches, apart from some small variations in technique, as will quickly be seen if you read the instructions before tackling them.

One last, important word of advice: the basic stitches should always be worked as evenly as possible. This not only makes the work easier to do but also gives a more professional finish. The secret? The tension control as the yarn passes through the fingers of the hand not holding the hook.

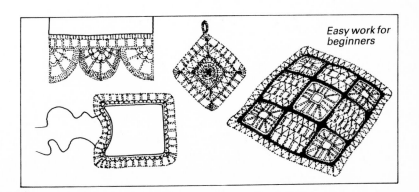

Easy work for beginners

IMPORTANT NOTE

All stitches throughout this book are referred to by their American terms. A table of English and American equivalents is given below:—

American

Slip stitch (sl st)
Single crochet (sc)
Half double crochet (hdc)
Double crochet (dc)
Treble (tr)
Double treble (dtr)

English

Slip stitch (sl st)
Double crochet (dc)
Half treble (htr)
Treble (tr)
Double treble (dtr)
Triple treble (trtr)

Abbreviations in addition to those referred to above:—

Beginning (beg)
Centimeters (cm)
Chain (ch)
Decreasing or decrease (dec)
Inch(es) (in)
Increasing or increase (inc)

Pattern (pat)
Repeat (rep)
Round (rnd)
Space (sp)
Stitch (st)
Yarn over (yo)

Turning chain

As explained in the book, in order to keep the sides of all work straight, a certain number of chain stitches must be added at the end of each row to bring the work into position for the next row. The work is then turned so that the reverse side is toward you. The number of turning chain required depends upon the type of stitch with which you will begin the next row. The following table gives the number of turning chain for each type of stitch used when the next row is to be worked in the same stitch:—
Single crochet – 1 chain
Half double or double crochet – 2 chain
Treble – 3 chain
Double Treble – 4 chain
In some cases, the turning chain also forms the first stitch of the next row.

The stitches

BASIC STITCHES, INCREASING, DECREASING AND FINISHING

Basic steps

The hook is held in the right hand between the thumb and forefinger, just like a pen. It rests on the middle finger which acts as a guide. The thread or yarn is controlled by the left hand, passing over the index finger, under the 2nd and 3rd finger and round the little finger. The 3rd finger is kept slightly crooked inwards, towards the palm of the hand. As the work grows, it is held quite taut between the thumb and 2nd finger of the left hand.

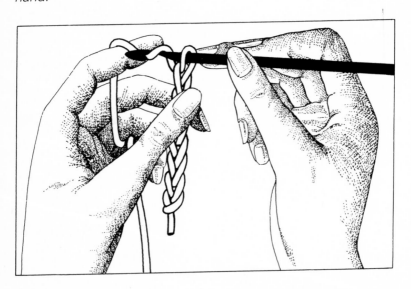

Starting work

The first thing to be done is to make a slip knot and put the hook through, as shown in the diagram, and pass the hook under the thread which is resting on the index finger. The instruction for this movement is 'yarn over hook'; pick up the thread

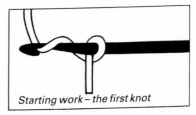

Starting work – the first knot

with the hook and pull it through the loop already on the hook. This makes the first chain stitch.

Chain stitch (ch)

The simple chain stitch is not only the basis of any piece of crochet work but is also an integral part of the creation of many other stitches.

Having made the initial knot, take the thread over the hook and pull it through the preceding loop until the chain is a reasonable length, in relation to the type of yarn being used.

It is important to remember that, to make a good basis to the work, the links of the chain must be of equal size, neither too loose nor too tight.

For circular work, or any shape that is worked continuously rather than back and forth, the last stitch of the length of chain is joined to the first with a slip stitch (sl st). This is done by inserting the hook into the first stitch, carrying the yarn over the hook and drawing it back through both loops.

Double chain stitch (dch)

Double chain stitch makes an excellent basis for crochet work. It is firmer than single chain stitch and can even be treated as a decorative edging in itself.

Work 2 chain,* insert hook into first chain, yarn over and pull through one loop on hook, yarn over hook and pull through both stitches on hook *. Stitch completed. Repeat from * to *, inserting hook into the front loop of the stitch previously completed until a chain of the required length is obtained.

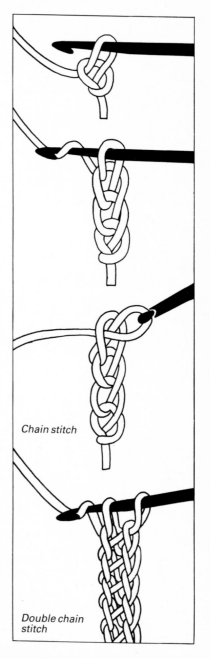

Chain stitch

Double chain stitch

17

Slip stitch (sl st)

This is the simplest of crochet stitches and is usually used as a finishing edge or to close a round before beginning the next one. It is worked from right to left, or back and forth. Work required length of chain.

*Insert hook into top loop of 2nd chain (i.e. skip the last chain worked), yarn over hook and pull through both loops on hook.

Repeat from * to end of chain. Chain 1, turn.

(This turning chain forms the first stitch of the following row.) Skip first slip stitch, repeat from first*.

Slip stitch (sl st)

Single crochet (sc)

Although it is so simple, this stitch is most effective for many kinds of work. It is a firm stitch and, worked in wool, its fabric-like texture lends itself to sweaters, jackets, skirts, capes, etc, while in cotton useful things can be made for the home.

Make a basic chain.
1. Insert hook under the two top loops in 2nd chain stitch from hook.
2. Yarn over hook and draw through chain stitch. There are now 2 loops on hook.
3. Yarn over hook and draw it through both loops on hook. This completes one single crochet.
4. Insert hook into next chain stitch. Repeat 2 and 3, working a single crochet (sc) into each chain to end of row. Work 1 chain.
5. Turn work, insert hook into first stitch of previous row and, repeating 2 and 3, work 1 single crochet into each stitch to end of row. Chain 1, turn.

Single crochet (sc)

Half double crochet (hdc)

Make a chain to the required length plus 2 ch, turn. Skip first 2 (turning) chain,* yarn over hook (yo), insert hook from front to back between 2 loops of next chain, yo, draw new loop through ch only (3 loops on hook), yo, draw new loop through the 3 loops on hook. This completes one half double crochet and leaves 1 loop to start next stitch. Repeat from * to end of chain. Ch 2, turn. Last 2 ch form 1st stitch on next row.

Work following rows, back and forth, in the same way but on next and subsequent rows skip the 1st half double crochet from hook and insert hook under *both* loops at top of each stitch on previous row. The last stitch of each row is worked into the turning chain of previous row.

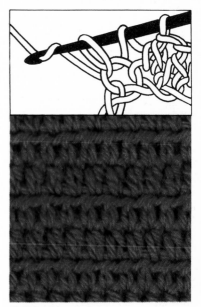

Half double crochet

Double crochet (dc)

Make a chain to the required length plus 2 ch, turn.

Miss first 2 (turning) chain, * yarn over hook (yo), insert hook from front to back between 2 loops of next chain, yo, draw new loop through ch only (3 loops on hook), yo, draw new loop of yarn through next 2 loops on hook (2 loops now on hook), yo, draw new loop through 2 remaining loops on hook. This completes one double crochet and one loop is left to start new stitch.

Repeat from * to end of chain. Ch 2, turn.

Work following rows, back and forth, in the same way but on next and subsequent rows skip the first double crochet from hook and insert hook under *both* loops at top of each stitch on previous row. The last stitch of each row is worked into the turning chain of previous row.

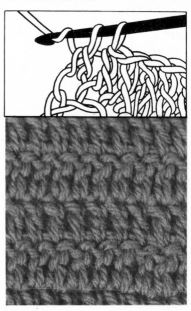

Double crochet

Treble (tr)

Make a chain to the required length plus 3 ch, turn.

Skip first 3 (turning) chain, * yarn over hook (yo) *twice*, insert hook from front to back between 2 loops of next chain, yo, draw new loop through chain only (4 loops now on hook), yo, draw new loop through next 2 loops on hook (3 loops now on hook), yo, draw new loop through next 2 loops on hook (2 loops now on hook), yo, draw new loop through 2 remaining loops on hook. This completes one treble and one loop is left to start new stitch.

Repeat from * to end of chain. Ch, 3, turn.

Work following rows back and forth in the same way but on next and subsequent rows skip the first treble from hook and insert hook under *both* loops at top of each stitch on previous row. The last stitch of each row is worked into the turning chain of previous row.

Treble

Double treble (dtr)

Make a chain to the required length plus 4 ch, turn.

Miss the first 4 chain from hook, *yarn over hook (yo) 3 times, insert hook from front to back between 2 loops of next chain, yo, draw new loop of yarn through chain only (5 loops now on hook), yo, draw new loop of yarn through next 2 loops on hook (4 loops now on hook), yo, draw new loop of yarn through next 2 loops on hook (3 loops now on hook), yo, draw new loop of yarn through next 2 loops on hook (2 loops now on hook), yo, draw new loop of yarn through 2 remaining loops on hook. This completes one double treble and one loop is left to start new stitch.

Double treble

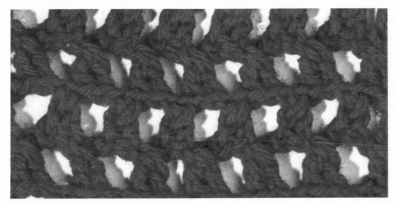

Crossed double crochet

Repeat from * to end. Ch 4, turn.
Work following rows back and forth in the same way but on next and subsequent rows miss the first double treble from hook and insert hook under *both* loops at top of each stitch on previous row. The last stitch of each row is worked into the turning chain of previous row.

Crossed double crochet

Make a chain with an even number of stitches to desired length, turn.
Row 1: 1 dc in 6th chain from hook (first 2 ch count as 1 dc), ch 1, crossing back over dc just made work 1 dc in 4th ch from beg. * Skip 2 ch, 1 dc in next ch, ch 1, crossing back over dc just made work 1 dc in first ch of 2 skipped ch. Rep from * end 1 dc in last ch. Ch 4, turn.
Row 2: Skip first 2 dc, 1 dc in next dc, ch 1, 1 dc in last skipped dc, * skip 1 dc, ch 1, 1 dc in next dc, ch 1, 1 dc in skipped dc. Rep from *, end 1 dc in 3rd ch of turning ch 4.

Lattice stitch

Start with a chain in multiples of 4 plus 3.

Row 1: 1 sc in 3rd ch from hook, *ch 5, skip next 3 ch, 1 sc in next ch. Rep from * across. Ch 5, turn.
Row 2: 1 sc in 3rd ch of ch-5 loop, *ch 5, 1 sc in 3rd ch of next ch-5 loop. Rep from * across end ch 3, 1 dc in last sc. Ch 5.
Row 3: 1 sc in 3rd ch of next ch-5 loop, ch 5, 1 sc in 3rd ch of turning ch 5. Ch 5, turn.
Repeat Rows 2 and 3 for pat.

Lattice stitch

Trellis, Filet or Mesh stitch

This is the foundation on which filet crochet is based. By filling in the spaces, with double crochet, representational or geometrical patterns can easily be created.

Start with a chain in multiples of 3 plus 2.

Row 1: skip 7 ch, 1 dc in next ch * ch 2, skip 2 ch, 1 dc in next ch, rep from * across. Ch 5, turn.

Row 2: Skip 1 dc and 2 ch, * 1 dc in next dc, 2 ch, skip 2 ch, rep from * to last pat, skip 2 ch, 1 dc in next ch. Ch 4, turn.

Rep Row 2 for pat st.

A smaller basic mesh can be obtained by following these instructions but working 1 ch instead of 2 and skipping 1 ch only. In this case, only 3 ch will be required at row endings to turn.

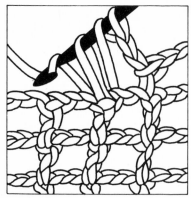

Trellis, Filet or Mesh stitch

Blocks and spaces in Mesh stitch

2 or 3 double crochet worked over 2 or 3 chain is called a block. 2 or 3 chain carried over a block and finished with a double crochet is called a space.

It is important to remember that the turning chain of previous row counts as the last stitch to be worked at end of each row. This is standard and is seldom specified in patterns as it is assumed that the worker has already mastered the basic technique.

Having made a practice piece in Mesh stitch, now make some blocks over some of the spaces as follows:

* 1 dc into dc of previous row, 2 dc into ch space, 1 dc into next dc of previous row.

Practice making spaces and blocks to end of row. Ch 3, turn. Repeat as required.

Blocks and spaces in Mesh stitch

To make blocks on blocks, 1 dc is worked into each of the 4 dc of previous row.

Very attractive designs can be made in filet crochet by drawing up a pattern or even a picture on graph paper. Each square on the paper will represent one block or space.

Afghan or Tunisian stitch

An afghan hook is used for this stitch (see earlier description) and the technique varies from ordinary crochet in that all the stitches are left on the hook in the first stage (A) of each row and then worked off the hook in the second stage (B).

At no time is the work turned.

Make a chain to the desired length, plus 1 turning ch. (On first row only, insert hook through *one* top loop only instead of two.)

Row 1: A. Insert hook through top loop of second chain from hook, yo, draw loop through. Repeat in each chain stitch to end, leaving all loops on hook. (See top part of diagram.)

B. Work all loops off hook by working yarn over, draw through first loop on hook,* yarn over and draw through 2 loops. Repeat from * until only 1 loop remains on hook which becomes the first stitch of next row.

Main pattern row: A. Ch 1,* insert hook into second *vertical* bar, yo, and draw a loop through. Repeat from * on each bar along work, ending by inserting hook under last bar and the stitch immediately behind it, yo, and

Afghan or Tunisian stitch

draw a loop through (this makes a firm edge).

B. As for Row 1B.

This main pattern row is repeated until work reaches the desired size.

To finish off neatly, work 1 slip stitch into each bar across work.

Increasing – Decreasing – Finishing

Increasing, decreasing and completion (buttonholes, edgings, etc.) are the only techniques left to be learned in order to be able to follow any pattern or to make up your own designs. There is nothing difficult about these skills – all that is needed is a little patience at first and your work will soon have that neat and regular appearance that everyone admires so much in crocheted garments or articles for the home. The finishing is particularly important as an irregular line of increasing or decreasing, a buttonhole that is too small or too large or an untidy edge will ruin the final result of any piece of work.

Increasing

This is done when more stitches are required to widen the work. It may be done on the outside edges or within the working of a row or round.

Increasing on outside edges

At the end of each row where an increase is required, work as many additional chain stitches as necessary, plus the usual number of turning chain, depending upon which stitch you are using.

Increasing within rows (or rounds)

Perfect internal increasing is obtained by ensuring that all in-creases are carefully worked above one another and in the same direction. It is a good idea to thread pieces of colored cotton in the positions where increases are to be worked. Thus, if the shaping is to be made towards the right, 2 stitches must be worked into the stitch preceding the cotton marking. If the shaping is to be towards the left, the extra stitch must be worked after the marking.

A double increase can be made by working 3 stitches into one instead of 2 stitches into one.

Decreasing

This is done when fewer stitches are required to narrow the work. This may be done on the outside edges or within the working of a row or round.

Increasing on outside edges

Increasing within rows

Decreasing is used for shaping armholes, necklines and flares.

Decreasing on outside edges

This is achieved simply by omitting the required number of stitches at the end of one row, if a sharp increase is required, or by omitting single stitches at the ends of several rows for a sloping effect.

To avoid irregularity, work a slip stitch into stitch after last one to be worked, make required number of turning chain and work first stitch of new row in the stitch following the slip stitch.

For example, if you wish to decrease 2 stitches, work to end of row, omitting last 2 stitches; work 1 sl st into next-to-last stitch, work turning chain, turn, omit slip stitch just worked, work next stitch into next stitch of previous row and continue as desired.

Decreasing on outside edges

Decreasing within rows

Decreasing within rows (or rounds)

As with increasing, internal decreases must be carefully worked above one another. Pieces of colored cotton should be threaded in the exact positions where decreases are to be worked. In the next row (or round), insert the hook into stitch preceding the marking, yarn over hook, pull one loop through, insert hook into stitch immediately following the marking, yo, pull one loop through all 3 loops on hook. This completes one decrease.

Increasing on mesh or filet with 1 dc, ch 2 pat

To increase the number of spaces at the beginning of a row to be worked, make a chain consisting of three times as many stitches as the number of new spaces you wish to make, plus 2 chain. Work back, incorporating the chain stitches as though they were part of the previous row.

To increase one space at the end of a row, work 2 chain and a double treble as follows: yo 3 times, insert hook into base of last double

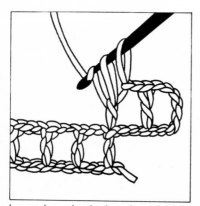 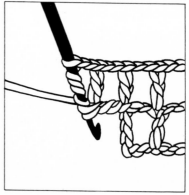

Increasing at beginning of row (left), and at end of row (right) on mesh

crochet, draw a loop through, * yo, draw through 2 loops. Repeat from * until all loops have been worked off the hook. Repeat entire process for each additional space desired.

Decreasing on mesh and filet with 1 dc, ch 2 pat

To decrease the number of spaces at the end of a row, it is only necessary to continue on the row being worked up to the point desired, make the necessary turning chain, turn and start the new row.

To decrease the number of spaces at the beginning of a row, work slip stitches into the first stitches of previous row until desired point is reached to start new row of spaces, work turning ch to replace first st and continue.

For example, if only one square is to be eliminated, work 3 slip stitches over previous space, 6 slip stitches if two squares are to be dispensed with and similarly until the required width of work is achieved.

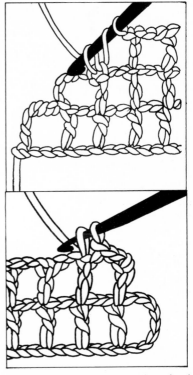

Decreasing on mesh at end of row (top), and at beginning of row (above)

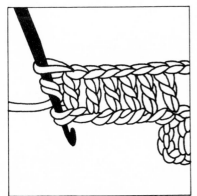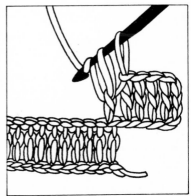

Increasing on blocks at end of row (left), and at beginning of row (right)

27

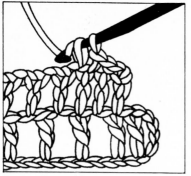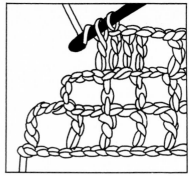

Decreasing on blocks at beginning of row (left), and at end of row (right)

Increasing of blocks on mesh or filet

To increase the number of blocks at the end of a row, work a double treble into the base of each newly worked stitch until the required number of blocks has been reached.

To increase the number of blocks at the beginning of a row, make a chain consisting of three times as many stitches as the number of new blocks you wish to make, plus 2 turning chain. Work back, making the new blocks on the chain just made.

Decreasing of blocks on mesh or filet

To decrease one or more blocks on mesh at the end of a row, continue on the row up to the width required, work 2 turning chain, turn and work back over previous row.

Increasing on outside edges of afghan stitch

To increase one stitch at beginning of a row, insert hook into chain between the 2 vertical bars of the chain stitch on previous row, yo, pull loop through.

To increase one stitch at end of a row, make 2 chain stitches and include the *first* of these (i.e. the one farthest from the hook) on the return row, thus forming an extra stitch.

Increasing within rows of afghan stitch

Mark the exact spot with a piece of colored cotton where you wish to have the internal widening.

For shaping towards the left, pick up a stitch from the chain which links the stitch you have marked to the following stitch.

For shaping towards the right, pick up a stitch linking the one you have marked to the preceding stitch.

Decreasing on outside edges of afghan stitch

To decrease a stitch at the end of each row, merely leave the last stitch of the first stage (A) unworked; work the second stage (B) as usual, draw the yarn through the last 3 stitches together.

Increasing on outside edges of afghan stitch

Increasing within rows of afghan stitch

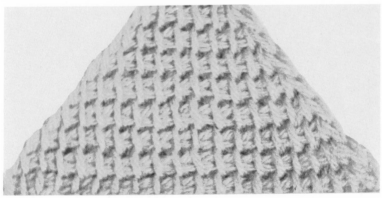

Decreasing on outside edges of afghan stitch

29

Decreasing within rows of afghan stitch

If it is necessary to decrease more than one stitch at a time, merely work as many slip stitches as necessary from the beginning of the row.

Decreasing within rows of afghan stitch

Mark the exact spot with a piece of colored cotton where you wish to have the internal narrowing.

For shaping towards the left, pick up the two vertical bars of the 2 stitches which precede the marking, yo, and draw the yarn through to make one loop.

For shaping towards the right, work 3 stitches together immediately after the marking on stage (B).

Buttonholes

Buttonholes are easy to do but it is important to know how to do them well as a garment may be spoiled if the buttonholes are untidy.

Horizontal buttonholes

Work 2 or more chain stitches at the point where you require a horizontal buttonhole. Skip as many stitches in the previous row as you have made chain stitches and work normally to end of the row. On the return row, work your pattern into the chain stitches previously made.

Vertical buttonholes

Split the work into two parts until the required length for each hole is achieved. Make sure you work exactly the same number of rows in each part and when the necessary height of the space has been reached, the work can then be joined into one piece, as before.

Horizontal buttonholes in afghan stitch

At the point in the work where a buttonhole is required, wind the yarn around the hook two, three or four times, according to the length of buttonhole to be made. Skip the same number of stitches on previous row and continue with the work. On the return row, work each of the loops off the hook one by one.

Horizontal buttonhole

Vertical buttonhole

Horizontal buttonhole in afghan stitch

Vertical buttonholes in afghan stitch

These are made exactly as in the case of ordinary crochet, by dividing the work as each buttonhole is reached. (See vertical buttonholes.)

Vertical buttonhole in afghan stitch

31

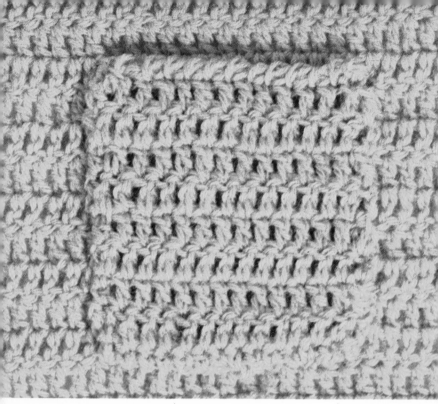

Patch pocket

Pockets

As with all the finishing touches, the pockets play a very important part in the ultimate success of a garment. The simplest is the pocket which is sewn on after the garment has been completed. The alternative is made as an integral part of the garment.

Patch pockets

When you have completed a garment, pockets may be made to whatever size you choose. The same stitch is normally used as that in which the whole garment is made or in which the edgings have been completed.

Integral pockets

When the point is reached where the pocket is to start, i.e. where the slit is to come, discontinue working. Decide on the width you wish the pocket to be and work an edging, if desired, such as you will ultimately have on the edges of the main parts of the garment for the width of the pocket. When this is complete, break off the yarn and fasten off. Now make the pocket lining. Make a loose chain of the same number of stitches as you have worked on the pocket edging, working in single crochet to the required depth of the pocket. Insert this piece of fabric where the work has been discontinued and continue working, as

Integral pocket

Edging in reverse single crochet

before, incorporating the stitches at the top of the pocket lining.

Edgings and borders

The edgings and borders illustrated in this chapter are the simplest and most commonly used to finish crochet work of any kind. They can also be used to decorate handkerchiefs, blouses, household linens, etc, the only difference being that finer yarns and hooks will be needed.

Reverse single crochet

This is a very popular finish. It is durable as it not only decorates an edge but reinforces it and helps to prevent stretching or bagginess. It may also be used to edge a knitted garment.

Working into the edge of the main fabric, ensuring that the stitches are regularly spaced, work in sc for the full length. Do not turn.

Now work as for regular sc but work from left to right of the work.

Scalloped edging

Scalloped edging

This is very simple but gives an attractive finish to almost any work. It consists of only one row. Working into the edge of the main fabric, start with a slip stitch and work *ch3, skip 2 sts, 1 sc into next st, repeat from * to end. Fasten off.

Shell edging

There are several variations of shell edges. This is the simplest and consists of one row only.
*1 sc into first st, ch 3, 3 dc into next st, skip 2 sts. Repeat from * to end. Fasten off.

Twisted cord edging

This edging gives an elastic but firm finish. It consists of two rows.
Row 1: sc, turn.
Row 2: *Insert hook into first st of previous row, yo, pull loop through keeping it fairly loose, turn the hook round so that the 2 loops on it are twisted, yo, complete stitch like a normal sc. Repeat from * to end. Fasten off.

Picot edging

There are many ways to make picot edgings but this is one of the simplest. It consists of one row only. 1 sl st into first st, *ch 5, sl st into 3rd ch from hook, (this makes a picot), ch 2, skip 2 sts, 1 sl st into next st. Repeat from * to end. Fasten off.

Working a sample piece

The texture of fabric produced depends upon three factors
1) the thickness of the yarn being used;
2) the size of the crochet hook;
3) control of tension.

It is always advisable, therefore, to make a sample before embarking on a piece of work, one of the advantages of crochet being that the measurements can easily be checked while work is in progress.

Start with 12 ch, in the yarn and hook of your choice. Work a few rows in the stitch you wish to use and, if the texture is right, you can calculate the number of stitches you will need for the measurements required. If the texture is too close, a larger hook is needed; if the texture is too open, then a smaller hook should be tried.

When you have achieved the correct texture and you are sure it is suitable for the article you wish to make, you can calculate the number of stitches required to work 4 in (10 cm) and the number of rows to work 4 in (10 cm). Having made a note of this, you can begin work from a measured design – even a simple paper pattern can be adapted.

Shell edging

Twisted cord edging

Picot edging

35

FIRM-TEXTURED STITCHES

Uses

All crochet stitches are merely combinations of the basic stitches already described. The closely worked stitches give a firm fabric and are particularly suitable for thicker garments in wool. Finer yarns can, of course, be used too. The firm texture is durable and such things as jackets, coats, capes, skirts and even trousers can be made very successfully. With a little ingenuity and some time spent on precise measurements, many acceptable and attractive items can be made for men, women and children alike. Using more than one color, either in the main body of the garment or in the borders, delightful effects can be obtained which give the appearance of tweed, Scottish tartan, stripes, checks, etc, according to personal taste.

The stitches described here are especially effective when worked in a tightly spun knitting worsted with a H hook.

Crossed single crochet

Make a chain with an even number of stitches.
Row 1: Insert hook into 4th ch from hook (first 2 ch count as 1 sc), yo, pull loop through, skip 1 ch, insert hook into next ch, yo, pull loop through (3 loops on hook), yo and pull through all loops on hook, ch 1, *insert hook into st already worked, yo, pull through, skip 1 ch, insert hook into next ch, yo, pull through, yo and pull through all loops on hook, ch 1. Repeat from * to end of row, ending with a sc in last stitch already worked. Ch 2, turn.
2nd and following rows: *Insert hook under ch st of previous row, yo, pull loop through, insert hook under next ch st, yo, pull loop through, yo and pull through all 3 loops, ch 1. Repeat from * working into the last stitch worked and then into the next ch st of previous row to end of row, end 1 sc in last st. Ch 2, turn.

Crossed single crochet

Elongated single crochet

Row 1: Starting in second ch from hook, * 1 sc, ch 1, skip 1 ch. Repeat from * to end of row, ending with 1 sc. Ch 1, turn.
Row 2 and following rows: * Insert hook under ch st of previous row and work 1 sc picking up the back loop of st directly below on row before previous row, ch 1. Repeat from * to end of row, ending with 1 sc in turning ch. Ch 1, turn.

Ridge stitch

Row 1: 1 sc in each ch to end of row, ch 1, turn.
Row 2: 1 sc in each st, inserting hook in *back* horizontal thread at top of st of previous row.

Crazy single crochet

Make foundation ch in multiple of 3 plus 2.
Row 1: Skip 1 ch, *work 3 sc into next ch, skip 2 ch. Repeat from * to last ch, end 3 sc in last ch. Ch 1, turn.
Row 2 and following rows: *3 sc into 2nd sc of 3-sc on previous row, repeat from * across. Ch 1, turn.

Elongated single crochet

Crazy single crochet

Ridge stitch

Alternating stitch no 1

Make foundation ch of uneven number of sts plus 2 turning ch.
Row 1: Starting in third ch from hook, *1 dc, 1 sc. Rep from * to end of row, end 1 dc. Ch 1, turn.
Row 2 and following rows: Work 1 dc on each sc of previous row and 1 sc on each dc. When row ends with a sc work 2 turning ch, and when it ends with a dc work 1 turning ch.

Alternating stitch no 1

Alternating stitch no 2

Make foundation ch in multiple of 3 plus 1 turning ch.
Row 1: Starting in second ch from hook, *1 sc, 1 hdc, 1 dc. Rep from * to end of row. Ch 2, turn.
Row 2: *1 hdc, 1 dc, 1 sc. Rep from * to end of row. Ch 2, turn.
Row 3: *1 dc, 1 sc, 1 hdc. Rep from * to end of row. Ch 1, turn.
Repeat these 3 rows as required.

Alternating stitch no 2

Alternating post stitch (front post dc and back post dc)

Make a chain with an even number of stitches.
Row 1: Skip first 3 ch, dc to end.
Row 2: Ch 4 (this includes 2 turning ch), skip last dc in previous row, *1 front post dc (yo, insert hook behind vertical bar of next dc in previous row, pull loop through and finish as for normal dc), 1 back post dc (yo, insert hook in front of vertical bar of next dc in previous row, pull loop through and finish as for normal dc).
Rep from * to end of row, finishing with 1 hdc in second turning ch at beg of previous row. Ch 2, turn.
Row 3: Skip the hdc worked in previous row, *1 back post dc, 1 front post dc, to end of row, finishing with 1 hdc on the second ch at beg of

Alternating post stitch

previous row. Ch 2 turn.
Rep second and third rows for pat, skipping first hdc instead of first dc on second row.

Basket-weave stitch

Make foundation ch in multiples of 8 plus 2 ch to turn.
Row 1: 1 dc into 3rd ch from hook, 1 dc into each ch to end. Ch 2, turn.
Row 2 (right side): *4 front post dc, 4 back post dc, counting ch 2 at beg of row as first front post dc. Rep from * across. Ch 2, turn.
Rows 3, 4 and 5: as Row 2.
Row 6: *Work 4 back post dc, 4 front post dc, counting ch 2 at beg of row as first back post dc. Rep from * across. Ch 2, turn.
Rows 7, 8 and 9: As Row 6.
Rep Rows 2 to 9 for pat.

Basket-weave stitch

Ridged double crochet no 1

Work foundation ch of any number.
Row 1 and all odd rows (right side): 1 dc into 3rd ch from hook, 1 dc into each st. Ch 2, turn.
Row 2 and all even rows: *1 front post dc (see Alternating post stitch for explanation of front post dc) into each st of previous row starting around second dc. Ch 2, turn.
These 2 rows form the pattern.

Ridged double crochet no 1

Ridged double crochet no 2

Work foundation ch of even number.
Row 1 and all odd rows (wrong side of work): Starting in third ch from hook, dc to end of row. Ch 1, turn.
Row 2: *1 sc in first dc, 1 front post dc around next dc (see instruction for Alternating post st). Rep from * to end of row. Ch 2, turn.
Row 4: *1 front post dc around first

Ridged double crochet no 2

dc, 1 sc. Rep from * to end of row.
Ch 2, turn.
Repeat Rows 2 through 5 for pat.

Ridge stitch with chain

Make foundation ch in multiples of 3
plus 1 turning ch.
Rows 1 and 2: Starting in second ch
from hook, sc to end of row. Ch 1,
turn.
Row 3 (wrong side): *2 sc, insert
hook from back to front around 3rd
sc of row before last, yo and pull loop
through, elongating it to the same
level as row on which you are working. Complete st as for normal sc.
Rep from * to end of row. Ch 1, turn.
Row 4: Sc to end of row. Ch 1, turn.
Row 5: As Row 3, making sure that
the picked up stitch is always directly
over the previously elongated stitch,
thus giving a vertical chain effect.
Rep Rows 4 and 5 to form pattern.

Ridge stitch with chain

Fancy stitch no 1

Make foundation ch of uneven number of sts plus 1 turning ch.
Row 1: Sc to end of row. Ch 1, turn.
Row 2: *1 sc, 1 hdc. Rep from *
ending with a sc. Ch 1, turn.
Row 3: Work 1 sc into *both* loops of
each stitch of previous row. Ch 1,
turn.
Rep Rows 2 and 3 for pat.

Fancy stitch no 2

Make a foundation ch in multiple of 4
plus 3 plus 2 turning ch. Ch 2 at beg
of each row counts as 1 dc.
Row 1 (right side): Starting in fourth
ch from hook, 1 dc in each ch across.

Fancy stitch no 1

Ch 2, turn.

Row 2: 1 dc in each dc. Ch 2, turn.

Row 3: *3 dc, **yo, insert hook around 4th dc of Row 2, draw yarn through and elongate loop**. Rep from ** to ** twice into same st, yo and draw through 4 loops on hook, yo and draw through rem loops. This makes one cluster.* Rep from * to * to end of row, end with 3 dc. Ch 2, turn.

Row 4: 1 dc in each dc and 1 dc on each cluster. Ch 2, turn.

Row 5: 1 dc, *1 cluster, working around next dc of Row 4, 3 dc. Rep from * ending with 1 cluster and 1 dc. Ch 2, turn.

Row 6: as Row 4.

Rep Rows 3 to 6 for pat. The effect should be to alternate clusters in each odd numbered row.

Fancy stitch no 2

Fancy stitch no 3

Make foundation ch of any number of sts plus 2 turning ch. Ch 2 at beg of each row counts as 1 dc.

Row 1: Starting in third ch from hook, dc across. Ch 2, turn.

Row 2: *yo, insert hook under second st of previous row (insert hook from front to back between first and second st, bringing it out between second and third st from back to front), draw yarn through, elongating loop to about ½ in (1 cm), yo and complete st as for dc. Rep from * around each dc across. Ch 2, turn. (This will be the right side of work.)

Row 3: As Row 2 except that hook is inserted from the back to the front between first and second dc of previous row, bringing it out towards the back between second and third st. (This will be the wrong side of work.)

Rep Rows 2 and 3 for pat.

Fancy stitch no 3

Fancy single crochet

Make foundation ch in multiples of 3 plus 2.
Row 1: In second ch work *(1 sc, ch 1, 1 sc), skip 2 ch. Rep from * across, end (1 sc, ch 1, 1 sc) in last ch. Ch 1, turn.
Row 2: *(1 sc, ch 1, 1 sc) into each ch-1 of previous row.* Rep from * to * across. Ch 1, turn. Rep Row 2 for pat.

Ridged crazy single crochet

Make foundation ch in multiples of 2 plus 1 turning ch.
Row 1: Starting in second ch, sc across. Ch 1, turn.
Row 2: *1 sc, 1 raised dc (a raised dc = work as for regular dc but insert hook into stitch just worked, bringing it forward after second sc of previous row). Ch 1, turn.
Rep these 2 rows for pat.

Close bobble stitch

Make foundation ch in multiples of 3 plus 1 plus 1 turning ch.
Row 1: Starting in second ch, 1 sc, *ch 3, skip 2 ch, 1 sc. Rep from * across. Ch 2, turn.
Row 2: *1 bobble in ch-3 space (a bobble = **yo, insert hook under ch-3 of previous row and draw yarn through. Rep from ** 3 times more. There are now 9 loops on hook. Yo, draw yarn through 8 loops. 2 loops now on hook. Yo, draw yarn through both loops), ch 3, 1 sc on next sc of previous row, ch 1. Rep from * across ending with 1 sc on last sc of previous row. Ch 2, turn.
Row 3: *1 bobble in ch-3 sp, ch 3, 1 sc into bobble of previous row, ch 1. Rep from * across ending with 1 sc in bobble of previous row. Ch 2, turn. Rep Row 3 for pat.

Fancy single crochet

Ridged crazy single crochet

Ridged basket-weave

See alternating post stitch (page 38) for explanation of front post dc and back post dc.

Make foundation ch in multiples of 6 plus 2 turning ch.

Row 1 (wrong side): Starting in third ch from hook, dc to end of row. Ch 2, turn.

Row 2: Starting around first dc, *3 front post dc, 3 back post dc, rep from * across, end 1 dc in turning ch. Ch 2, turn.

Row 3: Skip first dc, 1 back post dc, *3 front post dc, 3 back post dc, rep from * ending with 2 back post dc, 1 dc in turning ch. Ch 2, turn.

Row 4: Skip first dc, 1 front post dc, *3 back post dc, 3 front post dc, rep from * ending with 2 front post dc, 1 dc in turning ch. Ch 2, turn.

Row 5: Skip first dc, *3 back post dc, 3 front post dc, rep from * to end of row, end 1 dc in turning ch. Ch 2, turn.

Continue in this way, moving the rib one st to the right on right side of work and one st to the left on wrong side of work.

Close bobble stitch

Shell stitch

A shell is made by working 5 dc in 1 ch or 1 sc.

Make foundation ch in multiples of 6 plus 4 plus 2 turning ch.

Row 1: Starting in third ch from hook, 2 dc, *skip 2 ch, 1 sc in next ch, skip 2 ch, shell in next ch, rep from * to last 3 ch, skip 2 ch, 1 sc in last ch. Ch 3, turn.

Row 2: 2 dc in sc working through back loop only, *1 sc in center dc of shell working through both loops, shell in next sc working through back loop only, rep from * to last half shell, 1 sc in top of turning ch. Ch 3, turn.

Rep 2nd row for pat.

Ridged basket-weave

V-stitch

Make foundation ch in multiples of 3 plus 1 plus 2 turning ch.
To make one V-motif: *yo, insert hook into st, draw yarn through making a loose loop, rep from * twice more into same st, yo, draw yarn through all loops on hook;* ch 1, rep from * to * in same st.
Row 1: Starting in third ch from hook, *work 1 motif, skip 2 sts*, end 1 motif in last st. Ch 2, turn.
Next and following rows, work a motif in each ch-1 space of previous row. Ch 2, turn.

Shell stitch

Cornflower stitch

Make a foundation ch in multiples of 4 plus 1.
Row 1: Starting in third ch from hook, *3 dc into same st, skip 1 st, 1 sc, skip 1 st, rep from * ending with a 3 dc in next st, skip 1 st, 1 sc in last st. Ch 2, turn.
Next and following rows: 3 dc into each sc of previous row, work 1 sc between first and second of each 3 dc group in previous row. Ch 2, turn.

V-stitch

Double flower stitch

Make foundation ch with an even number of sts.
Row 1 and odd number rows: (right side) insert hook into second st from hook, yo, drawn yarn through, insert hook into next st, yo, draw yarn through, skip next st, insert hook into next st, yo, draw yarn through, yo, draw yarn through all loops on hook. (This completes one flower.) Work 1 ch fairly loosely. Insert hook into closing stitch at top of flower just worked, yo, draw yarn through, insert hook into base st just worked, yo, draw yarn through, skip 1 st,

Cornflower stitch

insert hook into next st, yo, draw yarn through, yo and draw through all loops on hook, 1 loose ch. Rep from * ending with 1 sc. Ch 2, turn.

Row 2 and even numbered rows: *work 2 double sc into the closing st of flower motif in previous row (a double sc is made by inserting hook into st, yo, draw yarn through, yo, draw yarn through one loop, yo, draw through both loops). Rep from * across ending with 1 sc in turning ch. Ch 2, turn.

Rep these 2 rows for pat.

Daisy stitch

Make a foundation ch in multiples of 8 plus 1, plus 1 turning ch. (Start with at least 18 ch.)

Row 1: starting in second ch from hook, *1 sc, skip 3 sts, into next st work (3 dc, 1 tr, 3 dc), skip 3 sts. Rep from * ending with 1 sc in last st. Ch 3, turn.

Double flower stitch

Row 2: Without drawing yarn through last loop (unfinished dc), work 1 unfinished dc in each of next 3 dc, yo, draw through all 4 loops on hook, *ch 2, 1 sc in next tr, ch 2, 1 unfinished dc in each of next 3 dc, 1 unfinished tr in next sc, 1 unfinished dc in each of next 3 dc, yo, draw through all 8 loops on hook*, repeat from * to * across, end ch 2, 1 sc in next tr, ch 2, 1 unfinished dc in each of next 3 dc, 1 unfinished tr in last sc, yo, pull through all 5 loops on hook. Ch 3, turn.

Row 3: 3 dc in st at base of turning ch-3, *1 sc in next sc, (3 dc 1 tr, 3 dc) in closing st of unfinished sts on previous row*, repeat from * to *, end 1 sc in next sc, (3 dc, 1 tr) in turning ch of previous row. Ch 3, turn.

Row 4: *1 unfinished dc in each of next 3 dc, 1 unfinished tr in next sc, 1 unfinished dc in each of next 3 dc,

Daisy stitch

45

yo, draw through all 8 loops on hook, ch 2, 1 sc in next tr, ch 2*, repeat from * to *, end last sc of repeat in turning ch of previous row. Ch 1, turn.

Row 5: 1 sc in first sc, *(3 dc, 1 tr, 3 dc) in closing st of unfinished sts of previous row, 1 sc in next sc, repeat from * across, end last sc in turning ch. Ch 3, turn.

Repeat Rows 2 through 5 for pat.

Forget-me-not stitch

Make foundation ch with an even number of sts plus 1 turning ch.

Row 1: (wrong side). Starting in second ch from hook, sc to end of row. Ch 2, turn.

Row 2: Insert hook into last ch worked, yo, draw yarn through, insert hook into first sc, yo, draw yarn through, insert hook into second sc, yo, draw yarn through (4 loops on hook); yo and draw yarn through all loops on hook (1 opening forget-me-not completed), * ch 1, insert hook into st which closes opening flower, yo, draw yarn through, insert hook into sc already worked, yo, draw yarn through, similarly work 1 half-finished sc into each of next 2 sc (5 loops on hook); yo and draw yarn through all 5 loops (this completes one whole forget-me-not), repeat from * across. Ch 2, turn.

Row 3: * 2 sc into each st that closes forget-me-nots in previous row. Ch 2, turn. Rep Rows 2 and 3 for pat.

Forget-me-not stitch

Crossed bar stitch

Make loose foundation ch in multiples of 3 plus 1.

Row 1: 1 hdc into 2nd ch from hook, ch 1, * 1 unfinished hdc into same st (unfin hdc = yo, insert hook into next st, yo, draw yarn through), skip 1 st,

Crossed bar stitch

46

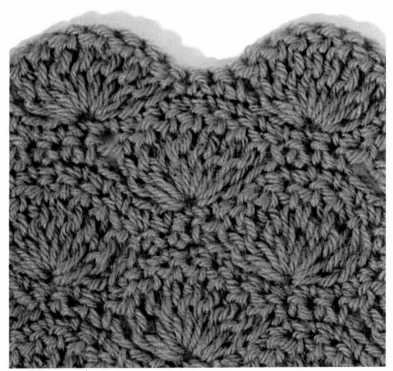

Fan stitch

1 unfin hdc in next st, yo, draw yarn through all 5 loops on hook, ch 1. Rep from * ending with 1 hole in last st. Ch 2, turn.

Row 2: 1 hdc into ch loop of previous row, ch 1, * 1 unfin hdc into same ch loop, 1 unfin hdc into next ch loop, yo, draw yarn through all 5 loops on hook, ch 1. Rep from * ending with 1 hdc in last hdc. Ch 2, turn. Rep Row 2 for pat.

Fan stitch

Make foundation ch in multiples of 10 plus 3, plus 1 turning ch.
Row 1: (wrong side). Starting in second ch from hook, sc to end of row. Ch 1, turn.

Row 2: * 3 sc, skip 3 sts, 7 tr into next st, skip 3 sts. Rep from * ending with 3 sc. Ch 1, turn.

Row 3: Sc to end of row. Ch 3, turn.

Row 4: Skip 1 sc of previous row, 5 tr into next sc, * skip 3 sts of previous row, 1 sc into each of next 3 sts (over 3rd, 4th and 5th sts of the fan), skip 3 sts, 7 tr into next st. Rep from * ending with 5 tr in penultimate st, 1 dc in last st. Ch 1, turn.

Rep Rows 1 through 4 for pat.

Alternating popcorn stitch

Make a foundation ch in multiples of 3 plus 1 turning ch.
Row 1: Starting in second ch from hook sc to end of row. Ch 1, turn.

Row 2: 1 sc, * 1 popcorn (popcorn = 5 unfinished dc into same base st as sc just worked, yo and draw yarn through all 6 loops on hook. 1 unfin dc = yo, insert hook, yo, draw yarn through, yo, draw yarn through 2 loops only), 2 sc. Rep from * to end of row, end 1 sc in last sc. Ch 1, turn.
Row 3: Sc across (1 sc on each popcorn and 1 sc on sc in between). Ch 1, turn.
Row 4: 2 sc, * 1 popcorn, 2 sc, * end 1 popcorn. Ch 1, turn.
Rep Rows 1 through 4 for pat.

Alternating popcorn stitch

Knotted single stitch

Make a foundation ch to desired length plus 2 ch.
Row 1: 1 sc in second ch from hook, * insert hook in foundation ch just worked, yo, draw through, insert hook in next ch, yo, draw through, yo, draw through all 3 loops on hook, repeat from * across. Ch 1, turn.
Row 2: 1 sc in first st, * insert hook in same st as st just worked, yo, draw through, insert hook in next st, yo, draw through, yo, draw through all 3 loops on hook, rep from * across. Ch 1, turn.
Repeat Row 2 for pat.

Knotted single crochet

Antonella's stitch

Make foundation ch with even number of sts plus 1 turning ch.
Row 1: Starting in second ch, sc across. Ch 2, turn.
Row 2: *insert hook into first st, yo, draw yarn through, insert hook into next st, yo, draw yarn through, yo, draw yarn through 2 loops, yo, keeping closing st loose draw yarn through rem 2 loops. Rep from * across every pair of 2 sts. Ch 1, turn.
Row 3: 1 sc into front loop and 1 sc into back loop of each closing st of

Antonella's stitch

Rib stitch

previous row. Ch 2, turn. Rep Rows 2 and 3 for pat.

Rib stitch

Make foundation ch in multiples of 6.
Row 1: (wrong side). Starting in second ch from hook, * 5 sc, 1 dc. Rep from * across, ending with 5 sc. Ch 1, turn.
Row 2 and even numbered rows: * 1 sc into each sc of previous row, 1 front post dc (front post dc = yo, insert hook from front to back of horizontal bar of dc in previous row, complete stitch as for normal dc). Rep from * across. Ch 1, turn.
Row 3 and odd numbered rows: * 1 sc into each sc of previous row, 1 back post dc (bk post dc = yo, insert hook from back to front of horizontal bar of dc in previous row, complete as for normal dc). Rep from * across. Ch 1, turn.
Rep Rows 2 and 3 for pat.

Column stitch

Make foundation ch with even number of sts (last st = 1 turning ch).
Row 1: Starting in second ch, * 1

double sc (dsc = insert hook into st, yo, draw yarn through, yo, draw yarn through 1 loop, yo, draw through both loops), ch 1, skip 1 st.
Rep from * across, end with 1 dsc in last st. Ch 2 turn.
Row 2 and following rows: Skip first dsc, ch 1, 1 dsc into each dsc, ch 1, over each ch-1 of previous row. Rep from * across. Ch 2, turn.

Column stitch

Plaited stitch

Plaited stitch

Make a foundation ch in multiples of 4 plus 3 plus 2 turning ch.
Row 1: Starting in third ch from hook, * 3 dc, ch 1, skip 1 st. Rep from * ending with 3 dc. Ch 3, turn.
Row 2: 1 dc in first dc, * ch 1, 1 dc in next ch-1 sp, 1 dc in ch skipped on foundation ch, 1 dc in same ch-1 sp, rep from * across, end ch 1, 1dc in last dc. Ch 3, turn.
Row 3: * 1 dc in next ch-1 sp, 1 dc in center dc of 3-dc group on next to last row, 1 dc in same ch-1 sp, rep from * across, end 1 dc in last ch-1 sp, 1 dc in center dc of 3-dc group on row 1, 1dc in same ch-1 sp. Ch 3, turn.
Row 4: 1 dc in first dc, * ch 1, 1dc in next ch-1 sp, 1 dc in center dc of 3-dc group on row before last, 1 dc in same ch-1 sp, repeat from * across, end ch 1, 1 dc in last dc. Ch 3, turn.
Repeat rows 3 and 4 for pat.

Transverse stitch

Make foundation ch in multiples of 3 plus 1 plus 1 turning ch. (This stitch is worked from the *right side* throughout).

Row 1: Starting in second ch from hook, * 1 sc, ch 2, skip 2 sts. Rep from * across, ending with 1 sc.
Row 2: Without turning work, ch 1, * 1 reverse sc into first st (reverse sc = insert hook between vertical bars of sc in previous row, yo, draw yarn through, yo, draw yarn through both loops), ch 2. Working from left to right, rep from * ending with 1 reverse sc.
Row 3: Without turning work, ch 2, * 1 sc into ch loop, ch 2. Rep from * ending with 1 sc into last ch loop, ch 1, and 1 sc into last sc.

Transverse stitch

Row 4: Without turning work, ch 2, skip first sc in previous row, 1 reverse sc into next ch-1 sp, ch 2, * 1 reverse sc in next ch-2 sp, ch 2. Rep from * ending with 1 reverse sc into last ch-1 sp.
Rep Rows 3 and 4 for pat.

Vera's stitch

Make foundation ch with an odd number of stitches, plus 1 turning ch.
Row 1: Starting in second ch from hook, sc across. Ch 2, turn.
Row 2: * Insert hook into first st, yo, draw yarn through, insert hook into second st, draw yarn through, yo, draw yarn through 2 loops, yo, draw yarn through rem 2 loops, keeping st very long. Rep from * across each pair of 2 sts, ending with 1 sc. Ch 1, turn.
Row 3: 1 sc in first st, 2 sc into each long st of previous row. Ch 2, turn.
Rep Rows 2 and 3 for pat.

Two-color interweave

Make a foundation ch in first color in multiples of 5 (last 5 sts = 1 base st,

Vera's stitch

1 turning ch and 3 ch to form first loop in second row).
Row 1: (First color.) Into 5th ch from hook, * 1 shell (shell = 2 dc, ch 1, 2 dc into same st), ch 2, skip 4 sts. Rep from * ending with 1 sc. Ch 1, turn.
Row 2: (Second color) 1 sc, * ch 5, 1 sc into ch-4 loop in base ch, keeping each shell in first col towards back of work.
Rep from * ending with 1 sc. Ch 4, turn.
Row 3: (Second color) * 1 shell by inserting under ch st in top of first col shell and the ch-5 loop in second col, ch 2.

Two-color interweave

Rep from * ending with 1 sc. Ch 1, turn.

Row 4: (First color) 1 sc, * ch 5, 1 sc through ch-2 loop in first col (3 rows back), keeping shells of previous row towards back of work. Rep from * ending with 1 sc. Ch 4, turn. Rep Rows 3 and 4, working 2 rows in each color, for pat.

Two colors with clusters

Make foundation ch in first color with even number of sts (last 2 sts = turning ch).

Row 1: Starting in third ch from hook (right side – first color) hdc across. Ch 2, turn.

Row 2: 1 front post hdc into each hdc (front post hdc = yo, insert hook horizontally from front to back behind bar between first and second sts of previous row, bringing it out in space between second and third sts, draw yarn through, yo, draw yarn through all 3 loops; the base ridge will form on right side of work). Ch 1, turn.

Row 3: (Second color) sc. Ch 1, turn.

Row 4: * 1 sc, 1 dc cluster into next

Two-color with clusters

st (dc cluster = ** yo, insert hook, draw yarn through, yo, draw yarn through 2 loops. Rep from ** twice more. Yo, close by drawing yarn through all 4 loops), ch 1. Rep from * ending with 1 extra ch in 1st color.

Row 5: (First color) * 1 hdc into each sc and 1 hdc into each ch st of previous row. Rep from * across. Ch 2, turn. Rep Rows 2–5 for pat.

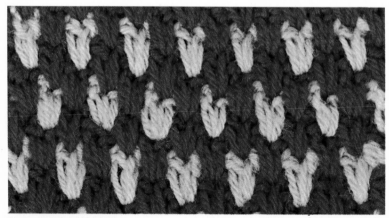

Two-color double crochet

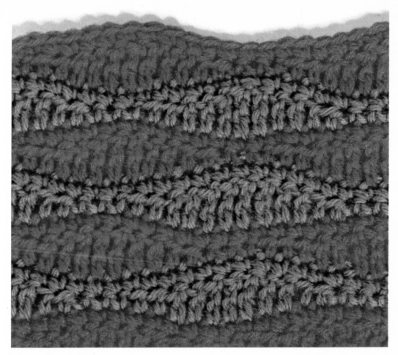

Two-color wavy chevrons

Two-color double crochet

Make foundation ch in first color in multiples of 4 plus 1 plus 1 turning ch.

Row 1: Starting in second ch from hook (first color) sc across. Ch 3, turn.

Row 2: 1 dc into first sc, * skip 3 sc, 2 dc into next sc.

Rep from * ending with 2 dc in last st. Ch 2, turn.

Row 3: * 2 dc into second of the 3 skipped sc of Row 1. Rep from * ending with 2 dc in second turning ch of Row 1. Ch 2, turn.

Row 4: (Second color) 2 dc *between* each 2 dc of Row 2. Ch 2, turn.

Row 5: (First color) 2 dc *between* each 2 dc of Row 3. Ch 2, turn.

Row 6: As Row 5, working between 2 dc of Row 4.

Row 7: (Second color) 2 dc *between* each 2 dc of Row 5.

Rep Rows 4–7 for pat.

Two-color wavy chevrons

Make foundation ch in first color in multiples of 14, plus 1 turning ch.

Row 1: (first color – wrong side). Starting on second ch from hook work 1 group over each 14 sts (group = 1 sc, 2 hdc, 2 dc, 3 tr, 2 dc, 2 hdc, 2 sc). Ch 1, turn.

Row 2: Starting on first st of previous row, sc across. Ch 4 in second color.

Row 3: (Second color). Starting on first st, work 1 reverse group over each 14 sts (reverse group = 1 tr, 2 dc, 2 hdc, 3 sc, 2 hdc, 2 dc, 2 tr). Ch 1, turn.

Row 4: Work as for Row 2. Rep these 4 rows for pat, changing color every 2 rows.

Star stitch

Make a foundation ch in first color in multiples of 6 plus 2.

Row 1: Starting in second ch from hook, sc across. Ch 1, turn.

Row 2: *1 sc, skip 2 sts, 7 dc in next st, skip 2 sts. Rep from * ending with 1 sc. Ch 3, turn in second color (these 3 turning ch form first dc of first star in next row).

Row 3: (Second color) 1 unfin dc in each of next 3 dc of previous row (unfin dc = yo, insert hook, draw yarn through, yo, draw yarn through 2 loops), yo, draw yarn through all 4 loops. *Ch 4, 1 sc in next dc (this is the central dc of 7 dc in previous row), ch 3, 1 unfin dc in each of next 3 dc, 1 unfin dc in next sc, 1 unfin dc in each of next 3 dc, yo, draw yarn through all 8 loops. Rep from * ending with 1 unfin dc in each of last 3 dc and 1 unfin dc in last sc, yo, draw yarn through all 5 loops. Ch 3, turn.

Row 4: 3 dc into st closing last 4 dc of previous row, *1 sc into sc of previous row, 7 dc into st closing 7 dc of previous row. Rep from * ending with 4 dc into st closing last star of previous row. Ch 1 in first color, turn.

Row 5: 1 sc in first dc, ch 3, *1 unfin dc in each of next 3 dc, 1 unfin dc in next sc, 1 unfinished dc in each of next 3 dc, yo, draw through all 8 loops on hook, ch 4, 1 sc in next dc,

Star stitch

ch 3, rep from * across, end 1 sc in last dc. Ch 1, turn.

Row 6: 1 sc in first st, *7 dc in closing st of 7-dc on previous row, 1 sc in next sc, rep from * across. Ch 3 with second color.

Repeat Rows 3 through 6 changing color every 2 rows.

Broken check in two colors

Make foundation ch in main color with an odd number of sts.

Row 1: (wrong side – first color) Starting in second ch from hook, sc across. Ch 1, turn.

Row 2: (right side – second color) *1 sc, 1 long sc (work sc by picking up st from foundation ch) Rep from * across. Ch 1, turn.

Row 3: (second color) Sc across. Ch 1, turn.

Row 4: (first color) *1 long sc (work under row below last), 1 sc*. Rep from * to * across. Ch 1, turn.

Row 5: (first color) Sc across. Ch 1, turn. Rep Rows 2–5, changing color every 2 rows.

Broken check in three colors

Make a foundation ch in first color with uneven number plus 1 turning ch.

Row 1: (First color) Starting in second ch from hook, sc across. Ch 2, turn.

Row 2: (First color) *1 dc, ch 1, skip 1 st. Rep from * across, ending with 1 dc. Ch 1 in second color.

Row 3: (Second color) *1 dc into skipped st of 2 rows below (referred to as dcb), ch 1, skip 1 st of previous row. Rep from * ending with 1 sc in turning ch. Ch 1 in third color.

Row 4: (Third color) *Skip 1 st, 1 dcb, ch 1. Rep from * ending with 1 dcb and ch 1 in first color; turn.

Rep Rows 3 and 4 for pat, changing color on each row.

Broken check in two colors

Broken check in three colors

Scottish tartan in two colors

Make foundation ch in first color in multiples of 14 plus 11.

Row 1: Starting in fourth ch work 3 dc, *ch 1, skip 1 st, 3 dc, ch 1, skip 1 st, 9 dc. Rep from * ending with ch 1, skip 1 st, 4 dc. Ch 3, turn.

Next and following rows: Skip first dc of previous row, 1 dc in each dc and ch 1 over each ch. Ch 3 in second color, turn.

Work 1 row in second color, 1 row in first color, 1 row in second color, 5 rows in first color until the work is the desired length.

In the first line of vertical holes, weave the second color under and over each chain stitch with a yarn needle threaded double. When one line has been woven, return, weaving through the same holes but going over instead of under, etc. When second line is finished, return, weaving through the same holes as in first line.

Work through next line of holes in the same way using second color and similarly across whole width of fabric.

Three-color stitch no 1

Make foundation ch in first color in multiples of 3 plus 1 turning ch.

Row 1: (first color) Sc across. Ch 1, turn.

Row 2: (right side) *2 sc, 1 dc. Rep from * across. Ch 1, turn.

Row 3: As Row 1.

Row 4: (second color) *2 sc, 1 dc worked around vertical bar of dc in Row 2. Rep from * across. Ch 1, turn.

Row 5: as Row 1.

Row 6: (third color) as Row 4.

Row 7: as Row 1.

Rep Rows 2 through 7 for pat.

Scottish tartan in two colors

Three-color stitch no 2

Make foundation ch in first color in multiples of 4 plus 5 (last 3 sts = 1 turning ch and 2 ch to form first dc in next row).
Row 1: (First color) Starting from fourth ch from hook work 2 dc, *ch 1, skip 1 st, 3 dc. Rep from * to end of row, ch 1.
Row 2: (Second color) Ch 2, *3 dc in skipped foundation ch, ch 1. Rep from * ending with ch 1, 1 dc into turning ch. Ch 1, turn.
Row 3: (Third color) *3 dc into second dc of 3-dc group 2 rows back, ch 1. Rep from * ending with ch 1 and 1 dc into turning ch 2 rows back.
Repeat Row 3 for pat, changing color on each row.

NOTE: Before working the following elaborations on basic Afghan stitch, it would be a good idea to refer back to the original instruction. Remember that this type of work tends to contract and should be worked loosely. When working stitches off hook, begin by drawing yarn through first loop on hook and then in pairs.
Finish Afghan stitch work with a slip-stitch row beginning with ch 1, 1 sl st into second bar and into each following bar. Fasten off.

Fancy Afghan stitch

Make foundation ch in multiples of 2 plus 1 turning ch.
Row 1: Simple Afghan stitch (insert hook through *one* top loop of ch instead of two). A and B = one row.
Row 2: A *insert hook under two vertical bars (starting with very first and second bars), yo, draw through. Insert hook in next horizontal st

Three-color stitch no 1

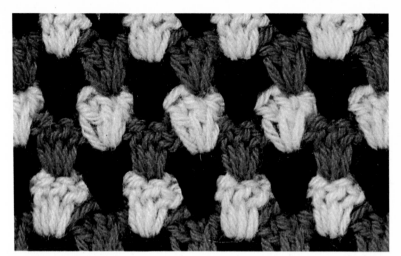

Three-color stitch no 2

Fancy Afghan stitch

between 2 vertical bars, yo, draw through. Rep from * to end.
B: As for Row 1B.
Rep Row 2 for pat.
To finish piece, work ch-1 and then 1 sl st into each vertical bar of previous rows.

Afghan rib

Make foundation ch in multiples of 6 plus 3, plus 1 turning ch.
Row 1: A and B – work in simple Afghan st.
Next and following rows: A – *3 Afghan sts, skip next sp between 2 vertical threads, 3 ribbed Afghan sts (ribbed A st = insert hook in sp *between* 2 vertical threads of st in previous row). Rep from *, end 3 Afghan sts.
B – work loops off in usual way.

Kairomanta stitch

Make foundation ch with an even number of sts, plus 1 turning ch.
Row 1: A and B – work in simple Afghan st. Ch 1.
Row 2: Ch 1, A – skip first vertical bar, insert hook under next vertical bar, yo, draw yarn through, *place hook behind yarn, yo twice, insert hook under next 2 vertical bars in previous row, bring yarn forward under hook, yo, draw yarn through 2 vertical bars*. Rep from * to * end yo, insert hook under last vertical bar, draw through.
B – 1 ch, *yo, work 2 sts off. Rep from * to end. Ch 1.
Row 3: A – Rep from * to * of Row 2.
B – As for 2B.
Rep Rows 2 and 3 for pat.

Afghan check

Make foundation ch in first color in multiples of 5.

Afghan rib

Kairomanta stitch

Row 1: (First color) A and B – work in simple Afghan st.

Row 2: (Second color) A – *Skip 2 sts, work 3 sts. Rep from * to end.

B – *work 3 sts off, ch 2. Rep from * ending with 2 ch sts, join to edge of work.

Row 3: (Second color) As Row 2 – A and B.

Row 4: (First color) A – *1 unfinished dc into each of 2 vertical bars (in first color) skipped in Row 2, work 3 sts. Rep from * to end.

B – Ch 1, work sts off as usual.

Rep Rows 2–4 for pat.

Afghan tweed

Make foundation ch in first color with an even number of sts, plus 1.

Row 1: (First color) A and B – work in simple Afghan stitch.

Row 2: (Second color) A – *work 1 st, skip 1 st. Rep from * across.

(First color) B – ch 1, *work 1 st off, ch 1. Rep from * until 1 st remains.

Row 3: (First color) A – *skip 1 st, 1 unfin dc into single vertical bar of st (in first color) skipped in Row 2A. Rep from * but leave last st un-worked.

Afghan check

Afghan tweed

(Second color) B – ch 1, *work 1 st off, ch 1. Rep from * until 1 st remains.

Row 4: (Second color) A – *1 unfin dc into single vertical bar of st (in same color) skipped in Row 3A, skip 1 st. Rep from * ending with 1 unfin dc into last st.

(First color) B – ch 1, *work 1 st off, ch 1. Rep from * until 1 st remains.

Rep Rows 3 and 4 for pat.

Broken Afghan stitch

Make foundation ch in an even number of sts.

Row 1: A and B – Work in simple Afghan st.

Row 2: A – skip 1 st, *insert hook under 1 vertical bar and 1 horizontal thread to the left of vertical bar, yo, draw yarn through. Rep from * to end.

B – Ch 1, *work loops off in usual way.

Rep Row 2 for pat.

Loop stitch

Although this is a simple stitch to do, it is very effective. It can be used as a trimming on collars and cuffs, to make dramatic boas to wear with evening dress, or warm jackets and

Broken Afghan stitch

housecoats.

For a really close texture, it is a good idea to use a crochet hook in a slightly smaller size than you would normally use for the thickness of the yarn. The best yarn for this stitch is a fairly heavy wool although baby wools can also look very pretty.

Make a ch to the desired length.

Row 1: 1 sc in second ch from hook and 1 sc in each remaining ch. Ch 1, turn.

Row 2: (wrong side) Hold yarn in usual way except that instead of it passing over the first finger it should go underneath. *Insert hook into next st, yo (picking yarn up from over middle finger, thus forming a loop the size of first finger), draw loop through, yo, draw through both loops, work a very tight ch to lock st firmly (this does not count as a st), slip loop from finger. Rep from * across. Ch 1, turn.

Row 3: 1 sc in base of each loop st across. Ch 1, turn.

Rep Rows 2 and 3 for pat.

An alternate method (replacing Row 2) of forming the loops is to cut a stiff strip of cardboard to the depth of loop required. Insert hook into back thread of st, pass yarn from front to back over the top of cardboard strip, pick up with hook, yo and draw yarn through both loops, work 1 tight ch.

Loop stitch

OPENWORK STITCHES

Dress elegantly with crochet

Openwork stitches can create a light, decorative effect and even the uncomplicated designs have a delicate air about them. There is almost no limit to the ways in which these stitches can be utilized, with a little imagination. Especially suitable for evening wear, summer sweaters, shawls, stoles and bed-jackets, the general effect is romantic and gracefully elegant. Baby clothes, too, lend themselves to this style of work. Materials can be of many kinds, depending on the article to be worked but perhaps the main quality is that the twist should be tight as in crochet cottons. Fine mohair mixtures are also very effective although mohair by itself is inclined to be too soft and stretchy.

Simple shell stitch

Make foundation ch with an even number of stitches plus 1 (last 2 ch = turning ch).
Row 1: (1 dc, ch 1, 1 dc) into third st from hook, *skip 1 st, (1 dc, ch 1, 1 dc) into next st. Rep from * across ending with 1 dc into last ch. Ch 3, turn.
Row 2 and following rows: *(1 dc, ch 1, 1 dc) into next ch space. Rep from * ending with 1 dc into turning ch of previous row. Ch 3, turn.

Simple shell stitch

Shell stitch no 1

Make foundation ch in multiples of 3 plus 1.
Row 1: 1 hdc into third ch from hook, *skip 1 st, 2 hdc into next st. Rep from * across, ending with 1 hdc in last st. Ch 3, turn.
Row 2 and following rows: 1 hdc between first 2 hdc in previous row,

Shell stitch no 1

*2 hdc between each 2-hdc group. Rep from * across, ending with 2 hdc between last 2-hdc group and last hdc, 1 hdc in turning ch of previous row. Ch 3, turn.

Shell stitch no 2

Make a foundation ch in multiples of 12 plus 4, plus 2 turning ch.
Row 1: 1 dc into third ch from hook, *ch 2, skip 2 ch, 1 dc into next ch. Rep from * across. Ch 3, turn.
Row 2: (1 dc, ch 2, 1 dc) into first ch-2 loop, *ch 2, skip 1 ch loop, 5 dc into next ch loop, ch 2, skip 1 ch loop, (1 dc, ch 2, 1 dc) into next ch-2 loop. Rep from * across. Ch 3, turn.
Row 3: *5 dc into ch-2 loop between 2 dc of previous row, ch 2, (1 dc, ch 2, 1 dc) into third dc of 5-dc group of previous row, ch 2. Rep from * ending with 5 dc into last loop. Ch 3, turn.
Row 4: *(1 dc, ch 2, 1 dc) into third dc of 5-dc group, ch 2, 5 dc into ch-2 loop between 2 dc, ch 2. Rep from * across, ending with (1 dc, ch 2, 1 dc) into third dc of last 5-dc group. Ch 3, turn.
Rep Rows 3 and 4 for pat.

Shell stitch no 3

Make a loose foundation ch in multiples of 7 plus 2.
Row 1: 1 dc in third ch from hook, 1 dc, *skip 2 sts, (3 dc, ch 1, 3 dc) in next base st, skip 2 sts, 2 dc. Rep from * across. Ch 3, turn.
Row 2 and following rows: *2 dc on 2 dc of previous row (3 dc, ch 1, 3 dc) into ch-1 in center of shell. Rep from * across. Ch 3, turn.

Shell stitch no 2

Shell stitch no 3

Shell stitch no 4

Shell stitch no 4

Make foundation ch in multiples of 3 plus 1 turning ch.
Row 1: Starting in second ch from hook, sc across. Ch 3, turn.
Row 2: (2 dc, 1 sc) into third sc, skip 2 sts, (2 dc, 1 sc) into each st ending with (1 dc, 1 sc) into last st. Ch 3, turn.
Row 3 and following rows: (2 dc, 1 sc) into first dc of previous row and rep into every second dc, ending with (1 dc, 1 sc) into last st. Ch 3, turn.

Alternating shell stitch

Make a foundation ch in multiples of 5.
Row 1: 3 dc into third ch from hook, skip 1 st, 1 sc *ch 3, skip 2 sts, 4 dc in next st, skip 1 st, 1 sc. Rep from * across. Ch 3, turn.
Row 2 and following rows: 3 dc into last sc worked in previous row, 1 sc into ch-3 loop (to left of shell in previous row), *ch 3, 4 dc into sc, 1 sc into ch loop. Rep from * across, ending with 1 sc into turning ch of previous row. Ch 3, turn.

Alternating shell stitch

Diagonal double crochet blocks

Diagonal double crochet blocks

Make foundation ch in multiples of 12 plus 4. *(From Rows 2–6 the turning ch of previous row forms the first dc of each row.)*
Row 1: 1 dc into fourth ch from hook, *ch 2, skip 2 ch, 1 dc. Rep from * across. Ch 3, turn.
Row 2: *2 dc into first ch-2 loop, 1 dc on second dc, 2 dc into next ch loop, 1 dc into third dc, 2 dc into next ch loop, 1 dc into fourth dc (10-dc group), ch 2, 1 dc on next dc and rep from * across. Ch 3, turn.
Row 3: 2 dc in first ch-2 loop, *1 dc into next 7 dc of previous row, ch 2, skip 2 dc, 1 dc in next dc, 2 dc in next ch-2 sp, repeat from * across, end 1 dc into next 7 dc, ch 2, skip 2 dc, 1 dc in turning ch. Ch 3, turn.
Row 4: *2 dc in ch-2 loop, 1 dc in next dc, ch 2, skip 2 dc, 1 dc in each of next 7 dc, repeat from * across. Ch 3, turn.

Row 5: 1 dc in each of next 4 dc, *ch 2, skip 2 dc, 1 dc in next dc, 2 dc in next ch-2 loop, 1 dc in each of next 7 dc, repeat from * across, end ch 2, skip 2 dc, 1 dc in next dc, 2 dc in next ch-2 loop, 1 dc in each of last 4 dc.
Row 6: *1 dc in each of next 7 dc, 2 dc in next ch-2 loop, 1 dc in next dc, ch 2, skip 2 dc, repeat from * across, end ch 2, skip 2 dc, 1 dc in turning ch. Repeat Rows 3 through 6 for pat.

Double crochet pyramid stitch

Make a foundation ch in multiples of 14 plus 15. (From rows 2–4, turning ch of previous row forms first dc of next row.)
Row 1: Starting in 4th ch from hook (turning ch-3, counts as 1 dc), 3 dc, *ch 1, skip 1 st, (1 dc, ch 1, skip 1 st), twice, 9 dc.* Rep from * to * ending with 4 dc. Ch 2, turn.

Double crochet pyramid stitch

Row 2: 4 dc on 4 dc, *1 dc into ch loop, ch 1, 1 dc into second ch loop, ch 1, 1 dc into third ch loop, 9 dc on 9 dc*. Rep from * to * ending with 4 dc. Ch 2, turn.

Row 3: 5 dc on 5 dc, *1 dc into first loop, ch 1, 1 dc into second loop, 3 dc on next 3 dc, (ch 1, skip 1 st, 1 dc) twice, ch 1, skip 1 st, 3 dc*. Rep from * to * ending with 5 dc. Ch 2, turn.

Row 4: 1 dc on first 6 dc, *1 dc into ch loop, 4 dc on 4 dc, 1 dc into first ch loop, ch 1, 1 dc into second ch loop, ch 1, 1 dc into third ch loop, 4 dc on 4 dc*. Rep from * to * ending with 6 dc.

Row 5: 4 dc, *ch 1, skip 1 st, (1 dc, ch 1, skip 1 st) twice, 3 dc in 3 dc, 1 dc in first loop, ch 1, 1 dc in second loop, 3 dc in 3 dc, rep from * across, ending with 4 dc in 4 dc. Ch 2, turn.

Row 6: 4 dc in 4 dc, *1 dc in ch loop, ch 1, 1 dc in second loop, ch 1, 1 dc in third loop, 4 dc in 4 dc, 1 dc in ch loop, 4 dc in 4 dc, rep from * across ending with 4 dc in 4 dc.

Repeat Rows 3 through 6 for pat.

Four-leaved clover stitch

Make a foundation ch in multiples of 8 plus 1, plus 2 turning ch. From rows 2–4, turning ch of previous row forms first dc of next row.

Row 1: Starting in third ch from hook 1 dc, *ch 1, skip 1 st, 1 dc, ch 1, skip 1 st, 5 dc*. Rep from * to * ending with 5 dc. Ch 2, turn.

Row 2: *5 dc on 5 dc, ch 1, 1 dc on 1 dc, ch 1*, end 1 dc on last dc. Ch 2, turn.

Row 3: 1 dc on 1 dc, *1 dc into ch, 1 dc on next dc, 1 dc into ch, 1 dc on first dc, ch 1, skip 1 st, 1 dc on third dc, ch 1, 1 dc on fifth dc*. Ch 2, turn.

Row 4: 1 dc on first dc, *ch 1, 1 dc on 1 dc, ch 1, 5 dc on 5 dc*. Ch 2, turn.

Rep from * to * to end of each row.
Rep Rows 1 through 4 for pat.

Four-leaved clover stitch

Block and cluster stitch

Block and cluster stitch

Make a foundation ch in multiples of 9 plus 1 plus 2 turning ch. On rows 2–5, turning ch of previous row forms first dc of next row.

Row 1: Starting in third ch from hook, work 1 dc, ch 2, *skip 2 ch, 7 dc, ch 2*, end 7 dc. Ch 2, turn.

Row 2: *2 dc, ch 1, skip 1 st, make a cluster on 4th dc – 1 cluster = (yo, insert hook, draw yarn through) six times into same st, yo, draw yarn through all 12 loops on hook) – ch 1, skip 1 st, 2 dc, ch 2, skip 2 sts*. Repeat between *'s ending with 1 dc. Ch 2, turn.

Row 3: *Ch 2, skip 2 ch, 2 dc on 2 dc, 1 dc on ch, 1 dc on cluster, 1 dc on ch, 2 dc on 2 dc. Ch 2, turn.

Row 4: *(1 dc, ch 1, skip 1 st) 3 times, 1 dc, ch 2, skip 2 ch*, end 1 dc. Ch 2, turn.

Row 5: *Ch 2, skip 2 ch, (1 dc in next dc, 1 dc in ch) 3 times, 1 dc in next dc*. Ch 2, turn.

Repeat Rows 2 through 5 for pat.

Open flower stitch

Open flower stitch

Make a foundation ch in multiples of 10 plus 3 plus 2 turning ch. On rows 2 and 4 turning ch at end of previous row forms first dc of next row.

Row 1: Starting in third ch from hook, *1 dc, ch 2, skip 2 sts*, end 1 dc. Ch 2, turn.

Row 2: 1 dc, ch 2, *1 dc, ch 2 and 2 unfinished tr on next dc, skip 1 dc, 2 unfinished tr on next dc, yo, draw yarn through all loops on hook, ch 2, 1 dc into st in which last 2 tr were worked, ch 2*, end 1 dc. Ch 1, turn.

Row 3: *1 sc, ch 2, skip 2 sts*. Ch 2, turn.

Row 4: 1 dc on first sc, ch 2, 1 dc on next sc, *(2 unfinished tr which are then finished tog, ch 3, 2 unfinished tr finished tog) into sc at center of 4 tr group, 1 dc on next sc, ch 2, 1 dc on next st*. Ch 2, turn.

Rep Rows 1 through 4 for pat.

Netting stitch

Make a foundation ch in multiples of 12 plus 3 plus 2 turning ch. On rows 2–6, turning ch of previous row forms first dc of next row.

Row 1: Starting in third ch from hook, *1 dc, ch 1, skip 1 st, 1 dc, ch 3, skip 1 st, (1 tr, skip 1 st) 3 times, 1 tr, ch 3, skip 1 st*. Rep from * to * ending with 1 dc, ch 1, skip 1 st, 1 dc. Ch 2, turn.

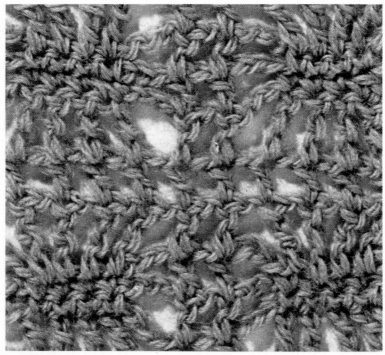

Netting stitch

Row 2: *1 dc on first dc, ch 1, 1 dc, on second dc, ch 3, 4 sc on 4 tr, ch 3*. Rep from * to * ending with 1 dc, ch 1, 1 dc. Ch 2, turn.

Row 3: *1 dc on first dc, ch 1, 1 dc on second dc, ch 3, 4 sc on 4 sc, ch 3*. Rep from * to * ending with 1 dc, ch 1, 1 dc. Ch 2, turn.

Row 4: *1 dc, ch 1, 1 dc, ch 1, 4 tr separated by ch 1 on the 4 sc, ch 1*. Rep from * to * ending with 1 dc, ch 1, 1 dc. Ch 2, turn.

Row 5: *1 dc, ch 1, 1 dc, ch 1, 4 dc separated by ch 1 on the 4 tr, ch 1*. Rep from * to * ending with 1 dc, ch 1, 1 dc. Ch 2, turn.

Row 6: *1 dc, ch 1, 1 dc, ch 3, 4 tr on the 4 dc, ch 3*. Rep from * to * ending with 1 dc, ch 1, 1 dc. Ch 2, turn.

Rep Rows 2–6 for pat.

Mesh stitch with picots

Make a foundation ch in multiples of 3 plus 1 plus 2 turning ch. Ch-3 at end of each row counts as 1 dc, ch-1 loop on following rows.

Row 1: Starting in third ch from hook, 1 dc, ch 1, skip 2 sts * 1 dc, 1 picot (= ch 3, 1 hdc into first ch), 1 dc worked into same st, ch 1, skip 2 sts * 1 dc in last st. Ch 3, turn.

Next and following rows: * (1 dc, 1 picot, 1 dc, ch 1), into each ch-1 loop. *

Irish loop lace stitch

Make a foundation ch in multiples of 7 plus 1 turning ch.

Row 1: 1 sc into second ch from hook, 5 ch, * skip 5 ch, 1 sc, ch 4 and 1 sc into next st, ch 5 *. Rep from * to *, skip 5 ch, 1 sc in last ch.

Row 2: ch 5, * in ch-5 loop work (1 sc, ch 4, and 1 sc), ch 5 * Rep from * to *, end ch 3, 1 dc in last sc.

Row 3: ch 5, skip first ch-4 loop, * work (1 sc, ch 4, 1 sc) in next ch-5 loop, ch 5, * rep from * to *, end 1 sc in third ch of turning ch-5. Repeat Rows 2 and 3 for pat.

Mesh stitch with picots

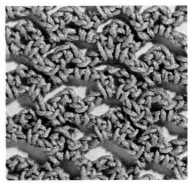

Irish loop lace stitch

Broken mesh stitch

Make a foundation ch in multiples of 9 plus 4 plus 1 turning ch.
Row 1: Starting in second ch from hook, 1 sc, * ch 3, skip 2 ch, 1 sc, ch 2, skip 2 ch, 1 dc, ch 2, skip 2 ch, 1 sc * ending with ch 3, skip 2 ch, 1 sc. Turn.
Row 2: ch 2, * 3 dc into ch-3 loop between first 2 sc, ch 2, 1 sc in dc, ch 2 *, end 3 dc in last ch-3 loop, 1 dc in sc. Turn.
Row 3: ch 2, * 1 dc in second of the 3-dc group, ch 2, 1 sc into ch-2 loop, ch 3, 1 sc into next ch loop, ch 2 *, end 1 dc in second of last 3-dc group, 1 dc in turning ch of previous row. Ch 1, turn.
Row 4: 1 sc in first dc, ch 2, 1 sc in next dc, ch 2, * 3 dc in next ch 3-loop, ch 2, in sc in next dc, ch 2 *, end 1 sc in turning ch of previous row. Ch 1, turn.
Row 5: 1 sc in first sc, * ch 3, skip 1 sc, 1 sc in next ch-2 loop, ch 2, 1 dc in second of 3-dc group, ch 2, 1 sc in next ch-2 loop, ch 3, 1 sc in next ch-2 loop *, end 1 sc in last sc.
Repeat Rows 2 through 5 for pat.

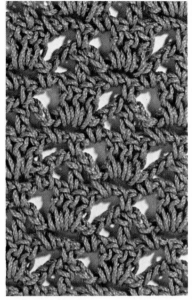

Broken mesh stitch

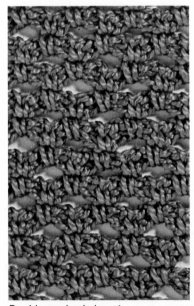

Double mesh stitch no 1

Double mesh stitch no. 1

Make a foundation ch in multipes of 3 plus 1 plus 1 turning ch.
Row 1: Starting in second ch * 1 sc, ch 4, skip 2 sts * end 1 sc in last ch. Ch 1, turn.
Row 2: * 1 sc in sc, ch 4, skip 4 ch *, end 1 sc in last sc. Ch 1, turn.
Row 3: 1 sc in first sc, ch 2, * 1 sc into ch loops of both Rows 1 and 2, ch 4 * end 1 sc into both ch loops, ch 2, 1 sc in last sc. Ch 1, turn.
Row 4: * Work 1 sc on sc of previous row, ch *. Rep from * to *. Ch 1, turn.
Row 5: 1 sc in first sc, * ch 4, skip 1 sc, 1 sc into ch-loops of both rows 3 and 4 *, end ch 4, 1 sc in last sc. Ch 1, turn.
Repeat Rows 2 through 5 for pat.

Double mesh stitch no. 2

Make a foundation ch in multiples of 8 plus 1 plus 1 turning ch.
Row 1: Starting in second ch from hook, * 1 sc, ch 3, skip 3 sts *, ending with 1 sc. Ch 1, turn.
Row 2: 1 sc on the first sc and 1 sc into the ch-3 loop, * ch 4, skip 1 sc, 1 sc into the loop before the next sc, 1 sc on the sc and 1 sc into next loop *, ending with 1 sc in the last loop, 1 sc on sc. Ch 1, turn.
Row 3: 1 sc on first sc, ch 2, * 1 sc into ch loop, ch 3, 1 sc on second of the 3 sc, ch 3 *, end 1 sc into ch loop, ch 2, 1 sc in last sc. Ch 4, turn.
Row 4: 1 sc into ch loop, 1 sc on next sc and 1 sc into next loop, ch 4, skip 1 sc *, end 1 sc into ch loop, 1 sc on next sc and 1 sc into next loop, ch 2, 1 dc in last sc. Ch 1, turn.
Row 5: 1 sc on first dc, * ch 3, 1 sc on second of 3 sc, ch 3, 1 sc into ch loop *, end 1 sc in turning ch of previous row. Ch 1, turn.
Repeat Rows 2 through 5 for pat.

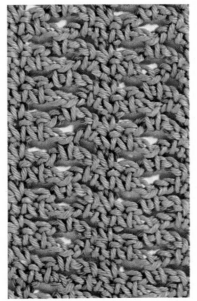

Double mesh stitch no 2

Hazelnuts on mesh

Hazelnuts on mesh

Make a foundation ch in multiples of 8 plus 9 plus 2 turning ch.

Row 1: Starting on 3rd ch, * 1 hdc, ch 1, skip 1 st *. Rep from * to * ending with 1 hdc. Ch 3, turn.

Row 2: Skip last hdc worked, * (1 hdc on next hdc, ch 1) 3 times, on next hdc work 1 hazelnut (hazelnut = ***yo, insert hook, draw yarn through to make a fairly long loop*** 3 times, yo, draw yarn through all 7 loops on hook), ch 1 *; rep from * to * ending with ** 1 hdc on next hdc, ch 1 ** 3 times, 1 hdc on last hdc. Ch 3, turn.

Row 3: Skip the last hdc worked, * 1 hdc on next hdc, ch 1 *. Rep from * to * working over each hazelnut as though it were a hdc. Ch 3, turn.

Row 4: Skip last hdc worked, 1 hdc on next hdc, * ch 1, 1 hazelnut on next hdc, ** ch 1, 1 hdc on next hdc ** 3 times*. Rep from * to * ending with ch 1, 1 hazelnut, ch 1, 1 hdc on next hdc, ch 1, 1 hdc on second of the 3 ch at start of previous row.

Row 5: As Row 3.

Repeat Rows 2 through 5 for pat.

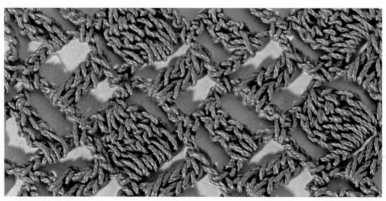

Open lacey stitch

Open lacey stitch

Make a foundation ch in multiples of 9 plus 4 plus 6 turning ch.
Row 1: Skip first 6 ch from hook, * on each of the next 2 ch work 1 unfinished tr, yo, draw yarn through all 3 loops on hook, ch 7, skip 1 ch, 1 sc into next ch, ch 1, skip 5 ch *, ending with 2 tr finished together (as above), ch 7, skip ch 1, 1 sc into last ch. Turn.
Row 2: ch 5, into the first ch-7 loop, work (5 unfinished tr, yo, draw yarn through all loops on hook, ch 7, 1 sc) ch 1, * 2 tr finished tog into next ch loop, ch 7, 1 sc, ch 1, into next ch loop work 5 tr finished tog, ch 7, sc, ch 1 *, ending with 1 sc in top of 2 tr closed tog at end of row. Turn.
Row 3: ch 5, into the first ch-7 loop work * (2 tr finished tog, ch 7 and 1 sc), ch 1 *, ending with 1 sc in top of 5 tr closed tog. Turn.
Repeat Rows 2 and 3 for pat.

Arabesque stitch

Arabesque stitch

Make a foundation ch in multiples of 4 plus 1 plus 2 turning ch.
Row 1: Starting in third ch from hook * work (1 dc, ch 1, 1 dc) in next st; skip 1 st, 1 sc, skip 1 st *, ending with 1 dc, ch 1 and 1 dc into last st. Ch 2, turn.
Next and following rows: * 1 sc into each ch-1 loop, into each sc work (1 dc, ch 1, and 1 dc). Ch 2 turn.

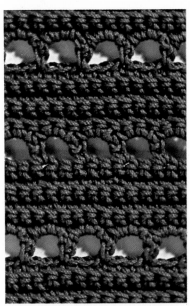

Ridged single crochet with openwork

Ridged single crochet with openwork

Make a foundation ch in multiples of 3 plus 1 plus 1 turning ch.
Row 1: Sc across. Ch 1, turn.
Row 2: 1 sc in each sc, working through back loops only. Ch 1, turn.
Rows 3, 4 and 5: As Row 2.
Row 6: 1 sc into first sc (inserting hook in *both* threads of st), * ch 5, skip 2 sc, 1 sc in next sc *.
Rep from * to *. Ch 1, turn.
Row 7: 3 sc into each ch loop ending with 1 sc into last sc. Ch 1, turn.
Rep Rows 2 through 7 for pat.

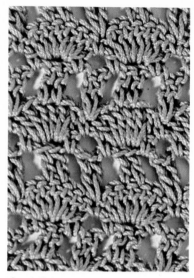

Graziella's stitch

Graziella's stitch

Make a foundation ch in multiples of 6 plus 3 plus 3 turning ch.
Row 1: Starting in fourth ch from hook, 2 dc in next ch, * ch 2, skip 2 ch, 2 dc in next ch *, ending with 2 dc in next to last ch, 1 dc in last ch. Ch 3, turn.

Row 2: * 1 sc, ch 2 * into each ch-2 loop, ending with 1 sc in turning ch. Ch 3, turn.
Row 3: * 1 sc into first ch-2 loop of previous row, 6 dc into next ch-2 loop *, ending with 1 sc in last loop. Ch 3, turn.

Lella's stitch

76

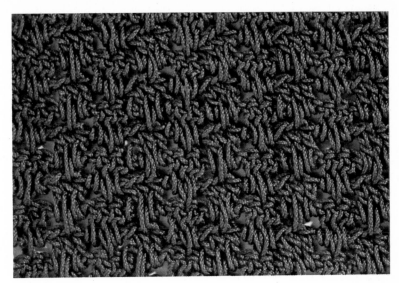

Martha's stitch

Row 4: 2 dc on first sc, * ch 2, 1 dc on third dc and 1 dc on 4th dc of 6-dc group of previous row, ch 2, 2 dc on sc *, ending with 1 dc in turning ch. Ch 3, turn.
Repeat Rows 2 through 4 for pat.

Lella's stitch

Make a foundation ch in multiples of 2 plus 1 turning ch.
Row 1: Sc across. Ch 2, turn.
Row 2: 1 dc on first st, * 2 crossed dc (crossed dc = skip 1 st, 1 dc on next st, 1 dc on skipped st) *. Rep from * to * ending with 1 dc on last st. Ch 1, turn.
Row 3: 1 sc into each st. Ch 2, turn.
Rep Rows 2 and 3 for pat.

Martha's stitch

Make a foundation ch in multiples of 4 plus 1 plus 3 turning ch.
Row 1: Starting in 4th ch from hook * 3 dc in same ch, ch 3, skip 3 ch * ending with 3 dc in the last st. Ch 3, turn.
Row 2: 1 sl st in first st, ch 3 * 1 dc into ch-3 loop of previous row, 1 dc in second of 3 sts skipped in last row, 1 dc into same loop as first dc, ch 3 *, ending with ch 3 and 1 sl st in last st. Ch 3, turn.
Row 3: * 1 dc into ch-3 loop, 1 dc in second of 3 dc group of first Row, 1 dc into same loop as first dc, ch 3 *, end 3 dc in last ch-3 loop in same manner. Ch 1, turn.
Rep Rows 2 and 3 for pat.

Smocking stitch

Make a foundation ch in multiples of 4 plus 1 plus 2 turning ch.

Row 1: (wrong side) Starting in third ch from hook, * (1 dc, ch 2, 1 dc) into same st, skip 3 sts *, ending with a V-motif in last ch. Ch 1, turn.

Row 2: * 3 hdc into the ch-2 loop, ch 1 *, 1 hdc in turning ch. Ch 2, turn.

Row 3: Work 1 dc in first st *, skip 3 hdc, insert hook between the second dc of the first V-motif and the first dc of the second V-motif on Row 1 and work (1 dc, ch 2, and 1 dc) *, 1 dc in turning ch. Ch 1, turn.

Row 4: 1 hdc in first st, ch 1, * 3 hdc into ch-2 loop, ch 1 *, 1 hdc in turning ch. Ch 2, turn.

Row 5: Rep from * of Row 1 but working the dc sts 2 rows below, as in Row 3, being sure to maintain positioning of V-motifs as on Row 1. Repeat Rows 2 through 5 for pat.

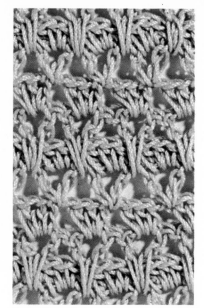

Smocking stitch

Ribbon insertion stitch

Make a foundation ch in multiples of 2 plus 1 plus 1 turning ch.

Rows 1, 2 and 3: Sc across. Ch 1, turn. At end of Row 3 ch 2, turn.

Row 4: * 1 dc, ch 1, skip 1 st *, ending with 1 dc.

Row 5: * 1 sc on dc, 1 sc into ch * end with 1 sc in dc.

Rep Rows 2 through 5 for pat.

Ribbon insertion stitch

Sayonara stitch

Make a foundation ch in multiples of 6 plus 1 plus 1 turning ch.
Row 1: * 1 sc, ch 2, skip 2 sts, (1 dc, ch 1 and 1 dc) into next st, ch 2, skip 2 sts * end 1 sc in last ch. Ch 5, turn.
Row 2: * (1 sc, ch 1) 4 times (inch-1 space) between the 2 dc of previous row, ch 2 * 1 dc in last st. Ch 5, turn.
Row 3: * (1 dc, ch 1, 1 dc) into center ch-1 loop of group of 4 sc, ch 2, 1 sc into ch-3 loop, ch 2 * 1 dc in third ch of turning ch-5. Ch 5, turn.
Rep Rows 2 and 3 for pat, working last st of each row into third ch of turning ch-5.

Sayonara stitch

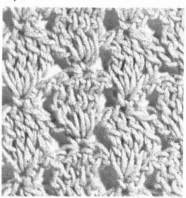

Sara's stitch

Make a foundation ch in multiples of 6 plus 1 plus 3 turning ch.
Row 1: Starting in 4th ch from hook, * 4 tr into same st, ch 2, skip 2 sts, 1 sc in next st, ch 2, skip 2 sts * end 4 tr in last st. Ch 3, turn.
Next and following rows: * 1 sc between second and third tr of each 4-tr group, ch 2, 4 tr on each 1-sc, ch 2 *. Ch 3 at end of each row.

Sara's stitch

Sylvia's stitch

Make a foundation ch in multiples of 6 plus 1.
Row 1: Starting in fourth ch from hook, * 4 dc, ch 2, skip 2 sts *. Rep from * to * ending with 4 dc. Turn.
Row 2: Ch 3, 1 dc in each of 4 dc, * insert hook into ch-2 loop and work 4 dc into it, ch 2, 1 sc between second and third dc of 4-dc group, ch 2 *. Rep from * to *, ending with 4 dc into last loop, 1 dc on each of last 4 dc. Turn.

Sylvia's stitch

Wanda's stitch

Row 3: Ch 3, 1 dc in each of 4 dc, * 1 dc in each of 4 dc on ch-2 loop, ch 2 *. Rep from * to * ending with 8 dc as at beg of row. Turn.

Row 4: Ch 3, 1 dc in each of 4 dc, * ch 2, 1 sc between second and third dc of next 4-dc group, ch 2, 4 dc in ch-2 loop, * end ch 2, 1 sc between second and third dc of 4-dc group, ch 2, 1 dc in each of last 4 dc. Turn.

Row 5: Ch 3, * 1 dc in each of next 4 dc, ch 2*, end 1 dc in each of last 4 dc. Turn.

Repeat Rows 2 through 5 for pat.

Wanda's stitch

Make a foundation ch in multiples of 2 plus 4 turning ch (turning ch-4 counts as 1 dc, ch 1).

Row 1: yo, insert hook into fifth ch from hook, draw yarn through, * yo, draw yarn through first 2 loops, yo, skip 1 st, insert hook into next st, yo, draw yarn through, yo, draw yarn through 2 loops, yo, draw yarn through all 3 loops on hook, ch 1, yo, insert hook in same st as last dc worked *. Rep from * to * ending with 1 dc in last ch.

Next and following rows: ch 4, yo, insert hook into first ch-1 of previous row, draw yarn through, * yo, draw yarn through 2 loops, yo, skip 1 st, insert hook into next st, yo, draw yarn through 2 loops, yo, draw yarn through all 3 loops, ch 1, yo, insert hook into same st as last dc worked, yo, draw yarn through *. Rep from * to *, ending with 1 dc in third ch of turning ch-4.

Openwork stitch no 1

Make a foundation ch in multiples of 6 plus 1 plus 2 turning ch.

Row 1: Starting in third ch from hook, 1 dc, * skip 2 sts, (2 dc, ch 1, 2 dc) into next st, skip 2 sts, 1 dc *. Ch 2, turn.

Next and following rows: Starting on first single dc work 1 raised dc (yo, insert hook from front to back of vertical bar of dc in previous row, bring hook forward, yo, and complete as for normal dc), * (2 dc, ch 1, 2 dc) into ch-1 loop, 1 raised dc on 1 dc *. Ch 2. turn.

Openwork stitch no 1

Openwork stitch no 2

Make a foundation ch in multiples of 8 plus 1 plus 1 turning ch. (Start with at least 18 ch).

Row 1: Starting in second ch from hook, 4 sc, * ch 1, skip 1 st, 7 sc *, ending with ch 1, 4 sc. Ch 2, turn.

Row 2: 1 motif into first st (motif = 1 dc, ch 1, 1 dc) skip 3 sts, * 3 open picots (** 1 sc, ch 3 ** 3 times, 1 sc) into ch loop, 1 motif on fourth of 7 sc *, ending with 1 motif in last sc. Ch 1, turn.

Row 3 and odd numbered rows: 2 open picots in ch loop of first motif, * 1 motif in center of second of 3 open picots, 3 open picots in ch loop of each motif *, ending with 2 open picots on the motif. Ch 3, turn.

Row 4 and even numbered rows: As Row 3, starting and ending with the motif. Ch 1, turn.

Openwork stitch no 2

Openwork stitch no 3

Make a foundation ch in multiples of 8 plus 1 plus 3 turning ch.
Row 1: Starting in fourth ch from hook, 1 dc, skip 3 ch, *(3 dc, ch 1, 3 dc) in next ch, skip 3 ch, (1 dc, ch 3, 1 dc) in next ch, skip 3 ch *, end (3 dc, ch 1, 3 dc) in next ch, skip 3 ch, 1 dc in last ch. Ch 5, turn.
Row 2: * (1 dc, ch 3, 1 dc) in ch-1 space, (3 dc, ch 1, 3 dc) in ch-3 space *, end (1 dc, ch 3, 1 dc) in ch-1 sp, ch 2, 1 dc in third ch of turning ch. Ch 3, turn.
Row 3: * (3 dc, ch 1, 3 dc) in ch-3 space, (1 dc, ch 3, 1 dc) in ch-1 sp *, end (3 dc, ch 1, 3 dc) in ch-3 sp, 1 dc in third ch of turning ch. Ch 5, turn.
Repeat Rows 2 and 3 for pat.

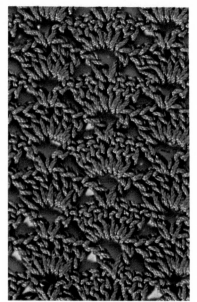

Openwork stitch no 3

Openwork stitch no 4

Make a foundation ch in multiples of 8 plus 5 plus 1 turning ch.
Row 1: * 5 sc, ch 2, skip 1 st, 1 dc, ch 2, skip 1 st * ending with 5 sc. Ch 4, turn.
Row 2: * 1 dc on third sc of 5-sc, ch 2, 1 sc into ch 2 loop, ch 1, 1 sc into next loop, ch 2 *, ending with 1 dc in third sc, ch 1, 1 dc in last st. Ch 1, turn.
Row 3: 1 sc in first sc, ch 1, 1 sc into loop (before the dc), ch 1, 1 sc into next loop, * ch 6, 1 sc into next ch-2 loop (before the dc), ch 1, 1 sc into loop (after the dc) *, ending with ch 1, 1 sc in third ch of turning ch. Ch 4, turn.
Row 4: * 1 dc into ch-1 loop between the 2 sc, ch 2, 5 sc into ch-6 loop, ch 2 *, ending with 1 dc into ch-1 loop between 2 sc, ch 2, 1 dc in last st. Ch 1, turn.

Openwork stitch no 4

Row 5: 1 sc in first sc, ch 1, * 1 sc in first ch loop (before the dc), ch 1, 1 sc in next ch loop (after the dc), ch 2, 1 dc in third sc of 5-sc group, ch 2 *, end 1 sc in first ch loop, ch 1, 1 sc in next ch loop, ch 1, 1 sc in last st. Ch 1, turn.

Row 6: 1 sc in first st, * ch 6, 1 sc in first ch loop, ch 1, 1 sc in next ch loop *, end ch 6, 1 sc in last st. Ch 1, turn.

Row 7; 1 sc in first sc, * 5 sc in ch-6 loop, ch 2, 1 dc in ch-1 loop, ch 2 *, end 5 sc in ch-6 loop, 1 sc in last sc. Ch 4, turn.

Repeat Rows 2 through 7 for pat.

Openwork stitch no 5

Make a foundation ch in multiples of 3 plus 1 plus 1 turning ch.

Row 1: Starting in second ch from hook, *1 sc, ch 2, skip 2 sts*, ending with 1 sc. Turn.

Row 2: Ch 3, *1 dc into first ch-2 loop, ch 1, (2 dc, ch 1, 2 dc) into second ch-2 loop, ch 1*, end 1 dc in last ch-2 loop, 1 dc in last dc. Turn.

Row 3: Ch 1, skip first dc, *1 sc before the next dc, ch 2, 1 sc after the dc, ch 2, 1 sc into ch loop between the 4 dc, ch 2*, end 1 sc before and after last dc with ch-2 between. Turn.

Row 4: Ch 3, *(2 dc, ch 1, 2 dc) in ch-2 loop over 1 dc, ch 1, 1 dc in sc at center of 4-dc group, ch 1*, end (2 dc, ch 1, 2 dc) in last ch-2 loop, 1 dc in last sc. Turn.

Row 5: Ch 1, 1 sc in first st, *ch 2, 1 sc into ch-loop between the 4 dc, ch 2, 1 sc before the single dc, ch 2, 1 sc after the dc*, end ch 2, 1 sc into ch loop between 4-dc, ch 2, 1 sc in last st. Turn.

Row 6: Ch 3, *1 dc in sc between 4-dc, ch 1, (2 dc, ch 1, 2 dc) in ch-2 loop above single dc, ch 1*, end 1 dc in sc between 4-dc, ch 1, 1 dc in last st.

Rep Rows 3 through 6 for pat.

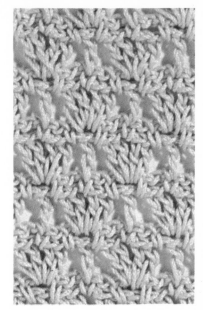

Openwork stitch no 5

Openwork stitch no 6

Openwork stitch no 6

Make a foundation ch in multiples of 4 plus 1 plus 1 turning ch. (Start with at least 14 ch.)

Row 1: Starting in second ch from hook, work *1 sc, ch 4, skip 3 ch*, end 1 sc in last ch. Ch 2, turn.

Row 2: 5 dc in first ch-4 loop, *6 dc in next ch 4-loop*, end 5 dc in last ch-4 loop, 1 dc in last sc. Ch 1, turn.

Row 3: 1 sc in first dc, ch 2, *1 sc between third and fourth dc of 6-dc group (dc at beg of row and turning ch at end of row counts as part of first and last 6-dc group), ch 4*, 1 sc between third and fourth dc, end ch 2, 1 sc in turning ch. Ch 1, turn.

Row 4: 1 sc in first sc, *ch 4, 1 sc in ch-4 loop*, end ch 4, 1 sc in last sc. Repeat Rows 2 through 4 for pat.

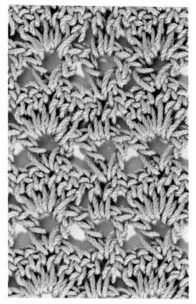

Openwork stitch no 7

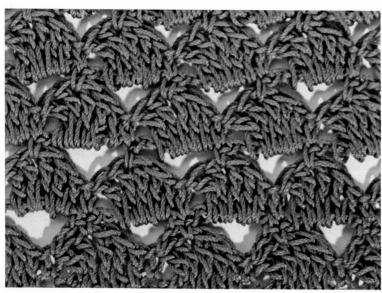

Openwork stitch no 8

Openwork stitch no 7

Make a foundation ch in multiples of 6 plus 1 plus 2 turning ch.
Row 1: Starting in third ch from hook, *(1 dc, ch 2, 1 dc) all into the same st, skip 2 sts*, ending with (1 dc, ch 2, 1 dc) in last ch. Turn.
Row 2 and even numbered rows: Ch 2, *(1 dc, ch 2, 1 dc) into first ch-2 loop, (3 dc, ch 1, 3 dc) into second loop*, end (1 dc, ch 2, 1 dc) in last loop. Turn.
Row 3 and odd numbered rows: Ch 2, *(1 dc, ch 2, 1 dc) into ch-2 loop, (1 dc, ch 2, 1 dc) into the ch-1 loop between the 2 3-dc groups*, end (1 dc, ch 2, 1 dc) in last ch-2 loop.
Repeat Rows 2 and 3 for pat.

Openwork stitch no 8

Make a foundation ch in multiples of 6 plus 1 plus 1 turning ch.
Row 1: Starting in second ch from hook, *1 sc, 1 dc, 4 tr*, ending with 1 sc. Ch 2, turn.
Row 2: 1 dc on 1 sc, ch 3, *1 sc between second and third tr, ch 6*, ending with 1 sc between second and third tr, ch 3, 1 dc in last sc. Ch 3, turn.
Row 3: 3 tr in ch-3 loop, *1 sc on the sc, (1 dc, 4 tr) into ch-6 loop*, ending 1 sc on sc, (1 dc, 2 tr) in ch-3 loop, 1 tr on last dc. Ch 1, turn.
Row 4: *1 sc in first st, ch 6, 1 sc between second and third tr*, end 1 sc in last tr. Ch 1, turn.
Row 5: *1 sc in sc (1 dc, 4 tr), in ch-6 loop*, end 1 sc in last sc. Ch 2, turn.
Repeat Rows 2 through 5 for pat.

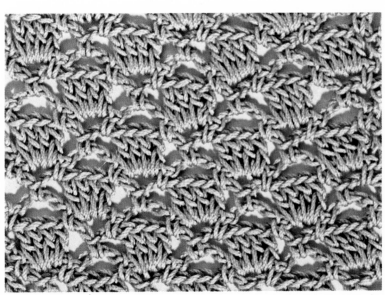

Openwork stitch no 9

Openwork stitch no 9

Make a foundation ch in multiples of 7 plus 6 plus 3 turning ch.

Row 1: 1 dc in 4th ch from hook, *ch 2, skip 1 st, 1 sc in next st, ch 2, skip 1 st, 1 dc in each of next 4 dc*, ending with 2 dc (instead of 4) in last repeat. Ch 5, turn.

Row 2: 1 sc into first ch-2 loop, *ch 3, 1 sc into next loop, ch 4, 1 sc into next loop*, ending with ch 3, 1 sc in next loop, ch 2, 1 dc into ch-3 at beg of previous row. Ch 1, turn.

Row 3: 1 sc into first loop, ch 2, 1 fan (fan = 4 dc) into next ch-3 loop, *ch 2, 1 sc into center of next ch-4 loop, ch 2, 1 fan into next ch-3 loop*, ending with ch 2, 1 sc into 3rd of 5 turning ch of previous row. Ch 4, turn.

Row 4: 1 sc into first ch-2 loop, *ch 4, 1 sc into next ch-2 loop, ch 3, 1 sc into next ch-2 loop*, ending with ch 4, 1 sc into next ch-2 loop, ch 2, 1 hdc on last st. Ch 3, turn.

Row 5: 1 dc in first loop, *ch 2, 1 sc into center of next ch-4 loop, ch 2, 1 fan in next ch-3 loop*, ending with ch 2, 1 sc into center of next loop, ch 2, 1 dc into second of 4 ch of previous row. Ch 5, turn.

Repeat Rows 2 through 5 for pat.

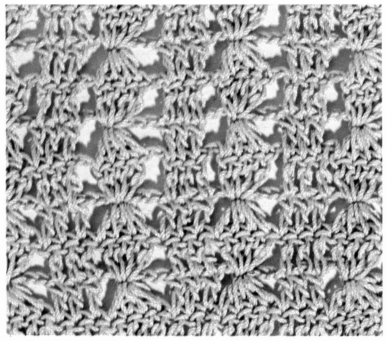

Openwork stitch no 10

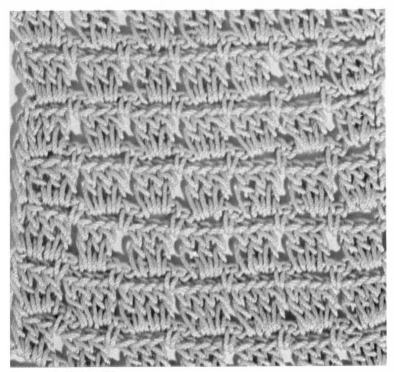

Openwork stitch no 11

Openwork stitch no 10

Make a foundation ch in multiples of 6 plus 1 plus 2 turning ch.
Row 1: Starting in third ch *4 dc into 1 st, skip 1 st, 3 dc, skip 1 st*, ending with 4 dc into last st. Ch 2, turn.
Row 2: *On 4-dc group of previous row work 4 unfinished dc, yo, draw yarn through all 5 loops on hook, ch 2, 3 dc, ch 2*, end 4 unfinished dc closed tog on last 4 dc. Ch 2, turn.
Row 3: *Into st finishing off the 4-dc group in previous row work 4 dc, 3 dc into the 3 dc*, end 4 dc into closing st of 4 dc. Ch 2, turn.
Rep Rows 2 and 3 for pat.

Openwork stitch no 11

Make a foundation ch in multiples of 4 plus 1 plus 1 turning ch.
Row 1: Starting in second ch, *1 sc, ch 3, skip 3 sts*, end 1 sc in last ch. Ch 2, turn.
Row 2: *3 dc into ch-3 loop, ch 1*, end 1 dc in last sc. Ch 1, turn.
Row 3: 1 sc in first dc, ch 3, *1 sc into ch-1 between 3 dc, ch 3*, end 1 sc in last sc. Ch 2, turn.
Rep Rows 2 and 3 for pat.

Openwork stitch no 12

Make a foundation ch in multiples of 8 plus 5 plus 1 turning ch.

Row 1: Starting in second ch from hook *1 sc, ch 4, skip 3 ch*, 1 sc. Ch 2, turn.

Row 2: *4 dc into next ch-4 loop, ch 2, 1 sc into next ch-4 loop, ch 2*, ending with 4 dc in last ch-4 loop, 1 dc on the sc. Ch 1, turn.

Row 3: 1 sc in first dc, ch 4, *1 sc into ch-2 loop after the 4 dc, ch 4, 1 sc into ch loop before the next 4 dc, ch 4*, ending with 1 sc in last st. Ch 5, turn.

Row 4: *1 sc in ch-4 loop, ch 2, 4 dc in next ch-4 loop, ch 2*, end 1 sc in last ch-4 loop, ch 2, 1 dc in last sc. Ch 1, turn.

Row 5: 1 sc in first dc, *ch 4, 1 sc in ch-2 loop before 4 dc, ch 4, 1 sc in ch-2 loop after 4 dc*, end ch 4, 1 sc in third ch of turning ch 5. Ch 2, turn.

Repeat Rows 2 through 5 for pat.

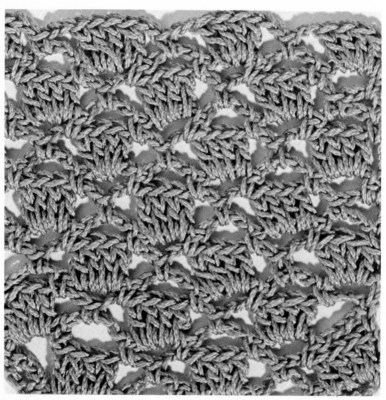

Openwork stitch no 12

Motifs,
medallions and
patchwork

STRIPS AND GEOMETRIC SHAPES

Stitches for medallions to build up into afghans, curtains, bedspreads, tablecloths, etc.

The stitches covered in this chapter are designed for particular purposes. The basic stitches are simple but they are used here to make small shapes – squares, circles, hexagons, etc. and ornamental motifs of various kinds – which, when joined together, may be made into highly individual and useful items.

The results are only bounded by our own imagination and all the shapes described here can, of course, be made into anything you wish to make. For instance, if we describe how certain medallions can be made into a bedspread, there is nothing to stop you using the component parts for placemats or even, perhaps, an evening shawl. The only distinction we have felt it necessary to make is between work carried out in wool (or similar man-made fibers) and in cotton as the former is usually bolder, modern and very often in bright colors while the latter is more elaborate and elegant.

Another consideration to be borne in mind is the time the work will take to complete. Whereas a cushion cover or a set of placemats may be finished fairly quickly, the undertaking and completion of, say, a pair of full length curtains or a double bedspread in a fine cotton needs determination and time. The rewards are great, however, for a beautifully crocheted bedspread, for instance, is a precious possession.

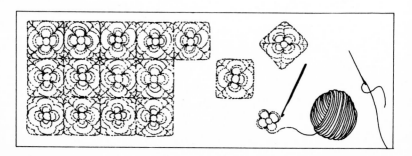

Stitches in wool for bedspreads, afghans, etc.

Hazelnut stitch no 1

Hazelnut stitch no 1

Make a foundation ch in multiples of 2 plus 1 plus 2 turning ch.
This stitch gives the same effect on both sides.
Row 1: Starting in third ch from hook, *(yo, draw yarn through) 3 times into same st, yo, draw yarn through all loops on hook (1 hazelnut completed), ch 1, skip 1 st*, end 1 hazelnut in last ch. Ch 3 (third ch counts as ch-1 loop on row after next), turn.
Row 2: As Row 1, working 1 hazelnut in each ch loop and ch-1 above hazelnuts of previous row, end ch 1, 1 dc in turning ch. Ch 2, turn.
Row 3: 1 hazelnut in each ch-1 loop across. Ch 3, turn.
Repeat Rows 2 and 3 for pat.

Hazelnut stitch no 2

Hazelnut stitch no 2

Make a foundation ch in multiples of 3 plus 1 turning ch.
Row 1: Starting in second st from hook, work 1 sc in each st across. Ch 1, turn.
Row 2: 1 sc, *1 hazelnut (hazelnut = 5 unfinished dc worked into the same st, yo, draw yarn through all

91

Large star stitch

loops on hook), 2 sc*, end 1 hazelnut, 1 sc. Ch 1, turn.
Row 3: Sc across. Ch 1, turn.
Row 4: As Row 2, but moving the motif by working 2 sc, *1 hazelnut, 2 sc*. Ch 1, turn.
Rep Rows 1 through 4 for pat.

Large star stitch

Make a foundation ch in multiples of 5.
Row 1: In 5th ch from hook work 2 unfinished tr, yo, draw yarn through all 3 loops on hook, *ch 4, 5 unfinished tr into the loop at bottom of same ch, skip 4 foundation ch, 3 unfinished tr into next st, yo, draw yarn through all 9 loops on hook*. Rep from * to *, ending with ch 2.
Row 2: 2 unfinished tr into ring at base of ch, yo, draw yarn through all 3 loops on hook, *ch 4, 2 unfinished tr into ring at base of ch, 3 unfinished tr into same stitch as last 2 tr, 3 unfinished tr into ring in center of next flower, yo, draw yarn through all 9 loops on hook*. Rep from * to *, ending with ch 4.

Raised shell stitch

Make a foundation ch in multiples of 4 plus 1 plus 1 turning ch.
Row 1 (right side): Starting in second ch from hook, work 1 sc in each ch

across. Ch 1, turn.

Row 2: 1 sc in first sc, skip 3 sts, *(1 sc, 5 dc) in next sc, skip 3 sts*, ending by skipping 3 sts, 1 sc in last st. Ch 2, turn.

Row 3: 3 dc in first sc, *skip next shell keeping it in front of the work, (1 sc, 5 dc) in 1 sc at end of same shell*, ending by skipping last shell, 1 sc in last st. Ch 2, turn.

Repeat Row 3 for pat being sure to keep raised shells on right side of work by alternately working behind the shells of previous row on one row and working in front of shells on the next.

Raised shell stitch

Strips, squares and other shapes from circles

2-color hexagon

2-color hexagon

Using first color, ch 8 and join with sl st to form ring.
Round 1: 18 sc into ring, ending with 1 sl st on first st.

Round 2: Ch 1, 1 sc on first sc of previous rnd, *ch 5, skip 2 sts, 1 sc on next st*. Rep from * to *, ending with sl st on first sc (6 loops).
Round 3: 1 sl st into first loop, ch 5, 7 dtr into next loop, 8 dtr into each

following loop, ending with 1 sl st into 5th ch.

Round 4: 1 sc on 5th ch and on each of the 7 dtr of previous round, *ch 3, 1 sc on each of the 8 dtr*. Rep from * to *, ending with ch 3, 1 sl st into first sc. Fasten off.

Round 5: Join second color in first ch-3 loop, ch 4, [2 unfinished tr, yo, draw yarn through all 3 loops (1 2-tr cluster), ch 5, 3 unfinished tr, yo, draw yarn through all 4 loops (1 3-tr cluster)] all into first ch-3 loop. *(Ch 3, 1 3-tr cluster on 3rd sc) twice, ch 3, (1 3-tr cluster, ch 5, 1 3-tr cluster) into next ch-3 loop*. Rep from * to *, ending with (ch 3, 1 3-tr cluster) twice into 3rd sc, ch 3, 1 sl st into closing st of first cluster, break yarn.

Round 6: Using first color, (3 sc, ch 3, 3 sc) into first ch-5 loop, *3 sc in each of next 3 spaces, (3 sc, ch 3, 3 sc) in next space*. Rep from * to *, ending with 3 sc in each of next 3 spaces, 1 sl st on first sc.

Round 7: 1 sl st into second sc, ch 4, 1 2-tr cluster into same st as sl st just worked, *ch 3, (1 3-tr cluster, ch 5, 1 3-tr cluster) into next loop, ch 3, 1 3-tr cluster on following second sc, (ch 3, 1 3-tr cluster) 3 times into every 3rd sc*. Rep from * to *, omitting 1 cluster at end of round and working ch 3, 1 sl st into closing st of first cluster.

Round 8: 3 sc into next ch-3 space, *(3 sc, ch 3, 3 sc) into next ch-5 space, 3 sc in each of next 5 ch-3 spaces. Rep from *, ending with 3 sc in each of last 4 ch-3 sps, 1 sl st in first sc.

Round 9: Using second color, 3 sc into first ch-3 loop, *1 sc on each of next 21 sc, 3 sc into next loop*. Rep from * to *, ending with 1 sc on each of next 21 sc, 1 sl st on first sc. Fasten off.

Diamond in single crochet

Ch 3.

Row 1: 1 sc into 2nd ch from hook, 1 sc into next ch. Ch 1, turn.

Row 2: 2 sc into first st, 1 sc into next st. Ch 1, turn.

Row 3: 2 sc into first st, 1 sc on each of next 2 sts. Ch 1, turn.

Row 4: 2 sc into first st, 1 sc on each of next 3 sts. Ch 1, turn.

Continue in sc, increasing 1 st at beg of every row until Row 15 (16 sts). Ch 1, turn.

Row 16: 1 decrease (= insert hook into first st, yo, draw yarn through, insert hook into second st, yo, draw yarn through, draw yarn through all 3 loops on hook), 14 sc. Ch 1, turn.

Row 17: 1 dec, 13 sc.

Continue in sc decreasing 1 st at beg of every row until Row 28 has been worked. Ch 1, turn.

Row 29: 1 dec, 1 sc. Ch 1, turn.

Row 30: 1 dec. Without breaking yarn, work a finishing row of sc around the edge of lozenge, working ch-1 between sc at each corner and ending with a sl st into first edging sc.

Fasten off.

Diamond in single crochet

Halved diamond

Ch 2.
Row 1: 1 sc into second ch from hook. Ch 1, turn.
Row 2: 2 sc on 1 sc of previous row. Ch 1, turn.
Row 3: 2 sc. Ch 1, turn.
Row 4: 2 sc in first st, 1 sc. Ch 1, turn.
Row 5: 3 sc. Ch 1, turn.
Row 6: 2 sc into first sc, 2 sc.
Continue in sc, increasing 1 st on one side only on every even numbered row until Row 15 has been worked. Starting with Row 16, decrease 1 st at beg of every even numbered row. Without breaking the yarn, work the finishing sc only along the edge where the increases and decreases have been worked.

Halved diamond – lower or upper part

Begin working as for complete diamond, finishing after completion of Row 15. Complete by working the finishing sc along the two edges where the increases and decreases have been worked.

Halved diamond (lengthwise)

Halved diamond (lower or upper part)

Square shape from circles

Ch 4 and join with a sl st to form a ring. (First circle.)

Round 1: Work 15 dc into ring (starting with ch 3 which equals one dc), closing the round with 1 sl st on third ch of starting ch-3.

Round 2: *1 dc in each dc, ch 1, * (starting with ch 4 which is equal to 1 dc plus ch 1), closing the round with 1 sl st.

Round 3: *1 dc in each dc, ch 2 * (starting with ch 5), closing the round with 1 sl st.

Round 4: As Round 3.

Round 5: As Round 2.

Round 6: *1 dc on the dc of previous round * 15 times, (starting with ch 3), close the round.

Round 7: Turn the work around and work in opposite direction, * 1 sc in next dc, skip 1 dc * 8 sc will have been worked altogether. Close the round.

Round 8; * Ch 5, 1 sc into second ch from hook, 1 tr into 3rd ch, 1 dc into 4th ch, 1 dc into 5th ch, skip 1 sc of previous row, 1 sl st on next sc. * When 4th petal has been worked, break the yarn.

Work a second circle, joining it to the first circle on Round 3 as follows: * 1 dc, ch 1, take hook out of loop and insert it in one of the holes in Round 3 of the first circle. Pick up the working loop again and draw it back through first circle hole, ch 1 *. Rep from * to * 3 times in all (linking up 3 holes) and complete Round 3. Now work Round 4, working dc on the dc of previous round, as instructed for the previous circle; the joins do not hamper the dc sts as they occur on the chains, as indicated. Both horizontally and vertically the joins are always on 3 holes, thus leaving 1 hole free between one join and the next. Four circles are required to complete a square. These can be made, too, with 16 circles or more, depending upon whether you wish to make a cushion cover or a bedspread.

Square shape from circles

Square woolen medallion

Ch 6 and join with a sl st to form a ring.

Round 1: 8 sc into ring.

Round 2: * 1 dc, ch 3*. Work from * to * 8 times altogether.

Complete this and every following round with 1 sl st. The first st of each round will be substituted by ch 3.

Round 3: *4 dc into first loop, ch 1*. Work from * to * 8 times.

Round 4: * 1 sc into ch-1, ch 5*.

Work from * to * 8 times.

Round 5: (3 dc, ch 1, 3 dc, ch 1) into each loop.

Round 6: * (3 dc, ch 2, 3 dc) into first ch, ** skip 3 dc, 1 sc into next ch-1, ch 3 **. Rep from ** to ** twice more, thus forming one side of square*. Work from * to * 4 times altogether.

Rounds 7 and 8: 1 sc into each st of previous row, working 3 sc into ch loops on each of 4 corners. Close with 1 sl st, break yarn and finish off.

Square woolen medallion

Multi-colored zigzag strip

Make a foundation ch of 16 sts plus 4. Change color every 6 rows.

Row 1: Starting in 5th ch from hook, *3 dc into same st, skip 2 sts *. Rep from * to * 4 times in all, 3 dc on next st, skip 2 sts, 1 dc on last st (5 clusters). Ch 3, turn.

Row 2: Skip the 1 dc and last cluster worked, *1 cluster between 2 clusters of previous row *. Rep from * to * 4 times in all, (1 cluster, ch 1, 1 dc) into ch-4 loop at beg of Row 1. Ch 4, turn.

Row 3: 1 cluster in the ch-1 next to the dc, * 1 cluster between 2 clusters * 4 times, 1 dc on 3rd ch at beg of Row 2. Ch 3, turn.

Rep Rows 2 and 3 until 11 rows have been worked.

Row 12: Skip 1 dc and last cluster worked, * 1 cluster between 2 clusters* 4 times in all, 1 cluster into ch-4 loop at beg of previous row. Ch 3, turn.

Row 13: Skip last cluster worked, * 1 cluster between 2 clusters * 4 times in all (1 cluster, ch 1, 1 dc) into ch-3 loop at beg of previous row. Ch 4, turn.

Row 14: 1 cluster on the ch next to the dc of previous row, * 1 cluster between 2 clusters * 4 times in all, 1 dc on 3rd ch at beg of previous row. Ch 3, turn.

Row 15: Skip the dc and last cluster worked, * 1 cluster between 2 clusters * 4 times in all (1 cluster, ch 1, 1 dc) into ch-4 loop at beg of previous row.

Rep Rows 14 and 15 until Row 23 has been worked. Ch 3, turn.

Row 24: 1 cluster on the ch next to the dc, * 1 cluster between 2 clusters * 4 times in all, 1 dc on 3rd ch at beg of previous row. Ch 4, turn.

Row 25: 1 cluster in space between last dc worked and 5th cluster of previous row, * 1 cluster between 2 clusters * 4 times in all, 1 dc on 3rd ch at beg of previous row.

Repeat from second row.

Multi-colored zigzag strip

'Old America' design medallion in 3 colors, wrong side

'Old America' design medallion in 3 colors

Ch 4 in first color and join with sl st to form a ring.

Round 1: Ch 3 (2 dc, ch 2) into ring, * 3 dc, ch 2 into ring* 3 times, ending with 1 sl st in top of starting ch 3. Start each round with ch-3 to replace first dc.

Round 2: (Second color) *(3 dc, ch 2, 3 dc, ch 2) into ch loop * rep 3 more times, ending with 1 sl st. Break the thread.

Round 3: (First color) *(3 dc, ch 2, 3 dc) into corner (ch 2, 3 dc, ch 2) between one corner and the next *, ending with 1 sl st. Break the thread.

Round 4: (Third color) * (3 dc, ch 2, 3 dc) into corner, ch 2, 3 dc into following loop, ch 2, 3 dc into loop just before the corner, ch 2 *, rep 3 more times, end 1 sl st. Break wool and fasten off.

'Old America' design: (above) a strip for a rug

dc, ch 1) into corner loop; (4 dc, ch 1) into each ch-1 loop between dc groups * rep from * to * 4 times in all.

Round 4: (Fourth color) *(4 dc, ch 1, 4 dc) into corner ch; 4 dc into ch before next 4-dc group in previous round, 4 dc into ch after same 4-dc*, rep from * to * 4 times in all. Fasten off.

'Old America' design – strip for a rug

Ch 5, in first color, and join with a sl st to form a ring.

Round 1: into ring, work (3 hdc, ch 1) 4 times. Close this round and all following rounds with a sl st. Break thread.

Round 2: (Second color) (3 hdc, ch 1, 3 hdc, ch 1) into each ch loop. Break thread. (4 corners worked).

Round 3: (Third color) * (3 hdc, ch 1, 3 hdc) into corner ch, ch 1 (3 hdc, ch 1) into ch between one corner and the next *.

Work from * to * 4 times altogether. Break thread.

Round 4: (4th color) * (3 hdc, ch 1, 3 hdc) into corner ch (ch 1, 3 hdc, ch 1, 3 hdc, ch 1 on side between corners *.

Work from * to * 4 times altogether. Break thread.

The medallion just completed is joined to next and following medallions on Round 4. Work 3 rounds but, on Round 4, after working 3 hdc, ch 1 on the first corner, remove hook from work, insert it from back to front in one of the corner ch of previously completed medallion, pick up dropped stitch from medallion being worked, yo, draw thread through loop and stitch. (This will result in a strip of medallions which can be made to length required,

4-color medallion in 'Old America' design

Ch 6 in first color and join with a sl st to form a ring.

Round 1: *start each round with ch 2.* Work 4 dc and ch 1 into ring 4 times to form 4 leaves. Close this round and all following rounds with a sl st on second starting ch. Break the thread.

Round 2: (Second color) (4 dc, ch 1, 4 dc, ch 1) into each of 4 ch-1 loops dividing the dc groups. Break the thread.

Round 3: (Third color) *(4 dc, ch 1, 4

(Left) 4-color medallion

Multi-colored strip of half-medallions for a rug

according to length or width of article being made.) Rounds 5 through 7 are worked around entire joined strip.

Round 5: (5th color) Starting from the top of strip, work * 1 corner (3 hdc, ch 1, 3 hdc), ** ch 1, 3 hdc ** 3 times, ch 1, 1 corner; rep from ** to ** 3 times (3 hdc, ch 1) once into the ch-1 joining corner of first medallion*, rep from ** to ** 3 times on a long side of second square. Rep around entire strip working joinings as described above. Break thread.

Round 6: (6th color) As Round 5, increasing 1 3-hdc group on each side of square.

Round 7: (7th color) As Round 5, increasing 1 3-hdc group on each side of square.

Multi-colored strip of half-medallions for a rug

Make 13 ch in first color.

Row 1: (wrong side) 1 dc into 9th ch from hook, ch 4, 1 sc into last ch. Ch 3, turn.

Row 2: (right side) 9 dc into first ch loop, 1 dc into 1 dc, 10 dc into second ch loop. Ch 6, turn.

Row 3: 1 dc on 3rd dc, * ch 2, skip 1 st, 1 dc on next st*. Rep from * to *, ending with ch 2 and 1 dc into 3rd ch of previous row (10 spaces). Ch 3, turn.

Row 4: * 3 dc into ch-2 loop, 1 dc on 1 dc * Rep from * to *, ending with 3 dc into turning of previous row. Ch 6, turn.

Row 5: Continue as for Row 3 (20 spaces). This row completes the motif. Break thread.

Row 6: (wrong side, i.e. working in same direction as Row 5).

With second color 1 sc into 8th dc from edge, ch 4, skip 1 dc, 1 dc into middle dc of first motif, ch 4, skip 1 dc, 1 sc on next dc. To start each following row, work ch 2 and 1 sl st at the end of every row into the next dc of previous motif.

Row 7: (right side) 9 dc into first ch loop, 1 dc into middle dc, 10 dc into second ch loop. End this row and all following rows with 1 sl st on next dc of previous motif.

Row 8: ch 2, *1 dc, starting on third dc, ch 2, skip 1 dc. Rep from * to *,

ending with ch 2 and 1 sl st on next dc of first motif (10 spaces).

Row 9: *3 dc into ch loop, 1 dc into 1 dc*. Rep from * to *, ending with 1 sl st into next dc of previous motif.

Row 10: As Row 8 (20 spaces).

Rep Rows 6 through 10, changing color every 5 rows.

Medallion for 4-leaved clover design

Ch 12 and join with sl st to form a ring.
Round 1: ch 2 (= 1 hdc), 27 hdc into circle, closing round with 1 sl st on second starting ch.
Round 2: ch 2, 1 hdc into closing st of previous round, 1 hdc on each of next 5 hdc, 2 hdc on next hdc, * 2 hdc on next st, 5 hdc, 2 hdc on next st *, closing round with 1 sl st into second starting ch.
Round 3: ch 2, 1 hdc into closing st of previous round, 7 hdc * 2 hdc into next st, 8 hdc *, close round as before.
Round 4: 2 ch, 10 hdc, * ch 1, 1 hdc into same st as last st, 10 hdc *, ending with ch 1 and 1 hdc into second ch at beg of round. There will

Medallion for 4-leaved clover design

now be 11 hdc on each side.

Round 5: ch 2, 11 hdc, * ch 3, 12 hdc (the first of these is worked into same st as last hdc and the 12th is worked after the last st of previous round)*, ending with ch 3 and 1 hdc into 2nd ch at beg of round.

Round 6: ch 2, 12 hdc, *ch 5, 13 hdc (work first and 13th as described for first and 12th in Row 5)*, ending with ch 5 and 1 hdc into second ch at beg of round.

Round 7: ch 2, 13 hdc, * ch 7, 14 hdc *, ending with ch 7 and 1 hdc into second ch at beg of round.

Round 8: ch 2, 14 hdc, * ch 9, 15 hdc *, ending with ch 9 and 1 sl st into second ch at beg of round.

Round and square medallions for curtains, coverlets and tablecloths

Small circle

Start from the middle with 14 ch joined into a ring with a sl st into first ch.

Round 1: 3 ch (= 1 dc), 31 dc into ring. Close the round with 1 sl st on 3rd starting ch (32 dc).

Round 2: 8 ch (= 1 dc plus 5 ch). Skip 1 dc *1 dc, ch 5, skip 1 dc of previous row *, 15 times. Close the round with 1 sl st on 3rd starting ch (16 loops).

Round 3: 1 sl st on each of first 3 ch of the ch-5 loop in order to be in center of loop, ch 3 (= 1 dc) (1 dc, ch 2, 2 dc) into same st. Working into 3rd ch of each ch-5 loop, work (2 dc,

109

Small circle

ch 2, 2 dc) to end of round. Close round with 1 sl st into 3rd starting ch (16 looped motifs worked).

Round 4: 1 sl st on each of first 2 dc of previous round in order to reach the first ch-2, ch 3 (= 1 dc into ch-2 space), 2 dc with 1 picot, 3 dc, work (3 dc, picot, 3 dc) in each ch-2 space around. Close the round with 1 sl st into 3rd starting ch (16 motifs). Fasten off.

Large circle

Start exactly as for small circle and work first 3 rounds.

Round 4: 7 dc into each ch-2 space.

Round 5: 4 sl st on first 4 of the 7 dc of previous row to be in center of first motif, ch 8 (= 1 dc plus ch 5), * 1 dc on 4th of the 7 dc of next motif, ch 5. * Rep from * to * to end of round, closing with 1 sl st on 3rd ch.

Round 6: ch 3 (= 1 dc). Into each ch-5 loop of previous round work * 7 dc and 1 dc into the dc between the 2 loops *, closing the round with 1 sl st on third starting ch.

Round 7: Sl st to fourth dc, ch 8 (= 1

Large circle

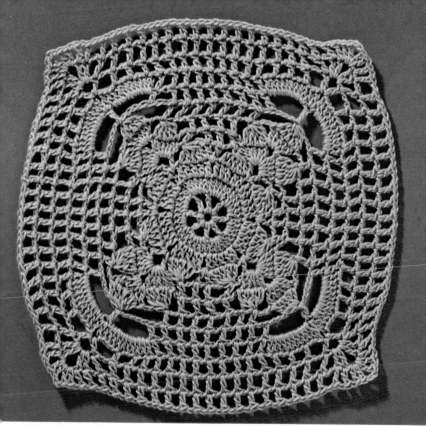

Medallion with lacy flowers

dc plus 5 ch), work * 1 dc, ch 5, 1 dc on dc between the 7 dc of previous round, ch 5 *, closing the round with 1 sl st into 3rd starting ch.

Round 8: Rep Round 3.

Round 9: Rep Round 4. Break thread and finish off.

Medallion with lacy flowers

Ch 6 and join with sl st into first ch to form a ring.

Round 1: ch 5, *1 dc, ch 2* 7 times into ring, ending with 1 sl st into 3rd starting ch.

Round 2: ch 3 (= 1 dc), *5 dc into each ch-2 loop*, ending with 1 sl st into 3rd starting ch.

Round 3: ch 3, *1 dc into each dc of previous round, with ch 1 between every 5 sts, to correspond with the 5-dc groups in previous round, ending with ch 1, and 1 sl st into 3rd ch.

Round 4: ch 3, 4 unfinished dc, yo, draw yarn through all loops, *ch 2 (1 dc, ch 1, 1 dc) into ch 1 of previous row, ch 2, 5 unfinished dc, yo, draw yarn through all loops, ch 2 (1 dc, ch 2

– these will form a corner – 1 dc) into ch 1 of previous row, ch 2, 5 unfinished dc, yo, draw yarn through all loops*, rep from * to * 3 times but instead of working the last 5 dc on the 3rd rep, work 1 sl st into closing st of first group of 5 dc.

Round 5: 1 sl st into first starting ch of previous round, ch 4, * 1 dc on 1 dc, ch 1, 1 dc on 1 dc, ch 1, 1 dc on second ch, ch 2 (5 dc, ch 2, 5 dc) into 2 corner ch, ch 2, skip st joining 5 dc, 1 dc into next ch, ch 1.* Rep from * to * 3 times but instead of working the last dc and ch 1 on the 3rd rep, work 1 sl st into 2nd starting ch.

Round 6: 1 sl st into first ch, ch 3, * 1 dc on 1 dc, ch 1*. Rep from * to * twice, ** ch 2, 5 unfinished dc, yo, draw yarn through all loops, ch 2, 5 dc into corner, ch 2, 5 unfinished dc, yo, draw yarn through all loops, ch 2, 1 dc on second ch of previous round, * ch 1, 1 dc on 1 dc *, rep from * to * 3 times more **, rep from ** to ** twice more, ending with 5 unfinished dc, yo, draw yarn through all loops, ch 2, 5 dc into corner, ch 2, 5 unfinished dc, yo, draw yarn through all loops, ch 2, 1 dc into ch of previous row, ch 1, 1 sl st into second ch.

Round 7: Ch 3, 1 dc into 1 dc, ch 1, 1 dc, ch 1, 1 dc, ch 1, 1 dc into ch of previous row, *ch 6, into 5 corner dc work 5 unfinished dc, yo, draw yarn through all loops, ch 6, skip next 5-dc group, 1 dc into next ch, ** ch 1, 1 dc**. Rep from ** to ** 4 times more, ch 1, 1 dc into ch of previous row *. Rep from * to * twice more, ending with ch 6, into the 5 corner dc work 5 unfinished dc, yo, draw yarn through all loops, ch 6, 1 dc into ch of previous row, 1 dc, ch 1, 1 sl st into second starting ch.

Round 8: Work 9 dc with ch 1 between each dc on all sides of the square (7 central stitches on the 7 of previous row and 2 extra sts at the side of the base ch). Each corner should be made up of ch 6, 1 dc into corner st of previous row and ch 6.

Round 9: (9 dc over 9 dc of previous row, with ch 1 between each) on all 4 sides of the square. Work 10 dc into every ch 6 loop and (1 dc, ch 2, 1 dc) into each corner dc.

Round 10: (1 dc, ch 2, 1 dc) into each corner (15 dc with ch 1 between each) on all 4 sides of the square (the 9 central sts will be on the 9 dc of previous row), the 6 side sts (3 each side) will be on the 10 dc on previous row.

Round 11: (2 dc, ch 2, 2 dc) into each corner; (17 dc with ch 1 between each) on all 4 sides.

Round 12: (2 dc, ch 2, 2 dc) into each corner; (21 dc with ch 1 between each) on all 4 sides. Fasten off.

Hexagons, flowers, squares and stars in cotton

In the following sections, the written instructions for certain patterns have been complemented by illustrations in chart form. The charts greatly simplify even the most complicated designs, as they are very easy to follow. They are built up of symbols representing the various stitches and are read in exactly the same way as the pattern is worked, i.e. a pattern worked in the round should be read anticlockwise, from the center outwards; each circle represents one round, the beginning of which is indicated by the turning chain. Patterns worked in rows are read back and forth starting from the bottom left hand corner. The pattern repeat is denoted by rows grouped together by a bracket. Where a border is added to the main work, an arrow indicates where the thread should be rejoined.

The key to the symbols is given below.

Key

chain (ch)	(yo, draw yarn through) 3 times, yo, draw yarn through all 7 loops on hook
single crochet (sc)	
half double crochet (hdc)	(yo, draw yarn through) 5 times, yo, draw yarn through all 11 loops on hook
double crochet (dc)	slip stitch (sl st)
treble (tr)	picot (3 ch, sl st in first ch)
double treble (dtr)	yo twice, * insert hook into next ch loop, yo, draw yarn through, yo, draw yarn through 2 loops on hook, * yo, rep from * to * (yo, draw yarn through 2 loops on hook) 3 times
2 unfinished double crochet finished together	

Hexagon with star design

Hexagon with star design

Ch 6 and join with sl st to form a ring.
Round 1: Working into ring, * 1 dc, ch 2 *, rep 6 times. (Replace the first dc of a round with ch 3 but if the first st is a sc replace it with ch 1 only. Close each round with 1 sl st into last starting ch.)
Round 2: 3 sc into each loop.
Round 3: *1 hazelnut (5 dc into same st. Remove hook from work, insert it into first of 5 sts just worked, pick up working loop and draw it through), 1 ridged sc (sc but working into the *back* loop only instead of through both loops), 3 ridged sc into next st*.

Rep from * to * to end of round.
Round 4: * 2 ridged sc, 3 ridged sc into same st, 2 ridged sc.*
Round 5: * 1 ridged sc, 1 hazelnut, 1 ridged sc, 3 ridged sc into next st (= 1 corner), 2 ridged sc, 1 hazelnut *.
Round 6: * 4 ridged sc, 1 corner (3 ridged sc into same base st), 4 ridged sc.
Round 7: * 1 hazelnut, 1 ridged sc, 1 hazelnut, 2 ridged sc, 1 corner, 3 ridged sc, 1 hazelnut, 1 ridged sc.*
Round 8: * 6 ridged sc, 1 corner, 6 ridged sc.*
Round 9: * 1 ridged sc, 1 hazelnut, 5 ridged sc, 1 corner, 6 ridged sc, 1 hazelnut *.

Round 10: * 8 ridged sc, 1 corner, 8 ridged sc *.

Round 11: * 1 hazelnut, 8 ridged sc, 1 corner, 9 ridged sc.*

Round 12: *, ** 1 ridged dc (work into *back* of loop), ch 1, skip 1 st **, rep 5 times. 1 ridged dc, ch 2, 1 dc into same st, ch 1, skip 2 sts. Rep from ** to ** 4 times instead of 5 times *.

Round 13: 1 ridged sc on each st, working 3 sc into ch-2 loop at each corner.

Round 14: *, ** 3 ridged sc, 1 hazelnut, 1 ridged sc**, twice, 2 ridged sc, 1 corner. Rep from ** to ** twice*.

Round 15: *, ** 2 ridged sc, 1 hazelnut, 1 ridged sc, 1 hazelnut **, twice, 3 ridged sc, 1 corner, 1 ridged sc. Rep from ** to ** twice more.*

Round 16: *, ** 1 ridged sc, 1 hazelnut, 3 ridged sc ** twice. 1 ridged sc, 1 hazelnut, 2 ridged sc, 1

Stylized flower

corner, 2 ridged sc. Rep from ** to ** twice more*.

Round 17: Along each side work * 1 ridged dc, ch 1, skip 1 st *. Into each angle work 1 dc, ch 3, 1 dc.

Round 18: 1 ridged sc into each st, working 3 ridged sc into the same stitch on each angle. Break the thread and finish off.

Stylized flower

Ch 16 and join with sl st into first ch to form a ring.

Round 1: work 34 dtr into ring.

Round 2: 1 dc on each dtr of previous row.

Round 3: * 3 tr, ch 3, 1 picot, ch 3, skip 1 st *. Rep from * to * 8 times.

Bring working st up to first picot with 6 sl st. The 4 corners of the square are now worked separately, as follows:—

Round 4: 1 sc into picot, ch 6, 1 tr, ch 7, 1 dtr, ch 7, 1 dtr, ch 6, 1 sc.

Turn work round and work 10 dc into each loop. Turn work around again and work 1 dc on each st of previous row (40 dc), ending the round with 1 sl st into loop of Round 3.

Turn work around, ch 2, 1 sl st into ch

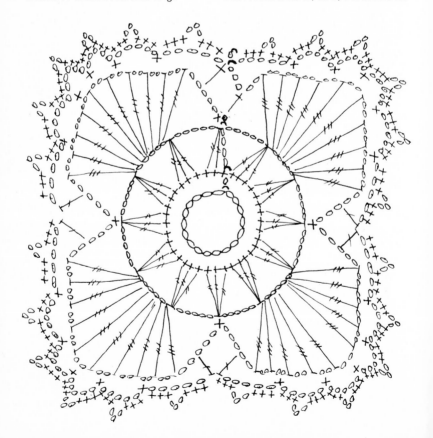

Left and above: Small square medallion

following the 3 tr of Round 3. Work 1 dc on each dc of previous row, ending with 1 sl st into ch loop of Round 3.

Having completed the 4 corners, finish the square off by working all around it as follows:—

Round 5: * 1 dc on the 5th dc of one corner ch 2, skip 1 st (1 dc and ch 2, skip 1 base st) until 5th last dc is reached*. Rep from * to * 4 times.

Round 6: (1 sc, 1 picot, 1 sc) into each space of previous row.

Small square medallion

Ch 18 and join with sl st into first ch to form a ring.

Round 1: Work 36 sc into the ring, ending with 1 sl st on first st.

Round 2: Ch 4 and 1 unfinished tr on each of next 2 sts of previous row, yo, draw yarn through all loops on hook (first petal), * ch 5, 1 petal (= 3 unfinished tr into next 3 sts, yo, draw yarn through all loops on hook)*. Rep from * to * to end of round, ending with ch 5 and 1 sl st on closing st of first petal.

Round 3: 1 sc on st in previous row, * ch 5, skip next ch-5 loop (1 dtr – inserting hook under ch – ch 2), 9 times into next ch-5 loop, ch 5, skip the next loop, 1 sc on closing st of next petal* until the last rep, ending with ch 2 and 1 dc worked into first sc (instead of ch 5 and 1 sc).

Round 4: ch 3, * 1 dc into next ch-5 loop, ** ch-5, skip next ch-2 space, 1

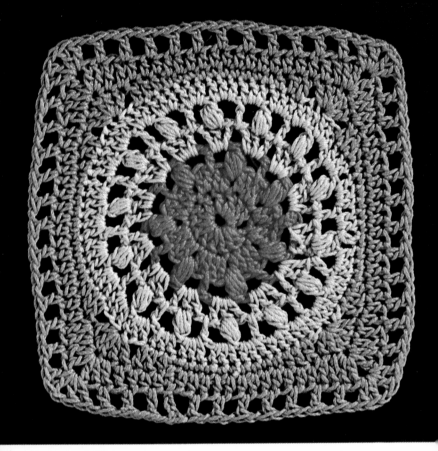

3-color medallion

sc into next space ** twice, ** ch 5 and 1 sc into next space ** twice, ch 5, skip next space, 1 sc into next space, ch 5, skip next space, 1 dc into ch-5 loop *, replacing last dc in final rep with 1 sl st into 3rd starting ch.

Round 5: * 3 sc, ch 3, 3 sc (1 scallop) * into each loop of previous row, ending with 1 sl st on first sc. Break the thread and fasten off.

To join the first square to the second and so on, work second square in the same way until Round 4 has been completed.

Round 5: 1 scallop into each of the first 3 loops of previous row, * 3 sc, ch 1, 1 sc inserting hook into ch-3 loop of corresponding scallop of first square, ch 1, 3 sc *, rep from * to * 6 times altogether, and then continue as for first square.

Medallion with interwoven center

3-color medallion

In first color, ch 3 and join with sl st into first ch to form a ring.

Round 1: Work 14 dc into ring.

Round 2: 2 dc into each dc of previous row (28 dc).

Round 3: In the spaces between each 2 dc work: * 1 dc, ch 2, 4 unfinished hdc, yo, draw yarn through all loops on hook, ch 1 *.

Rep from * to *.

Round 4: (Second color.) Into each ch space work 1 dc, ch 1, 1 dc, ch 1, 1 dc, ch 1.

Round 5: * ch 2 on middle dc of previous row, 4 unfinished dc, yo, draw yarn through all loops on hook, ch 1, 1 dc between the following 2 dc of previous row *, rep from * to *.

Round 6: 3 dc on each ch of previous row.

Round 7: (3rd color) * 10 sc, 1 hdc, 2 dc, skip 2 sts, 5 dc into next base st, skip 2 sts, 2 dc, 1 hdc *, rep from * to *.

Round 8: * 1 hdc, 2 dc (2 dc, ch 1, 2 dc) into corner st, 2 dc *, rep from * to *.

Round 9: * 1 dc, ch 1, skip 1 st * (2 dc, ch 1, 2 dc) into corner ch. Fasten off.

Medallion with interwoven center

Ch 18 and join with sl st into first ch to form a ring.

Round 1: Work 36 dc into ring, closing with 1 sl st into starting st. (The first ch 3 of the round are equal to the first dc. In all following rounds, if the first st is a sc or a tr, it is replaced by 1 or 4 ch respectively, at the beg of a round. Each round is completed with 1 sl st into the last starting ch of the round).

Break the yarn. Work 7 more identical rings, interweaving them as the work progresses. The interweaving is done before closing the foundation ch into a ring. Slip the length of ch through the previous ring and join with sl st into first ch. Then work the 36 dc into it by turning the new ring gradually, making sure that all the stitches are worked in the same direction.

On starting the 8th ring, slip the length of ch into the last ring worked and into the first, thus linking all the rings into a circle, and complete as before.

Rejoin yarn to point of attachment of 2 of the rings, pick up loops of dc from front and back rings simultaneously, work 1 sc * pick up loops of dc from front (first) and back (second) rings simultaneously and work 1 sc, ch 9, skip 6 sts of second ring, 1 sc into next st of the same ring, ch 9, insert hook through dc loops of second ring and third ring, at point of attachment,* rep 7 times..

Round 1: Work 14 sc into each loop.

Round 2: * (2 dc cluster = 2 unfin dc, yo, draw yarn through all 3 loops, ch 2) 7 times, skip 5 sts, 3 dc, ch 2, skip 6 sts *.

Round 3 * (Between first and second 2-dc clusters work 1 2-dc cluster, ch 2) 6 times, 1 dc into loop on right of the 3 dc of previous row (= 1 right increase), 3 dc on 3 dc, 1 dc into loop on left of the same 3 dc (= 1 left increase), ch 2*.

Round 4: * (Between first and 2nd 2-dc clusters work 1 2-dc cluster, ch 2) 5 times, 1 right inc, 5 dc, 1 left inc, ch 2 *.

Round 5: * (Between first and second 2-dc clusters work 1 2-dc cluster, ch 2) 4 times, 1 right inc, 7 dc, 1 left inc, ch 2*.

Rounds 6–8: As Round 5, bringing the number of dc in the 8 groups to 15 and the number of 2-dc clusters in the 8 groups to 1. At the same time, make 1 increase in the ch loops on each side of the dc.

Round 9: * 7 sc into first loop, 15 sc on the 15 dc, 7 sc into next loop.*

Round 10: * 1 sc on sc over last 2-dc cluster, ch 5, 1 sc on first of 15 sc, ch 14, 1 sc on last of 15 sc, ch 5 (1 dc, ch 3, 1 dc) on sc over last 2-dc cluster (corner) ch 5, 1 sc on first of next 15 sc, ch 14, 1 sc on last of 15 sc, ch 5.* Rep from * to * for entire round.

Round 11: * 7 sc into first loop, 7 sc into ch-5 loop (2 dc, ch 2, 2 dc) into corner, 7 sc into loop after corner, 15 sc into ch-14 loop, 7 sc into next loop.*

Round 12: Work 1 dc into each st for entire round, but on the 4 sts at each corner work (1 dc, ch 2) twice, 1 dc, ch 3, 1 dc, ch 2 (1 dc, ch 2) twice.

Round 13: 1 dc, ch 2, skip 2 sts*. Rep from * to * along each side, working each corner as follows: (1 dc, ch 2 on each dc) 3 times, 1 dc, ch

Medallion with central flower

3, 1 dc into ch-3 corner loop (1 dc, ch 2 on each dc) 3 times, ch 2.
Round 14: As Round 13.

Medallion with central flower

In starting from the middle of the flower, care must be taken always to work with right side facing you, without ever turning the work (not normally done, in any case, when working rounds). The petals of the flower should always be towards you.

Ch 6 and join with sl st into first ch to form a ring.
Round 1: Ch 6 (= 1 dc plus ch 3). Work (1 dc, ch 3) 7 times into circle. Complete round with 1 sl st on 3rd of 6 starting ch (8 loops).
Round 2: (1 sc, 3 dc, 1 sc) on each

ch-3 loop of previous round (first round of 8 petals).

Round 3: 1 sc on sl st of Round 1 (between 2 petals), ch 4 (1 sc on next dc of Round 1 (between 2 petals), ch 4) 7 times. Complete round with 1 sl st on sc of previous round (8 loops).

Round 4: (1 sc, 1 dc, 3 tr, 1 dc, 1 sc) into each 4 ch loop of previous round. (Second round of 8 petals).

Round 5: 1 sc on sl st of Round 3 (between 2 petals), ch 5 (1 sc on next sc of Round 3, between 2 petals, ch 5) 7 times. Complete round with 1 sc on first sc of previous round (8 loops).

Round 6: (1 sc, 1 dc, 5 tr, 1 dc, 1 sc) on each ch 5 loop of previous row. (3rd round of 8 petals).

Round 7: 1 sc on sl st of Round 5 (between 2 petals), ch 6 (1 sc on next sc of Round 5, between 2 petals, ch 6) 7 times. Complete round with 1 sl st on first sc of previous row. (8 loops).

Round 8: (1 sc, 1 dc, 3 tr, ch 1, 3 tr, 1 dc, 1 sc) on each ch-6 loop of previous round. (4th round of 8 petals). The flower has now been completed.

Round 9: 5 sl st on first 5 sts of first petal to bring work to the central ch of the petal, ch 4 (= 1 tr) (3 tr, ch 2, 4 tr, ch 2) into central ch, 2 dc between the 2 petals, ch 3, 1 sc into central ch of next petal, ch 3; 2 dc between next 2 petals, ch 2 (4 tr, ch 2, 4 tr, ch 2) into central ch of next petal, 2 dc between the 2 petals, ch 3, 1 sc into central ch of next petal, ch 3, 2 dc between the 2 petals, ch 2. Complete round with 1 sl st into 4th starting ch.

Round 10: 4 sl st on the 4 tr of previous round to bring work to the 2 corner ch (ch 4 = 1 tr), 4 tr, ch 2, 5 tr, ch 2) into 2 corner ch (2 dc, ch 2) into 2 ch of previous round (2 dc, ch 2) into next 3 ch (2 dc, ch 2) on central sc of petal (2 dc, ch 2) into 3 ch (2 dc, ch 2) into next 2 ch, ch 2 (5 tr, ch 2, 5 tr, ch 2) into 2 corner ch (2 dc, ch 2) into first 2 ch (2 dc, ch 2) into next 3 ch (2 dc, ch 2) on central sc of petal, (2 dc, ch 2) into next 3 ch (2 dc, ch 2) into next 2 ch. Complete round with 1 sl st on 4th starting ch.

Round 11: 5 sl st on the 5 tr of previous round to bring work to the 2 corner ch, ch 4 (= 1 tr), 4 tr, ch 2, 5 tr, ch 2) into 2 corner ch (2 dc, ch 2) into first 2 ch of previous round, (2 dc, ch 2) into next 2 ch, skip next 2 ch (2 dc, ch 2) between 2 dc of previous rnd, skip next 2 ch (2 dc, ch 2) into next 2 ch (2 dc, ch 2) into next 2 ch, ch 2 (5 tr, ch 2, 5 tr, ch 2) 3 times into 2 corner ch (2 dc, ch 2) into next 2 ch (2 dc, ch 2) into next 2 ch, ch 2, skip next 2 ch (2 dc, ch 2) between 2 dc of previous rnd, skip next 2 ch (2 dc, ch 2) into next 2 ch (2 dc, ch 2) into next 2 ch, ch 2. Complete round with 1 sl st on 4th starting ch.

Round 12: Rep Round 11.

Round 13: Rep Round 11, working ch-3 between the 2 dc instead of 2.

Round 14: Ch 3 (= 1 dc). Work 1 dc on every ch, dc and tr of previous rnd, except on the corners. On each 2 corner ch work 2 dc, ch 2, 2 dc. Complete round with 1 sl st on 3rd starting ch.

Break yarn and fasten off.

Medallion with 8-petal flower

Ch 12 and join with sl st into first ch to form a ring. (The first dc of each round must be replaced by ch 3 and the first tr by ch 4).

Round 1: Work 24 tr into ring, completing round and all following rounds with 1 sl st.

Round 2: 1 dc, ch 3 (3 dc, ch 3) 7 times, ending with ch 3, 2 dc.

Round 3: (3 dc, ch 3, 3 dc) into each ch-3 loop, ending with sl st into 3rd starting ch.

Round 4: Sl st on each of first 3 dc of previous row to bring work to first loop. (3 dc, ch 3, 3 dc, ch 3) into each ch-3 loop for entire round.

Round 5: Sl st on first 3 dc of previous row, *(3 dc, ch 1, 3 dc) into first loop, ch 2, 1 sc into the single ch of Round 3, ch 2*. Rep from * to * 7 more times.

Round 6: Sl st to center of first group, * 1 sc into middle of first group, ch 5, 1 cluster (cluster = ** yo, insert hook through 2 bars between the 2 groups ** 3 times, yo, draw yarn through all 7 loops on hook), ch 5 *. Rep from * to * 7 more times.

Round 7: 8 dc into each loop of previous row.

Round 8: * 1 sc into st corresponding with the sc of Round 6, ch 5, 2 dc to correspond with cluster between next 2 groups, ch 5, 1 sc in st corresponding with the sc of Round 6, ch 5 (2 tr, ch 3, 2 tr) to correspond with next cluster (corner), ch 5*. Rep from * to * 3 more times.

Round 9: * 1 sc on sc, 5 sc into next ch loop, 2 sc on 2 dc, 5 sc into next ch loop, 1 sc on sc (2 sc, 1 hdc, 3 dc) into next ch loop, 3 dc on next 2 dc (3 dc, ch 3, 3 dc) into corner loop, 2 dc on next 2 dc (3 dc, 1 hdc, 2 sc) into next ch loop*. Rep from * to * 3 more times.

Round 10: 1 dc into each st of previous row on all 4 sides, working (2 dc, ch 3, 2 dc) into each of the 4 corner ch loops.

Round 11: * (skip 2 sts, 2 dc, ch 2) 7 times on each side, working (3 dc, ch 3, 3 dc) into each corner ch loop, ch 2, skip 3 sts (2 dc, ch 2, skip 2 sts) twice.* Rep from * to * 3 more times.

Medallion with star design

Ch 10 and join with sl st into first ch to form a ring.

Round 1: Work (1 sc, 1 hdc, 3 dc, 1 hdc) into ring 5 times. Complete with 1 sl st into starting st.

Round 2: *Into sc of petal, insert hook from *back to front* (and from right to left, as usual) and work 1 sc, ch 4.* Rep from * to * 4 more times. (Petals will lie forward with the ch loops behind them.) Complete round with 1 sl st into opening st.

Round 3: (1 sc, 1 hdc, 5 dc, 1 hdc, 1 sc) into each ch-4 loop (5 petals), completing round with 1 sl st into starting st.

Round 4: As in Round 2, work from back to front (1 sc into sc of Round 2, ch 6) 5 times, completing round with 1 sl st into starting st.

Round 5: *1 dc on sc, ch 2 (1 dc, ch 2) into ch-6 loop 3 times. * Rep from * to * 4 times.

Round 6: * 1 dc on 1 dc, ch 2, 1 hazelnut (hazelnut = ** yo, insert hook into next st, yo, draw yarn through ** 5 times, yo, draw yarn through all loops on hook, ch 1), ch 1, 1 dc on 1 dc, ch 2.* Rep from * to * 7 more times.

Round 7: * 1 dc on dc, ch 2, 1 hazelnut to the right and 1 hazelnut to the left of hazelnut in previous row, ch 1, 1 dc on dc, ch. 2.* Rep from * to * 7 more times.

Round 8: 1 dc on dc, ch 2, 3 hazelnuts (1 to the right, 1 in between and 1 to the left of hazelnuts in previous row), ch 1, 1 dc on dc, ch 2*. Rep from * to * 7 more times.

Round 9: * 1 dc on dc, 4 hazelnuts (on hazelnuts in previous row), ch 1, 1 dc on dc, ch 2.* Rep from * to * 7 more times.

Round 10: * 1 dc on dc, ch 2, 1 dc on closing st of next hazelnut, ch 2, 3 hazelnuts, ch 1, 1 dc on closing st of next hazelnut, ch 2, 1 dc on dc, ch 2.*

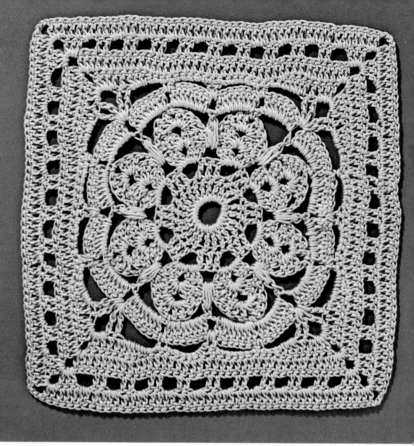

Medallion with 8-petal flower

Rep from * to * 7 more times.
Round 11: * 1 dc on dc, ch 2, 1 dc, ch 2, 1 dc on closing st of next hazelnut, ch 2, 2 hazelnuts, ch 1, 1 dc on closing st of 3rd hazelnut, ch 2, 1 dc on dc, ch 2, 1 dc on dc, ch 2*.
Rep from * to * 7 more times.
Round 12: * (1 dc on dc, ch 2) 3 times, 1 dc on closing st of next hazelnut, ch 2, 1 hazelnut, ch 1, 1 dc on closing st of second hazelnut, ch 2 (1 dc on dc, ch 2) 3 times*. Rep from * to * 7 more times.
Round 13: * (1 dc on dc, ch 2) 4 times, 1 dc on closing st of hazelnut, ch 2 (1 dc on dc, ch 2) 4 times*. Rep from * to * 7 more times.
Round 14: *(1 ridged sc – formed by working into the back loop only instead of through both loops – on

dc, 2 ridged sc into ch 2) 4 times, ch 3, skip 1 ch-2 loop, (1 sc, 1 picot*, 1 sc, ch 4) into next ch loop, 5 times.* Rep from * to * 3 more times. (A picot is worked as follows: ch 3 and 1 sl st into st already worked on.)

Round 15: *Ridged sc on ridged sc of previous round, 2 ridged sc into next ch-2, ch 5 (1 sc, 1 picot, 1 sc, ch 4) 4 times, ch 1, 2 ridged sc on next ch-2, 16 ridged sc *. Rep from * to * 3 more times.

Round 16: * Ridged sc into ridged sc, 2 ridged sc into next ch-2, ch 6 (1 dc, 1 picot, 1 sc, ch 4) 3 times, ch 2, 2 ridged sc into next ch-2, 18 ridged

Medallion with 8-petal flower

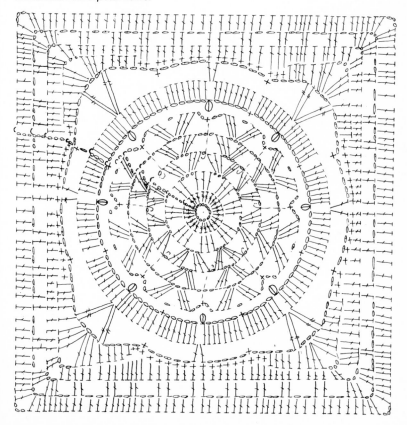

125

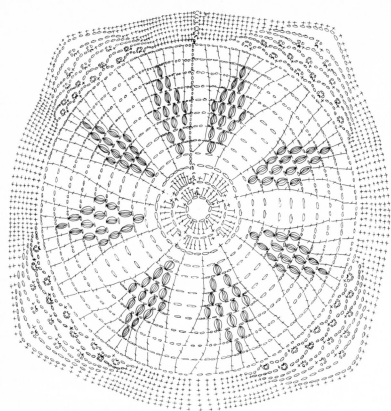

Medallion with star design

sc*. Rep from * to * 3 more times.

Round 17: * Ridged sc on ridged sc, 2 ridged sc into next ch-2, ch 6 (1 sc, 1 picot, 1 sc, ch 4) twice, ch 2, 2 ridged sc into next ch-2, 20 ridged sc *. Rep from * to * 3 more times.

Round 18: * ridged sc on ridged sc, 2 ridged sc into next ch-2, ch 7, 1 sc, 1 picot, 1 sc, ch 7, 2 ridged sc into next ch-2, 22 ridged sc*. Rep from * to * 3 more times.

Round 19: * 2 ridged sc on ridged sc, 2 ridged sc on next ch-2, ch 15 (= corner), 2 ridged sc into ch-2 of ch-7 loop worked after picot, 24 ridged sc *. Rep from * to * 3 times.

Medallion with star design

Round 20: 1 ridged sc into every st for entire round.

Medallion with 4-pointed star and 4 rays

Ch 6 and join with sl st into first ch to form a ring.

Round 1: Work 16 sc into ring, ending with 1 sl st into first st.

Round 2: Work in sc, increasing 4 sts evenly spaced (20 sts).

Round 3: (each point is worked back and forth by turning the work at the end of each row) ch 20, * 1 dc (for first st only, work into 6th ch from

Medallion with 4-pointed star and 4 rays

hook), skip 1 st *. Continue by inserting hook into next ch and repeat from * to * 3 more times, 3 dc, 4 sc, 1 sc into next sc.

Round 4: Turn the work, 15 ridged sc (work into *back* of loop only on sts just worked, 5 sc into st at the tip of the point, 15 sc along the other side, 1 sc into next base sc.

Round 5: Turn the work, * 7 sc on sts of previous row, ** ch 5, 1 sc on stitch already worked into **, 2 sc, rep from ** to **, 2 sc, rep from ** to **, 5 sc, ch 5, 1 sc into same st (tip), work along the other side in the same way (7 picots), 1 sc on next sc*. This completes work on first point of star.

Round 6: (Start first ray) Ch 11, 1 sl st into 6th ch from hook. A ring has been made into which work: 1 sc, ch 3, remove hook from working loop and insert it into the first picot of the first point, pick up working loop again, yo, draw yarn through, ch 2, * 1 sc into ring (the first link has been completed), ch 5 *, rep from * to * 4 times, 5 sc on next 5 ch (at start of first ray) and work 5 sc, 1 sc on base sc (this completes the ray), skip 1 base st. Rep Rounds 3, 4 and 5 to make a second point. On the last round, link first picot with 5th picot of ray, as already described. Work 4 points alternating with 4 rays altogether.

Break the yarn and put completed star on one side while the frame is begun. This is worked in rows, back and forth, in ridged dc.

Starting from one corner, ch 21.

Row 1: Work first dc into 4th ch from hook, 17 dc. Ch 3, turn.

Row 2: 18 dc.

Row 3: (working only on the middle stitches), ch 3, 6 dc.

Row 4: As Row 3. Break the yarn.

Turn the work, insert hook into last st (on the right), ch 9.

Row 5: Work 1 dc into 4th ch from hook, 5 dc on next 5 ch, 6 dc worked opposite the dc of Row 1 (they will therefore be worked on the other side of the foundation ch).

Row 6: ch 3, 12 dc on dc of previous row, ch 9.

Row 7: 1 dc on 4th ch from hook, 5 dc on next 5 ch, 6 dc on 6 dc of previous row (6 dc remain).

Row 8: As Row 6.

Rep Rows 6 and 7 until 6 rectangles of 2 rows of 12 dc, ch 3, have been worked (1 side of frame).

Make the second corner as follows: work as for Row 7, then return to beg of row with sl sts, rep Row 6 (the rectangle for the second corner is now complete), continue to make the other sides (as before) and alternate the corners (first and second). In the last repetition of Row 6 (before the third corner), ch 15 instead of 9.

To complete the frame, on the final row of the 4th corner, link up with the 6 dc of the first side (6 central sts will remain unused).

Now work 2 rounds around the inside of the frame which will link it to the star already made:

Round 1: 1 sc into inside corner of first rectangle, * ch 9, 1 sc into corner of second rectangle,* rep from * to * 4 times, ch 5, 1 sc into first rectangle of second side. Continue the round in this way, ending with 1 sl st into starting st.

Round 2: (5 sc, 1 ch-5 picot, 5 sc) into each ch-9 loop. At each corner, work 5 sc into the ch-5 loops. As you work this round, link the central star with the 4 picots of the 4 rays.

On the outside edges of the frame, work 2 finishing rounds. These are identical to those inside except that the corners are worked as follows: Round 1 – ch 9 and on Round 2 – 5 sc, 1 picot, 5 sc.

Medallion with triangular design

Starting from the center, ch 6 and join with sl st into first ch to form a ring.

Round 1: ch 3 (= 1 dc), work 2 dc into the ring, (ch 2, 3 dc) 3 times into the ring. Complete round with ch 2 and 1 sl st into 3rd starting ch.

Round 2: ch 3 (= 1 dc), * 1 dc on each dc in previous row (2 dc, ch 3, 2 dc) into each ch loop. * Rep from * to * for entire round, ending with 1 sl st on 3rd starting ch.

Rounds 3, 4, 5 and 6: Rep Round 2, increasing 4 dc on each side. (At completion of Round 6, there will be 23 dc on each side).

Round 7: * ch 3, 1 sl st on next dc, ch 3, skip next dc, 1 sl st on next dc *. Rep from * to * for entire round.
At each corner, ch 5 instead of 3.

There will now be 8 loops close together and 7 loops spaced by a dc on each side of square.

Round 8: 1 sl st into first loop (one of those spaced by a dc). * ch 5, skip 1 close loop, 1 sl st into next spaced loop.* Rep from * to * for entire round, working ch 5, 1 sl st, ch 5, 1 sl st, ch 5 into each corner loop.

There will now be 8 loops on each side and 1 loop on each corner.

Round 9: * 1 sl st into next loop and then, still in same loop, work (ch 5, 1 sl st) 3 times *. Rep from * to * along each side, working into all 4 corner loops as follows: (ch 6, 1 sl st) 4 times.

There will now be 3 small loops on each of the loops on all 4 sides and 4 on each corner loop.
Fasten off.

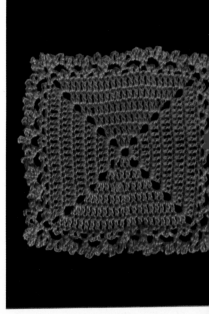

Medallion with triangular design

Medallion with star

Ch 8 and join with sl st into first ch to form a ring.

Round 1: Work 12 sc into the ring, closing with 1 sl st into first st of round.

(Replace the first sc of the round with ch 1. If, in the following instructions, the first st is a dc, a tr, or a dtr, these should be replaced with 3, 4 or 5 ch respectively. Each round must be closed with a sl st on the last of the starting ch.)

Round 2: Work in sc, with 4 evenly distributed increases.

Round 3: * 1 dtr, ch 2 *, rep 15 more times.

Round 4: 1 sc on each st.

Rounds 5, 6 and 7: Work in sc, with 6 evenly distributed increases.

(At the end of Round 7 there will be 66 sc).

Round 8: * 11 sc, turn; ch 3, turn; ch 3, 7 sc, turn; continue in this way, decreasing 1 sc at a time on both sides of the point until 1 sc remains. Return to base of point by sl stitching along the left side*. Rep 5 more times, but do not sl st, back after last point has been worked.

Round 9: * 1 sc on the tip of last point worked, ch 16 *, rep 5 more times.

Round 10: 1 sc into each ch and 3 sc into sc over each point.

Fasten off.

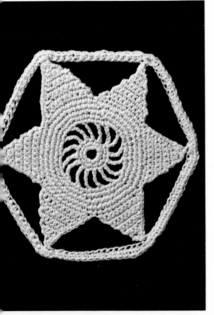

Medallion with star

BORDERS, EDGINGS AND INSERTIONS

Crochet for the finishing touches

Borders are simply strips of crochet made to finish off and embellish a garment or an object such as a tablecloth or handkerchief. They may be worked separately and then attached to the edge of the fabric or they may be worked directly on to the fabric itself. In either case, borders are worked lengthwise until they reach the length required.

Edgings tend to be more elegant and elaborate in style. They are always worked separately and are only attached to the garment or other item for which they are intended on completion.

Insertions are also decorative strips but – as the name implies – they are inserted into the fabric rather than being attached to the edges. The fabric may remain underneath (as with appliqué crochet) or it may be cut away.

If worked in fairly thick crochet cotton (No 10 or 20, for example) these borders, edgings and insertions are suitable for decorating towels, curtains and informal table linen. The finer crochet cottons (No 40 and 60 – or even finer) look extremely elegant when worked to these designs and are ideal for formal tablecloths and table napkins, luncheon cloths, handkerchiefs and light garments.

Borders

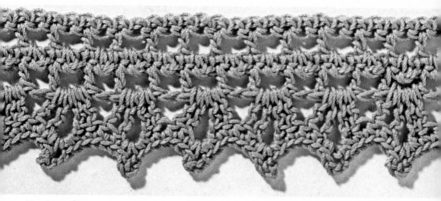

Border no 1

Border no 2

Border no 1

Make a foundation ch to required length.

Row 1: 1 sc in second ch from hook, sc into each remaining ch.

Row 2: Ch 3, * skip 1 st, 1 dc on next st, ch 1.* Rep from * to *, ending with 1 dc.

Row 3: Ch 1, * 1 sc on dc, 1 dc, 1 sc into ch-1 space*. Rep from * to *, ending with 1 sc.

Row 4: Ch 3, * skip 1 st, 1 dc on next st, ch 1*. Rep from * to *, ending with 1 dc.

Row 5: 1 sl st into first space (2 tr, ch 2, 2 tr) into same space, * skip 1 space (2 tr, ch 2, 2 tr) into next space *. Rep from * to *.

Row 6: Ch 1, 1 sc on each of first 2 tr, * (1 sc, ch 4, 2 sc) into ch-2 space, 1 sc into each of next 4 tr *. Rep from * to *, ending with 2 sc. Fasten off.

Border no 2

Make a foundation ch to required length.

Row 1: 1 sc into 6th ch from hook, * ch 5, skip 2 sts, 1 sc *. Rep from * to *, ending with 1 sc.

Row 2: Ch 3, * 1 sl st into 3 center ch of ch-5 loop, ch 3 *. Rep from * to *.

Row 3: Ch 1, 1 sc into each st to end of row.

Row 4: Ch 1, 5 sc, * ch 12, skip 8 base sts, 6 sc *. Rep from * to *.

Row 5: 1 sc, * on the ch-12 loop work: 5 dc into first 5 ch, 4 dc into next 2 ch, 5 dc into last 5 ch; 1 sc on each of the 6 dc of previous row.* Rep from * to *.

Row 6: Ch 3, skip 1 dc of previous row, * (1 dc into next dc, ch 1, skip 1 dc) twice, 1 tr on dc, ch 1, 2 tr on dc, ch 1, 2 tr, ch 1, 2 tr, ch 1, skip 1 dc of previous row, (1 tr on dc, ch 1, skip 1 dc) twice, 1 tr on tr *. Rep from * to *.

Row 7: Ch 2, * 1 sc on tr, 1 sc into 1 ch 3 times, 1 sc between 2 tr, ch 3, 1 sc into ch-1 separating the 3 groups of tr 5 times, 1 sc on tr, 1 sc into ch-1 3 times *. Rep from * to * on each loop.
Fasten off.

Border no 3

Make a foundation ch to required length.

Row 1: Into 4th ch from hook work * 1 dc, ch 1, skip 1 st *. Rep from * to *, ending with 1 dc.

Row 2: Ch 1, * ch 7, skip 1 dc, 1 sc into next dc *. Rep from * to *.

Row 3: Work 10 sc into each ch-7 loop.

Row 4: 1 sl st on first 5 dc, to bring working st to top of loop, * ch 7, 1 sl st into center top of next loop *. Rep from * to *, ending with 1 sl st into first of 10 sc of previous row.

Row 5: Ch 3, 3 dc into first ch-7 loop of previous row, * ch 2, 4 dc into next ch-7 loop *. Rep from * to *.

Row 6: ch 5, 3 dc into first ch-2 loop of previous row, * ch 2, 4 dc into next ch-2 loop *. Rep from * to *.

Row 7: Ch 3, * 3 unfinished tr into next ch-2 loop, yo, draw loop through all 4 loops on hook, ch 3, 1 sl st in middle of the 4 dc of previous row, ch 3 *. Rep from * to * but making 4 unfinished tr instead of 3.
Fasten off.

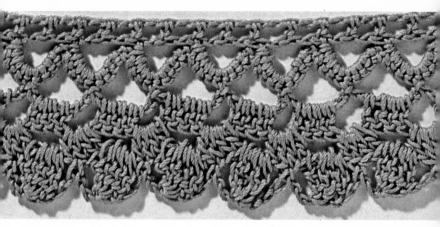

Border no 3

Border no 4

Make a foundation ch to required length.

Row 1: 1 sc into second ch from hook, 1 sc into each remaining ch.

Row 2: Starting in second ch from hook, work * 1 dc, ch 1, skip 1 *. Rep from * to * to end of row.

Row 3: *(1 dc into ch-1 of previous row, ch 1) 9 times, ch 5, skip 5 sts *. Rep from * to * to end of row.

Row 4: *(1 dc into ch-1 of previous row, ch 1) 6 times, (2 dc, ch 1, 2 dc, ch 1, 2 dc, ch 1) into ch-5 loop *. Rep from * to * to end of row.

Row 5: *(1 dc into ch-1, ch 1) 5 times, on the dc worked in the center of the ch sts work 1 dc on first dc, 2 dc on second dc, ch 1, 1 dc on first dc of second group, 2 dc on next dc, ch 1, 1 dc on next dc, 2 dc on second dc of 3rd group, ch 1 *. Rep from * to * to end of row.

Row 6: *(1 dc into ch-1 of previous row, ch 1) 3 times, on the 3 dc of previous row work 4 dc as follows: 1 dc on first dc, 2 dc on center dc, 1 dc on 3rd dc of first group; ch 1, rep twice more, ch 1 *. Rep from * to * to end of row.

Row 7: * 1 dc into ch-1 of previous row, ch 1, 1 dc into next ch, ch 1, 5 dc on next 4 dc of first group as follows: 1 dc on each of first 2 dc, 2 dc on 3rd dc, 1 dc on 4th dc; ch 1, 5 dc on 4 center dc, ch 1, 5 dc on last group, ch 1 *.

Rep from * to * to end of row.

Row 8: * 1 sc into ch between 1 dc and the next, 1 dc into each of next 5 dc, 1 sc into next ch, 5 dc into 5 center dc, 1 dc into next ch, 5 dc on 3rd dc group *. Rep from * to * to end of row.

Row 9: * 1 sc on dc, ch 4 *. Rep from * to * to end of row.

Fasten off.

Border no 5

Make a foundation ch to required length.

Row 1: 1 sc into second ch from hook, 1 sc into each remaining ch.

Row 2: * 2 dc, ch 1, skip 1 base st *. Rep from * to * to end of row.

Row 3: * 1 sc on dc, 1 tr on next st, 1 dc and 1 tr into ch, ch 3, skip 2 dc*. Rep from * to * to end of row.

Row 4: * 1 sc on tr, ch 6 *. Rep from * to * to end of row.

Row 5: *(1 dc, 6 tr, 1 dc) into each ch-6 loop *. Rep from * to * to end of row.

Row 6: 1 sc, ch 4 into each st *. Rep from * to * to end of row.

Fasten off.

Border no 6

Make a foundation ch to required length.

Row 1: * 1 dc, ch 1, skip 1 ch *. Rep from * to * to end of row.

Row 2: *(1 dc, ch 2, 1 dc) into first ch loop of previous row, ch 3, skip 3 sps (1 tr, ch 5, 1 tr) into next ch loop, skip 3 sps *. Rep from * to * to end of row.

Row 3: *(1 dc, ch 2, 1 dc) into ch-2 loop (4 tr, ch 5, 4 tr) into ch-5 loop*. Rep from * to * to end of row.

Row 4: *(1 dc, ch 3, 1 dc) into ch-2 loop (4 tr, ch 5, 4 tr) into ch-5 loop*. Rep from * to * to end of row.

Fasten off.

Border no 3

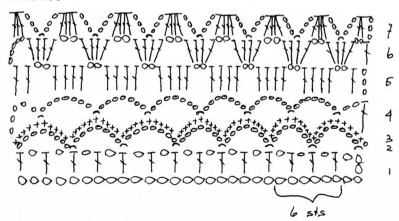

6 sts

136

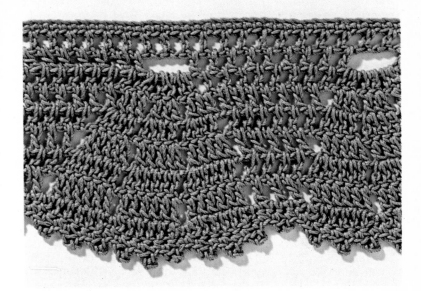

Border no 4

Border no 5

Border no 6

Border no 7

Border no 8

Border no 9

Border no 7

Make a foundation ch to required length.
Row 1: 1 sc into second ch from hook, 1 sc into each remaining ch.
Row 2: * 3 dc, ch 3, skip 3 sts *. Rep from * to * to end of row.
Row 3: * 1 sc into first ch loop, ch 3, 3 dc, ch 2, 3 dc into second ch loop, ch 3 *. Rep from * to * to end of row.
Row 4: * 1 sc on sc of previous row, ch 4 (3 dc, ch 2, 3 dc) into ch-2 loop, ch 4 *. Rep from * to * to end of row.
Row 5: *(2 dc, ch 2, 2 dc) on sc of previous row, ch 3 (1 dc, ch 1) 6 times, ch 3 *. Rep from * to * to end of row.
Row 6: * (1 dc, ch 2, 1 dc) into ch-2 loop of previous row, ch 1, 1 dc on next dc (ch 1, 1 dc on next base st) 10 times, ch 1 *. Rep from * to * to end of row.
Row 7: * 1 sc into ch-2 loop, ch 4, skip 1 loop *. Rep from * to * to end of row.
Fasten off.

Border no 8

Make a foundation ch to required length.
Row 1: 1 sc into second ch from hook, 1 dc into each remaining ch.
Row 2: * (1 tr, ch 3, 1 tr) into same base ch, skip 2 sts, 2 tr, skip 2 sts *. Rep from * to * to end of row.
Row 3: * 2 tr into ch-3 loop of previous row (1 tr, ch 3, 1 tr) into space between 2 tr *. Rep from * to * to end of row.
Row 4: * (1 tr, ch 1) into ch-3 loop 3 times, 1 tr, 1 sc into space between next 2 tr *. Rep from * to * to end of row.
Row 5: * 4 sc, ch 3, 1 sc *. Rep from * to * to end of row.
Fasten off.

Border no 9

Make a foundation ch to required length.
Row 1: 1 sc into second ch from hook, 1 sc into each remaining ch.
Row 2: * 1 sc, ch 5, skip 5 ch *. Rep from * to * to end of row.
Row 3: * 3 dc into ch-5 loop, 3 dc into second loop, ch 4 *. Rep from * to * to end of row.
Row 4: * ch 3, 7 dc into ch-4 loop *. Rep from * to * to end of row.
Row 5: * ch 3, 7 dc into ch-3 loop. Rep from * to * to end of row.
Fasten off.

Border no 10

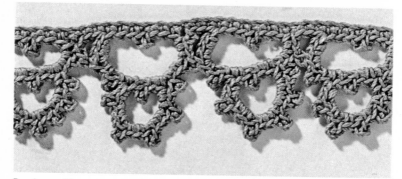

Border no 11

Border no 10

Make a foundation ch to required length.

Row 1: 1 sc into second ch from hook, 1 sc into each remaining ch.

Row 2: * 1 sc, ch 5, skip 5 sts *. Rep from * to * to end of row.

Row 3: * 1 sc into first ch-5 loop, ch 5, 1 sc into second loop *. Rep from * to * to end of row.

Row 4: * 5 dc into ch-5 loop, ch 3, 1 sl st into top of last dc worked (1 picot) 4 dc into same ch-5 loop, 1 sc into dc of previous row *. Rep from * to * to end of row.

Fasten off.

Border no 11

Make a foundation ch to required length.

Row 1: Starting in second ch from hook, work 3 sc, 1 picot (ch 3 and 1 sl st into the first of them), 3 sc, ch 12. Remove hook from work, insert it in the 3rd st to the right of picot, replace working st (of 12th ch) on hook and work 1 sl st. Into the loop thus formed, work 3 sc, 1 picot, 3 sc, 1 picot, 4 sc, 1 picot, 2 sc. Ch 10, remove hook and insert it in the middle of 4 sc just worked, replace working st (of 10th ch) on hook and work 1 sl st. Into the new loop work

(3 sc, 1 picot) 5 times. This will bring work back to the loop underneath. Into this work 2 sc, 1 picot, 3 sc, 1 picot, 3 sc. This will bring work back to the base ch *. Into this work 6 sc (1 into next 6 ch), 1 picot, 3 sc, ch 12, insert hook into 3rd st to the right of the picot, 1 sl st. Into the new loop formed work 3 sc, ch 2, make a link with the picot on nearby loop, ch 1, 3 sc, 1 picot, 4 sc, 1 picot, 2 sc. Ch 10, insert hook in the middle of 4 sc just worked, 1 sl st. Into the new loop formed work (3 sc, 1 picot) 5 times. Return to underneath loop with 2 sc, 1 picot, 3 sc, 1 picot, 3 sc. Work will now be back to the base chain *. Rep from * to * until all base ch have been worked.
Fasten off.

Border no 12

Make a foundation ch to required length.
Row 1: 1 sc into second ch from hook, 1 sc into each remaining ch. Ch 3, turn.
Row 2: * Skip 1 st, 1 dc, 1 dc into skipped st (yo, insert hook into st just skipped, yo, draw yarn through to front and complete as for normal dc), ch 1 *. Rep from * to * to end of row.
Row 3: Ch 3, * dc into ch-1, 1 dc into preceding dc (i.e. second dc skipped on previous row)*.
Row 4: * 1 sc between first and second groups of crossed dc, ch 7, skip 8 dc. *.
Row 5: *(1 tr, ch 1, 1 tr) into ch-7 loop, ch 2 (1 tr, ch 1, 1 tr, ch 3, 1 tr, ch 1, 1 tr) into next ch-7 loop, ch 2 *.
Row 6: * 1 sc into ch between the 2 tr, ch 2 (1 tr, ch 2, 1 tr) into next ch loop (1 tr, ch 1) 5 times into next ch-3 loop, 1 tr into next ch, ch 2 *.
Row 7: * 1 sc and 1 picot into each ch loop* (picot = ch 3 and 1 sc into first ch).
Fasten off.

Border no 12

141

Border no 13 with corners

Make a foundation ch to required length.

Row 1: 1 sc into second ch from hook, 1 sc into each remaining ch, working 3 sc into 1 sc where corners are to be made.

Row 2: * 1 dc, ch 3, skip 1 sc *. Rep from * to * to end of row.

Row 3: * 1 sc into center of ch-3 loop of previous row, ch 2, 7 tr into center of next ch-3 loop, ch 2 *. Rep from * to * working 9 tr into the corners.

Row 4: * ch 3, 1dc on sc of previous row, ch 3 (1 tr, ch 1) 7 times*. Rep from * to * on sides, working (1 tr, ch 1) 9 times on each corner.

Row 5: * 1 tr on tr, ch 3 *. Rep from * to * across entire row, including the corners.

Row 6: (3 sc, 1 picot [see Border no 12, row 7]) into every ch-3 loop. Fasten off.

Border no 13 with corner

Trimmings

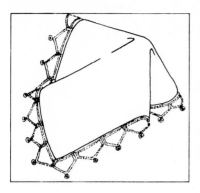

Trimming no 1 with corner

Trimming no 1 with corners

Make a foundation ch to required length.
Row 1: 1 sc into second ch from hook, sc into each remaining ch.
Row 2: sc, working 3 sc into 1 sc where corners are to be made.
Row 3: 1 sc, ch 5, * skip 3 sc, 1 sc into next sc, ch 5 *. Rep from * to * on sides, working an extra sc and ch 5 into central sc on each corner.
Row 4: (3 sc, 1 picot, 3 sc) into each ch-5 loop (picot = ch 3 and 1 sl st into first ch).
Fasten off.

Trimming no 2 with corner

Trimming no 2 with corners

Make a foundation ch to required length.
Row 1: 1 sc into second ch from hook, 1 sc into each remaining ch.
Row 2: sc, working 3 sc into 1 sc where corners are to be made.
Row 3: Ch 7, * skip 3 sts, 1 tr, ch 4 (3 unfinished tr, yo, draw yarn through all 4 loops on hook) into next st *. Rep from * to * on sides but on central st of each corner work ch 4, 3 unfinished tr, yo, draw yarn through all 4 loops on hook.
Row 4: * (1 sc, ch 3, 1 sc) into each ch-4 loop, 1 sl st between tr and tr cluster *. Fasten off.

Trimming no 3 with corners

Make a foundation ch to required length.

Row 1: 1 sc into second ch from hook, 1 sc into each remaining ch.

Row 2: Sc, working 3 sc into 1 sc where corners are to be made.

Row 3: * ch 4, skip 2 sts, 1 sc into next st *. Rep from * to * on sides but for each corner work 1 sc on st preceding central corner st, ch 4, 1 sc on st immediately following corner st.

Row 4: (ch 3, 2 dc, 1 picot [ch 3 and 1 sc on last dc worked], 3 dc) into first ch-4 loop (corner loop), * 1 sc into center of next ch-4 loop, 1 motif (3 dc, 1 picot, 3 dc) into next ch-4 loop *. Rep from * to * on each side. Fasten off.

Trimming no 3 with corner

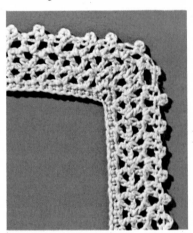

Trimming no 4 with corner

Trimming no 4 with corners

Make a foundation ch to required length.

Row 1: 1 sc on second ch from hook, 1 sc in each remaining ch.

Row 2: Sc, working 3 sc into 1 sc where corners are to be made.

Row 3: * Skip 2 sts, 1 scallop (1 dc, ch 2, 1 dc) into next st *. Rep from * to * on all sides but work 1 scallop, ch 2 and 1 scallop on central sc at each corner.

Row 4: * 1 scallop between 1 scallop and the next of previous row*.

Rep from * to * on the sides. At each corner work (ch 2, 1 scallop) twice into central ch-2 loop, ch 2.

Row 5: * 2 dc, 1 picot (ch 3 and 1 sl st into last dc worked) *.

Rep from * to * into each ch-2 loop. Fasten off.

Trimming no 5 with corners

Make a foundation ch to required length.

Row 1: 1 sc on second ch from hook, 1 sc in each remaining ch.

Row 2: Ch 9, * skip 2 sts (1 dtr, ch 2,

1 dtr) into next st *. Rep from * to *
on each side. Where corners are to
be made, work (1 dtr, ch 2, 1 dtr) 3
times into same st.
Row 3: Ch 4 * (4 unfinished dtr), yo,
draw yarn through all loops on hook,
ch 2) into each ch-2 loop*.
Row 4: * 3 sc into ch-2 loop, 1 sc into
top of dtr cluster, 1 picot (picot = ch
3 and 1 sl st into first ch)*.
Fasten off.

Trimming no 6 with corners

Make a foundation ch to required
length.
Row 1: 1 sc in second ch, 1 sc in
each remaining ch.
Row 2: Sc, working 3 sc into 1 sc
where corners are to be made.
Row 3: * Ch 5, skip 4 sts, 1 sc on
next st, ch 5, skip 4 sts, 1 dc into next
st, ch 3, 1 dc *. Rep from * to * on
each side but work 1 dc, ch 3, 1 dc on
central sc at each corner.

Trimming no 5 with corner

Row 4: * 6 sc into ch-5 loop, 1 sl st
on next sc, 6 sl st into next ch-5 loop
(1 hdc, 1 picot [ch 3 and 1 sl st into
first ch]) into next ch-3 loop, 1 hdc *.
Rep from * to * on straight sides but
work (1 hdc, 1 picot) 3 times and 1
hdc into each corner ch-3 loop.
Fasten off.

Trimming no 7 with corners

Make a foundation ch to required
length.
Row 1: Sc across.
Row 2: Sc, working 3 sc into st
where corners are required.
Row 3: * 1 dc, ch 2, skip 2 sts * along
each side, working (1 dc, ch 2, 1 dc)
into center st on each corner.

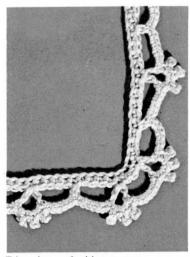

Trimming no 6 with corner

Row 4: * Ch 7, 1 sc into 4th ch from hook, ch 5, 1 sc into same 4th ch, ch 4 and 1 sc into same 4th ch (3 picots made), ch 3, skip 1 dc of previous row, 1 sc into next dc *. Rep from * to * to end of row.
Fasten off.

Trimming no 8 with corners

Make a foundation ch to required length.
Row 1: 1 sc into second ch, 1 sc in each remaining ch.
Row 2: Sc, working 3 sc into 1 sc where corners are to be made.
Row 3: * ch 3, skip 2 sts, 2 unfinished dc, yo, draw yarn through all 3 loops on hook, 1 picot (picot = ch 3 and 1 sl st into first ch), skip 2 sts *.
Rep from * to * on sides but turn corners as follows: on first of 3 sc work ch 2, 2 unfinished dc, yo, draw yarn through; on central sc work 1 picot, ch 2, 1 dc; on 3rd sc work 1 picot, ch 2, 1 dc.
Fasten off.

Trimming no 9 with corners

Make a foundation ch to required length.
Row 1: 1 sc into second ch, 1 sc in each remaining ch.
Row 2: 1 sc, ch 3, 1 sc, ch 3, 1 sc into 1 sc where corners are to be made, * 8 sc, ch 3 *. Rep from * to * on sides.
Row 3: *(1 tr, ch 7, 1 tr) into first ch-3 loop, 1 petal (petal = ch 4, and into first of these ch work 2 unfinished tr, yo, draw yarn through all loops on hook) *. Rep from * to * on sides but turn corners as follows: into first ch-3 corner loop work 1 tr, ch 7, 1 tr, ch 1, into second ch-3 corner loop work 1 tr, ch 7, 1 tr.
Fasten off.

Trimming no 7 with corner

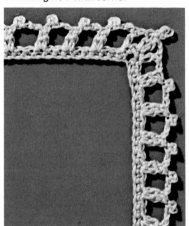

Trimming no 8 with corner

Trimming no 10 with corners

Make a foundation ch to required length.
Row 1: 1 sc into second ch from hook, 1 sc into each remaining ch.
Row 2: Sc, working 3 sc into 1 sc where corners are to be made.
Row 3: * (1 sc, ch 3, 3 dc) into 1 st, skip 2 sts *. Rep from * to * to end of row. Fasten off.

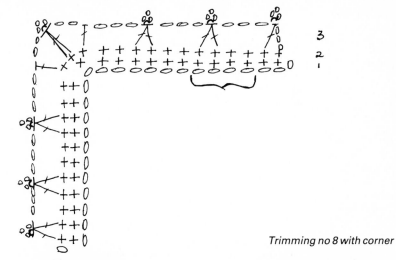

3
2
1

Trimming no 8 with corner

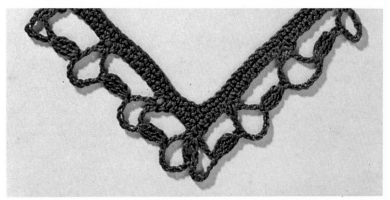

Trimming no 9 with corner

Trimming no 10 with corner

Edgings

Edging no 1

Edging no 2

Edging no 1

Ch 4.

Row 1: (2 dc, ch 2, 2 dc) on first ch, ch 5.

Row 2: (2 dc, ch 2, 2 dc) into ch-2 loop of previous row, ch 5.

Row 3: (2 dc, ch 2, 2 dc, ch 2, 4 dc) into ch-2 loop of previous row, 1 dc into last of 4 dc of previous row, 3 dc into ch-5 loop, ch 10.

Row 4: 4 dc on 4 dc of previous row, ch 2, 1 dc on next dc, ch 2 (2 dc, ch 2, 2 dc) into ch-2 loop, ch 5.

Row 5: (2 dc, ch 2, 2 dc) into ch-2 loop of previous row, ch 2, 1 dc on 4th of 2 dc, ch 2, 1 dc on next dc, ch 2, 3 dc into next ch-2 loop, 1 dc on first of 4 dc of previous row, ch 2, 16 dc into ch-10 loop (made at the end of Row 3), ch 5, 1 dc into ch-5 loop made in Row 1, 2 ch.

Row 6: 1 dc on 3rd of 5 ch, 1 dc on first of 16 dc, * 1 picot (picot = ch 5 and 1 sc into first ch), skip 1 st, 1 dc on next st *. Rep from * to * on the 16 dc, 4 dc into ch-2 loop, ch 2, 1 dc on next dc, ch 2, 1 dc on next dc, ch 2, 1 dc on next dc, ch 2, 1 dc on first of 4 dc of previous row, ch 2 (2 dc, ch 2, 2 dc) into next ch-2 loop, ch 5.

Rows 7 & 8: As Row 2.

Row 9: As Row 3.

Row 10: As Row 4.

When the edging is complete, work 1 row on the side which will be attached to the fabric as follows: 1 sc into center of ch-5 loop, ch 5.

Row 4: As Row 2.
Row 5: As Row 1.
Row 6: As Row 2.
Row 7: As Row 1.
Row 8: As Row 2, continuing with ch 14, 1 sl st into 3rd starting ch of Row 5, ch 2, 1 sc into first starting ch of Row 5. Turn.

Row 9: 24 dc into 14-ch loop, 18 dc.

Row 10: * 3 dc, ch 2, skip 2 sts *. Rep from * to * twice more; 3 dc, * ch 2, skip 1 dc, 1 dc into next st *. Rep from * to * 11 times more; ch 2, 1 sl st into 3rd starting ch of Row 3, ch 1, 1 sc into first ch of Row 3. Turn.

Row 11: * 2 dc into each ch-2 loop and 1 dc on each dc *.

Row 12: * 3 dc, ch 2, skip 2 sts *. Rep from * to * twice, 3 dc; * ch 2, skip 1 dc, 1 dc into next st *. Rep from * to * 18 times more, ch 1, 1 sl st into 3rd starting ch of Row 1. Turn.

Row 13: Ch 1, 1 sc into first ch-1 loop, 1 sc, * 1 picot (picot = ch 3, 1 sl st into first ch), 1 sc, 1 picot, 1 sc *, 1 sc into next loop, 1 sc. Rep from Row 2.

Edging no 2

Ch 18.

Row 1: 18 dc (Replace first dc of each row with ch 3).

Row 2: * 3 dc, ch 2, skip 2 sts *. Rep from * to * twice more, 3 dc.

Row 3: As Row 1.

Edging no 3

Ch 14.

Row 1: 1 tr into 9th ch from hook, ch 8, 1 sc into last ch. (Turn the work on each row.)

Row 2: ch 1, 11 sc into 8-ch loop, 1 sc on dtr, ch 1, 1 sc into second ch, ch 4.

Row 3: 1 dc into sc of previous row (ch 2, skip 1 base st, 1 sc into next st) 4 times, ch 4, 1 sc, ch 6.

Row 4: 1 sc into ch-4 loop, ch 5 and 1 sc into each ch-2 loop, ch 1, 1 sc on dc of previous row, ch 1, 1 sc into second ch, ch 6.

Row 5: 1 tr on second sc of previous row, ch 8, skip 1 loop, 1 sc into next ch loop.

Rep Rows 2–5.

Edging no 4

Ch 15.

Row 1: 12 dc, ch 1, skip 1 st, 2 dc. Turn.

Row 2: Ch 3, skip first st, 1 dc, ch 1, skip 1 st, 2 dc, ch 8, skip 9 sts, 1 scallop on last st (scallop = [1 dc, ch 2] 3 times, 1 dc all into the same st). Turn.

Row 3: 1 petal (petal = 1 sc, 1 hdc, 3 dc, 1 hdc, 1 sc all into same place) into each of 3 loops on scallop, ch 6, 1 dc into 7th ch, 1 dc into 8th ch, 2 dc on next 2 dc, ch 1, skip 1 ch, 2 dc. Turn.

Row 4: Ch 3, skip 1 st, 1 dc, ch 1, skip 1 st, 4 dc on 4 dc, 1 dc on first ch, 1 dc on second ch, ch 8, 1 scallop on second dc in center of second petal. Turn.

Row 5: 1 scallop into each of the 3 ch-2 loops, ch 6, 1 dc on 7th ch, 1 dc on 8th ch, 6 dc on 6 dc, ch 1, skip 1 st, 2 dc. Turn.

Row 6: Ch 3, skip 1 st, 1 dc, ch 1, skip 1 st, 8 dc on 8 dc, 1 dc on first ch, 1 dc on second ch, ch 8, 1 scallop on second dc of second petal. Turn.

Row 7: 3 scallops into 3 ch-2 loops, ch 6, 2 dc on 7th and 8th ch, 10 dc on 10 dc (12 dc in all), ch 1, skip 1 st, 2 dc. Turn.

Rep Rows 2–7.

Edging no 3

Edging no 4

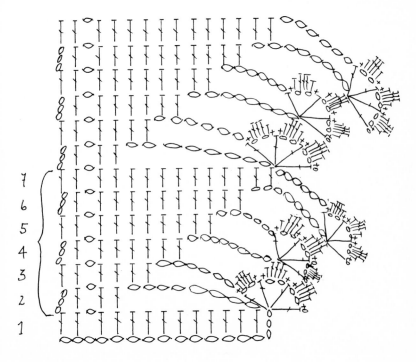

Edging no 4

Edging no 5

Edging no 6

Edging no 5

Ch 12.
Row 1: 1 sc into 8th ch from hook, ch 5, skip 3 ch (1 dc, ch 3, 1 dc) into last base ch. Turn.
Row 2: Ch 3, 9 dc into first ch loop of previous row, 1 sc into next loop, ch 5, 1 sc into last loop. Turn.
Row 3: Ch 7, 1 sc into first ch loop, ch 5, 1 dc into 5th of 9 dc of previous row, ch 3, 1 dc. Turn.
Repeat from Row 2.

Edging no 6

Ch 11.
Row 1: 1 dc into 5th ch from hook, ch 2 (1 dc, ch 2, 1 dc) into same st. (3 loops). Turn.
Row 2: Ch 1 (1 sc, 3 dc, 1 sc) into each of the 3 ch-2 loops, ch 3, 1 dc into 3rd ch. Turn.
Row 3: Ch 7, 1 dc into second dc of middle loop (ch 2, 1 dc) 3 times into same st. Turn.
Rep from Row 2.

Edging with chain lace crochet

Ch 23.
Row 1: Starting from the 7th ch from hook work 12 dc, ch 4, skip 4 ch, 1 sc. Ch 6, turn.
Row 2: 1 sc into first ch loop, ch 4, skip 2 dc, 9 dc in between dc of previous row. Ch 4, turn.
Row 3: Skip 2 sts, 6 dc in between dc of previous row, ch 4, 1 sc into ch-4 loop, ch 4, 1 sc into turning ch loop. Ch 6, turn.
Row 4: 1 sc into ch loop of previous

row, ch 4, 1 sc into next ch, ch 4, skip 2 dc, 3 dc in between dc of previous row. Ch 6, turn.

Row 5: 1 sc into first ch loop of previous row, ch 4, 1 sc into next ch loop, ch 4, 1 sc into next ch loop. Ch 6, turn.

Row 6: 1 sc into first ch loop, ch 4, 1 sc into next ch loop, ch 4, 3 dc into next ch loop.

Row 7: Ch 8, 1 dc into 7th ch from hook, 1 dc into next ch loop, 2 dc on dc, 2 dc into ch loop, ch 4, 1 sc into next ch. Ch 6, turn.

Row 8: 1 sc into ch loop, ch 4, 2 dc into next ch loop, 5 dc on dc, 2 dc into starting dc of previous row.

Row 9: Ch 8, 1 dc into 7th ch from hook, 1 dc into next ch, 8 dc in between dc of previous row, 2 dc into ch loop, ch 4, 1 sc into next ch loop. Ch 6, turn.

Rep Rows 2–9 until required length is achieved.

To complete the scalloped edge, work as follows:—

(2 dc, ch 3, 2 dc, ch 3, 2 dc) into ch loop at point of scallop (2 dc, ch 3, 2 dc) into loop at side on 6 dc row (Row 3); 1 sc on dc at side on 3 dc row (Row 4); ch 1, 1 sc into next dc at side on 3 dc row (Row 6); (2 dc, ch 3, 2 dc) into ch loop on 6 dc row (Row 7). Rep from * to * for entire length.

Row 2: 1 sc into a loop of 3 dc, * ch 6, 1 sc into first ch loop, 1 sc into next ch loop *. Rep from * to * for entire length.

Fasten off.

Rejoin yarn at top right hand corner of edging, right side facing, and work 1 row of sc along entire length.

Edging with fan design

Edging with chain lace crochet

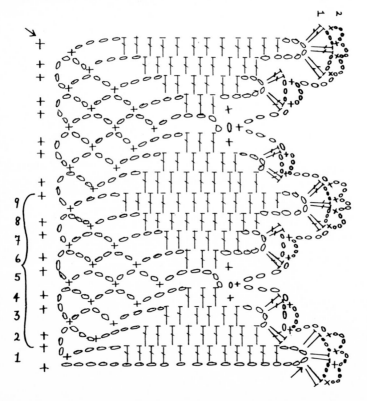

Edging with fan design

Ch 20.
Row 1: 1 dc into 8th ch from hook, 2 dc, ch 2, skip 2 sts, 3 dc. Ch 5, turn.
Row 2: 3 dc into ch-2 loop, ch 2, skip 3 dc, 3 dc into starting ch loop of previous row. Ch 5, turn.
Row 3: 3 dc into 3 ch, ch 2, skip 3 dc, 3 dc into ch, ch 10, 1 sc into first of the 20 foundation ch. Ch 2, turn.
(When working subsequent fans, link the ch-10 with a sc into the 4th picot of the previous fan.)
Row 4: 14 dc into ch-10 loop, ch 2, skip 3 dc, 3 dc into ch-2 loop, ch 2, skip 3 dc, 3 dc into base ch. Ch 5, turn.
Row 5: Skip 3 dc, 3 dc into ch-2 loop, ch 2, skip 3 dc, 3 dc into ch-2 loop, 14 dc worked by inserting hook in between 14 dc of previous row. Ch 2, turn.

(When working subsequent fans, after the 14 dc work 1 sc into the 7th picot of previous fan.)
Row 6: (1 dc, ch 1) 14 times, worked by inserting hook between 14 dc of previous row, ch 2, skip 3 dc, 3 dc into next ch loop, ch 2, 3 dc into next ch loop. Ch 5, turn.
Row 7: skip 3 dc of previous row, 3 dc into ch loop, ch 2, skip 3 dc, 3 dc into next ch loop, ch 1 (1 tr into ch-1, (ch 1) 14 times. Ch 2, turn.
(When working subsequent fans, after the 14 dc work 1 sc into the 9th picot of previous fan).
Row 8: * Ch 4, 1 sc into first ch, 1 sc on next tr of previous row *. Rep from * to * another 15 times, also working picots on the last 3 sts; ch 2, 3 dc into ch loop, ch 2, skip 3 dc into next ch loop. Ch 5, turn.
Row 9: 3 dc into ch loop, ch 2, skip 3 dc, 3 dc into ch-2 loop. Ch 5, turn.
Rep from Row 2.

Insertions

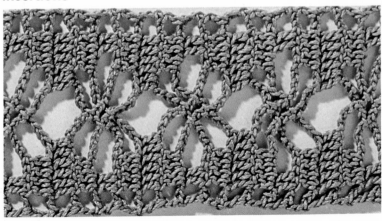

Insertion no 1

Insertion no 1

Ch 26.
Row 1: Starting on the 8th ch from hook work 6 dc, ch 9, skip 4 ch, 6 dc, ch 2, skip 2 ch, 1 dc into last ch. Turn.
Row 2: Ch 5 (= 1 dc plus ch 2), 4 dc on dc, ch 6, skip 2 dc, 1 sl st into 5th of ch-9 loop, ch 6, skip 2 dc, 4 dc on dc, ch 2, 1 dc into 3rd starting ch of previous row. Turn.
Row 3: Ch 5 (= 1 dc plus ch 2), 2 dc on dc, ch 6, skip 2 dc, 1 sl st into 5th ch of ch-6 loop, ch 3, 1 sl st into second ch of next ch-6 loop, ch 6, skip 2 dc, 2 dc on the 2 dc, ch 2, 1 dc into 3rd starting ch of previous row. Turn.
Row 4: Ch 5, 2 dc on dc, 2 dc on first 2 ch of ch-6 loop, ch 6, 1 sl st into second ch of ch-3 loop, ch 6, 2 dc on last 2 ch of ch-6 loop, 2 dc on dc, ch 2, 1 dc into 3rd starting ch of previous row. Turn.
Row 5: Ch 5, 4 dc on dc, 2 dc on first 2 ch of ch-6 loop, ch 9, 2 dc on last 2 ch of ch-6 loop, 4 dc on dc, ch 2, 1 dc into 3rd starting ch of previous row. Turn.
Rep from Row 2 for required length.

Insertion no 2

Ch 12.
Row 1: Starting on 4th ch from hook work 4 dc, ch 4, skip 4 ch, 1 dc into last ch, ch 3. Turn.
Row 2 and all following rows: 4 dc into ch-4 loop, ch 4, skip 4 dc, 1 dc into last ch, ch 3. Turn.
When required length has been reached, complete the 2 sides as follows:
Starting on second ch of 3 turning ch loop, work lengthwise:
* 1 tr, ch 4, 1 tr * into each space between the tr blocks, which will be at right-angles to this row.
Fasten off and work the other side in the same way.

Insertion no 3

Ch 20.
Row 1: Starting on 8th ch from hook work 1 dc, 2 ch, skip 2 ch, 4 dc, ch 2, skip 2 ch, 1 dc, ch 2, skip 2 ch, 1 dc into last ch. Turn.
Row 2: Ch 5 (= 1 dc plus 2 ch), 1 dc on dc, ch 2, 4 dc on dc, 2 dc on 2 ch, 1 dc on next dc, ch 2, 1 dc into 3rd starting ch of previous row, ch 10. Turn.
Row 3: Starting on 8th ch from hook work 1 dc, ch 2, skip 2 sts, 1 dc on next dc, 2 dc on 2 ch, 1 dc on first of next 7 dc, ch 2, skip 2 sts, ch 2, skip 2 sts, 1 dc. Turn.
Rep Rows 2 and 3 as required.

Insertion no 2

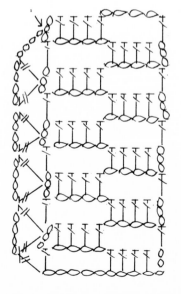

2

1

Insertion no 2

Insertion no 4

Ch 30.

Row 1: Starting on 6th ch from hook work 1 sc, ch 5, skip 5 ch, * 1 sc, ch 5, skip 5 ch *. Rep from * to *, ending with 1 sc, ch 5. Turn.

Row 2: * 1 sc into 3rd of 5 ch, ch 5 *. Rep from * to *, ending with 1 sc, ch 5. Turn.

Rows 3-7: As Row 2.

Row 8: Work loops as in Row 2 but when second loop has been made work 1 sc into next loop, ch 3, 4 dc into next loop, ch 3, 1 sc into next loop, ch 5. Turn.

Row 9: Work loops as in Row 2. Into loop preceding 4 dc group work ch 3, 4 dc into ch-3 loop, ch 3, 4 dc into next ch-3 loop, ch 3, continue with loops.

Row 10: Work loops as in Row 2. Rep central motif from Row 8 of 4 dc between the 2 dc groups of previous row.

Row 11: As Row 2.

Rep Rows 2–11 as required.

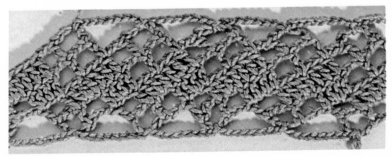

Insertion no 3

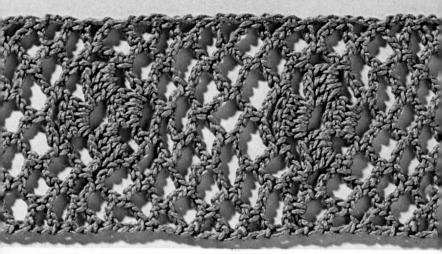

Insertion no 4

Insertion no 5

Insertion no 5

Ch 18.

Row 1: Starting on 6th ch from hook work 2 dc, ch 3, skip 3 ch (1 dc, ch 2, 1 dc) into next ch, ch 3, skip 3 ch, 2 dc, ch 1, skip 1 ch, 1 dc, ch 4. Turn.

Row 2: 2 dc on dc, ch 3 (2 dc, ch 2, 2 dc) into ch-2 loop, ch 3, 2 dc on dc, ch 1, 1 dc into 3rd starting ch of previous row. Turn.

Row 3: 2 dc on dc, ch 3 (1 dc, ch 2, 1 dc) into ch-2 loop, ch 3, 2 dc on dc, ch 1, 1 dc into 3rd starting ch of previous row. Turn.

Rep rows 2 and 3 as required.

Insertion no 6

Ch 30.

Row 1: Starting on 8th ch from hook work 1 dc, ch 2, 8 dc, ch 2, 8 dc, ch 1, 1 dc, ch 2, 1 dc. Ch 5, turn.

Row 2: 1 dc on 2nd dc, ch 2 on first 4 of 8 dc, ch 5, 1 dc into ch-2 loop, ch 5, skip 4 dc, 4 dc on next 4 dc, ch 2, 1 dc, ch 2, 1 dc on 3rd of 5 starting ch of previous row. Ch 5, turn.

Row 3: 1 dc, ch 2, 2 dc on first 2 dc of previous row, ch 5, 1 sc into 3rd ch of previous row, ch 5, 1 sc into next 3rd ch, ch 5, 2 dc on last 2 dc, ch 2, 1 dc, ch 2, 1 dc into 3rd of 5 starting ch. Ch 5. Turn.

Row 4: 1 dc, ch 2, 4 dc, ch 5, 1 dc into 3rd ch, ch 5, 4 dc (working 2 on 4th and 5th ch and the other 2 on the next 2 dc), ch 2, 1 dc, ch 2, 1 dc into 3 ch of 5 starting ch of previous row. Rep from Row 1 as required.

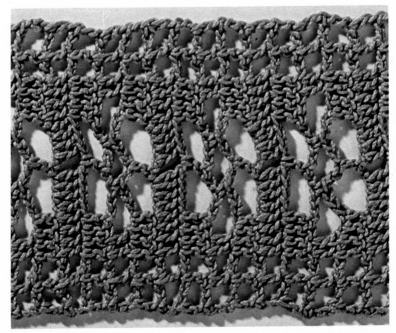

Insertion no 6

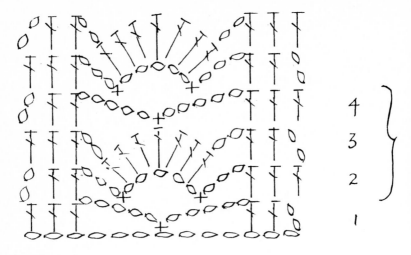

4

3

2

1

Insertion no 7

Insertion no 7

Insertion no 8

Insertion no 7

Ch 13.
Row 1: 3 dc, ch 5, skip 3 ch, 1 sc into next st, skip 3 ch, ch 5, 3 dc. Ch 2. Turn.
Row 2: 3 dc, ch 3, 1 sc into first ch loop, ch 5, 1 sc into 2nd ch loop, ch 3, 3 dc. Ch 2. Turn.
Row 3: 3 dc, ch 2, 7 dc into ch-5 loop, ch 2, 3 dc. Ch 2. Turn.
Row 4: 3 dc, ch 5, 1 sc into 4th of 7 dc, ch 5, 3 dc. Ch 2. Turn.
Rep from Row 2.

Insertion no 8

Make a chain of 12 sts and join with sl st into first ch to form a ring.
Row 1: Ch 1 (= 1 sc), 11 sc into ring, keeping these sts on one half of ring. Turn.

Row 2: Ch 3 (= 1 dc) into first sc (ch 1, 1 dc) into each sc, ending with 1 dc into starting ch of previous row. Turn.
Row 3: Ch 3 (= 1 dc) into first dc (ch 2, 1 dc) into each dc, ending with 1 dc into 3rd starting ch.
Without breaking the yarn, continue as follows:
Ch 12 and join with sl st into first ch to form another ring.
Row 1: Working into only half the ring, on the opposite side to previous ring, ch 1, 11 sc. Turn.
Row 2: Ch 3 into first sc (ch 1, 1 dc) into each dc, ending with 1 dc into starting ch. Work 1 sl st into last dc of Row 2 of previous motif. Do not turn.
Row 3: 1 sl st into last sc of Row 1 of first motif. Turn.
(No turning ch required as work is now level with top of dc) ch 2, 1 dc on each of foll 12 dc *.

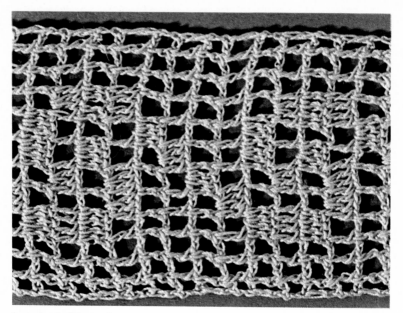

Insertion in filet crochet

Rep from * to * for entire length of insertion, each motif being made on alternate sides of ch rings.
Complete both sides of insertion by working 9 sc into each unworked half ring and 3 sc into each ch-2 loop.

Insertion no 9 in filet crochet

Ch 36 and work as shown in diagram to the required length. Each cross corresponds to 3 dc and each square to ch 2 and 1 dc.

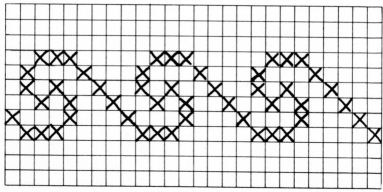

Diagram for the filet insertion

Patterns

GARMENTS AND ACCESSORIES

Creating things to wear

In this chapter we have combined ideas for patterns with some of the stitches described in previous sections. Exactly the same techniques apply whether you are making a square for a patchwork rug or a coat or a baby's garment. The items we have selected here should only be regarded as examples of the limitless variations an enthusiastic crocheter may devise and it is hoped that the suggestions offered will encourage you to adventure into the satisfying realm of designing articles for yourself, your family and friends.

Examples of garments for men, women and children are included, as are ideas for a wide range of accessories such as belts, collars, shopping bags.

For the garments, you will need to select the most suitable yarn and hook using our suggestions as a starting point, and find your gauge (number of sts and rows per inch). You must then determine the number of stitches you will need to work for your desired size. The adult articles have been designed for a medium size. Regard the following section of projects as your workbook for learning how to design.

Blue and white bib no 1

Materials: Crochet Cotton No. 5 in white and blue.
Aluminum crochet hook size 2.
With white cotton ch 30.
Row 1: 28 sc, 3 sc into same st, work 28 sc back on opposite side of ch.
Row 2: 28 sc, 2 sc into next st, 1 sc, 2 sc into next st, 28 sc.
Row 3: 28 sc, 2 sc into next st, 1 sc, 3 sc into next st, 1 sc, 2 sc into next st, 28 sc. Continue in sc for another 8 rows, increasing as in Row 3 into the same sts on each row. At the end of the last row, ch 10 and work a sc into each of them. Make a similar strip on the side. These form the neckband.
With blue cotton continue working as follows:
Row 1: * (1 sc, ch 1, 2 dc) into 1 st, skip 2 sts, * rep from * to *, ending with (1 sc, ch 1, 2 dc) into last st.
Row 2: * (1 sc, ch 1, 2 dc) into the sc of previous row. *
Rep from * to *.
Rep Row 2 for another 8 rows.

(Left) White and blue bib no. 2   (Right) Blue and white bib no. 1

Finish off as follows: * 4 sc, 1 picot (1 picot = ch 3, 1 sc into sc preceding the ch) *. Rep from * to * to end of row.

Fasten off.

Make two cords in white as follows: ch 60, 1 sc into each st.

Fasten off and sew neatly to ends of neckband.

White and blue bib no 2

Materials: Crochet Cotton No. 5 in white and blue.

Aluminum crochet hook size 2.

This is worked back and forth lengthwise.

With white cotton ch 75.

Work 16 rows in sc.

Continue in sc for a further 25 rows working on first 55 sts only.

At the end of last row, ch 20 and work on all 75 sts for another 16 rows (neck opening will have been formed).

Finish the bib off as follows:

Row 1: Sc around outside edge only, working 3 sc into each corner st.

Row 2: With blue cotton work * 3 dc into 1 st, skip 2 sts *.

Continue all round outside bib edge from * to *, working 5 dc into 1 st on each corner.

Rows 3 & 4: With white cotton, as Row 1.

Row 5: As Row 1, but continuing around inside neck edge.

Row 6: Reverse sc around entire edge of bib.

Make 2 cords in white as follows: Ch 60, 1 sc into each st.

Fasten off and sew neatly to each corner of neck opening.

White and red bib

Child's collar no 1

Materials: Crochet Cotton No. 5.
Aluminum crochet hook size B.
Ch 101.
Row 1: skip 1 ch, * 1 dc, ch 1, skip 1 base ch *. Rep from * to * (50 dc).
Row 2: * (2 dc, ch 2, 2 dc) into ch-1 loop, ch 4, skip 2 loops *. Rep from * to * (17 motifs).
Row 3: * (2 dc, ch 2, 2 dc) into ch-2 loop, ch 4 *. Rep from * to *.
Row 4: * (2 dc, ch 2, 2 dc) into ch-2 loop, ch 2, picking up the ch of rows 2 and 3 work 1 sc, ch 3 *. Rep from * to *.
Row 5: As Row 2.
Row 6: As Row 3.
Row 7: As Row 4.
Row 8: * (1 sc, ch 3) 3 times into first loop, 1 sc into second loop, 1 sc into 3rd loop, ch 3 *. Rep from * to *.
Finish off the collar by working along both sides and inside neck edge as follows: 1 row in sc and 1 row in reverse sc.
Fasten off.
Work two cords of 50 ch and sew them neatly to each inside corner of neck opening.

White and red bib

Materials: Crochet Cotton No. 5 in white and red.
Aluminum crochet hook size 2.
With white cotton ch 66.
Row 1: 10 hdc, * 3 hdc into 1 ch, 10 hdc into next 10 ch *. Rep from * to * 5 times – 6 points in all.
Continue working in hdc for another 11 rows, increasing on the central st of each increase in previous row.
Work on the 2 central points only for another 11 rows, still increasing on each increase in previous row.
Finish off as follows:
Row 1: (red cotton) * 3 dc into 1 st, skip 1 st, 1 sc, skip 1 st *. Rep from * to *.
Row 2: (white cotton) sc.
Row 3: Reverse sc.
Make 2 cords in white as follows: ch 60, 1 sc into each st.
Fasten off and sew neatly to each inside corner of neck opening.

Child's collar no. 1

Child's collar no 2

Materials: Crochet Cotton No. 5.
Aluminum crochet hook size B.
Ch 90.
Row 1: starting in second ch from hook, work in sc to end.
Row 2: * 2 dc in 1 st, ch 4, skip 3 sts. *. Rep from * to * 23 times.
Row 3: * 1 sc on first dc of previous row, ch 3, 1 sc on next dc, 4 sc into ch-4 loop. * Rep from * to *.
Row 4: * (3 unfinished tr, yo, draw yarn through all 4 loops on hook, ch 3) 3 times into ch-3 loop, ch 3, 1 sc into next ch-3 loop, ch 3 *. Rep from * to *.
Row 5: * (5 dc, ch 1, 1 4-ch picot, ch 1) into first ch-3 loop of previous row, 5 dc into second loop, ch 4 *. Rep from * to *.
Finish off the collar by working along both sides and inside neck edge as follows: 1 row in sc and 1 row in reverse sc.

Child's collar no. 3

Make 2 cords of 50 ch each and sew them neatly to inside corners of neck opening.

Child's collar no 3

Materials: Crochet Cotton No. 5.
Aluminum crochet hook size 2.
Ch 92.
Row 1: starting in second ch from hook, work in sc to end.
Row 2: * 1 dc, ch 5, skip 4 sc, (2 dc, ch 3, 2 dc) into next st, ch 5, skip 4 sts *. Rep from * to *.
Row 3: 1 sc on dc, ch 4, * 1 sc into ch-5 loop, ch 4, 8 dc into ch-3 loop, ch 4, 1 sc into next ch-5 loop *. Rep from * to *.
Row 4: 1 dc on sc, * ch 4, (1 dc, ch 1) 8 times on dc, ch 4, 1 dc between 2 sc of previous row *. Rep from * to *.
Row 5: 1 sc on dc, * 1 sc into next loop, ch 1, (1 dc, 1 ch-3 picot closed with sl st into dc just worked, ch 1) 8 times, ch 1, 1 sc into next loop *. Rep from * to *.
Work both ends of the collar in sc to link up with start of dc sts and picots. Finish off inside neck edge and both

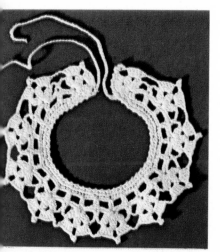

Child's collar no. 2

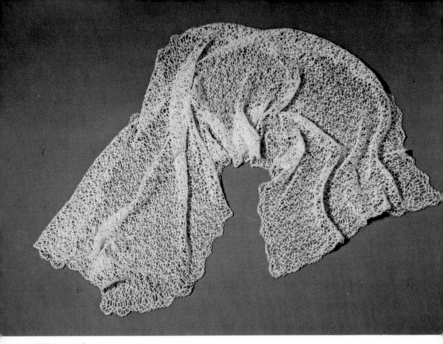

White stole

ends with 1 row of reverse sc.
Make 2 cords of 50 ch each and sew
them neatly to inside corners of neck
opening.

White stole

Materials: 12 oz (300 grams) 2-ply
mohair.
Aluminum crochet hook size 2.
Make a loose ch about 20 in (50 cm)
long.
Row 1: * 1 sc, ch 6, skip 6 ch *. Rep
from * to * to end of row, finishing
with 1 sc.
Row 2: 1 sc, ch 6, skip 1 loop, 1 sc
into second loop, * ch 6, skip 1 loop,
(1 tr, ch 1) 4 times into next loop, skip
1 loop, ch 6, 1 sc into next loop *.
Rep from * to *.

Row 3: * 1 sc on sc, ch 6, 1 sc into
first loop between first and second
tr, ch 6, 1 sc into second loop
between second and 3rd tr, ch 6, 1
sc into 3rd loop between 3rd and 4th
tr, ch 6 *. Rep from * to * to end of
row.
Row 4: Ch 3, * 1 sc, ch 6 *. Rep from
* to * into each loop of previous row.
Row 5: Rep from Row 2, moving the
motif by working the 4 tr into the
loop over the sc, between the 2
groups of dc. Continue repeating
from Row 2 until the stole measures
about 72 in (180 cm).
Complete by working an edging as
follows:
Row 1: * 1 sc, ch 6 *. Rep from * to *
on all 4 sides.
Row 2: * 1 sc into first loop, ch 6, 1
sc into next loop, ch 6, 1 sc into

Mohair scarf

next loop, ch 6, (1 tr ch 4) twice, 1 tr ch 6 *. Rep from * to *, working (1 tr, ch 4) 4 times, 1 tr into each corner loop instead of repeating the tr twice.

Row 3: * 1 sc, ch 6 *. Rep from * to * into each loop of previous row.

Fasten off.

Mohair scarf

Materials: 12 oz (320 grams) 2-ply mohair. Aluminum crochet hook size H.

Stitches used: single crochet, treble, fancy stitch.

Instructions for fancy stitch:

Row 1: * (1 tr, ch 2, 1 tr) into 1 st, skip 3 sts, ch 1, 1 sc, skip 3 sts *.

Row 2: * 1 sc into ch-2 loop, ch 1 (1 tr, ch 2, 1 tr) into 1 sc, ch 1 *.

Row 3: * (1 tr, ch 2, 1 tr) into 1 sc, ch 1, 1 sc into ch-2 loop.

Rep Rows 2 and 3.

Instructions for scarf: ch 60 and work in fancy stitch for about 52 in (130 cm).

To complete scarf, make a fringe of about 10 in (25 cm) on each short side.

To make fringe: cut a number of strands of yarn approximately 20 in (50 cm) long and place them in groups of 3 or 4 strands according to thickness required. With wrong side of edge to be fringed uppermost, insert a crochet hook (several sizes larger than the one used for main work) as near the edge as possible, fold strands in half to form a loop, put loop on hook, pull through edge of work, place hook behind all strands of yarn and draw through loop. Continue in this way along both edges, spacing the groups at regular intervals. If desired each cluster of strands can be divided in half and knotted so that half of one cluster is knotted to half of the next. This gives a very rich effect and makes the scarf hang well.

White triangular shawl

Materials: 18 oz (500 grams) 2-ply mohair. Aluminum crochet hook size H.

Stitches used: lattice stitch (see page 21), double, single crochet.

Center: this consists of 2 equal triangles which are joined with 2 dc into the loops down one side of each triangle. The 2 triangles are placed so that the ch loops of each go in opposite directions.

Triangle: In lattice stitch, make one loop to start, increasing one loop on each row until 23 loops have been made.

Work a second triangle in the same way and join it to the first.

Flower: Ch 6 and join with a sl st into first ch to form a ring.

Row 1: work 12 sc into ring.

Row 2: * 3 sc, ch 6 *.

Row 3: * 10 dc into ch-6 loop, 1 dc on second of 3 sc *.

Fasten off.

Work 12 flowers and sew them invisibly along the 2 equal sides of the triangle made by joining the 2 smaller triangles.

Picking up the stitches from the outside edges of the flowers, work a 4¾ in (12 cm) strip in lattice st right along the lower edge.

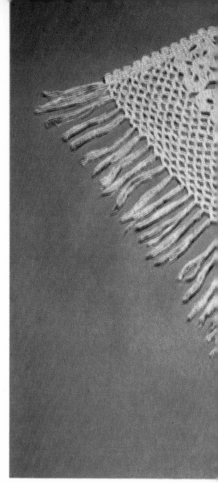

White triangular shawl

Detail of fringing

Black shawl in filet crochet

On the 2 equal sides, make a 6 in (15 cm) knotted fringe (see page 169). On the 3rd side work 1 row of sc and 2 rows as follows:
Row 1: * 1 sc, ch 3 and 1 sc *.
Row 2: * 1 sc on sc of previous row, 3 ch and 1 sc on sc of previous row *. Fasten off.

When the first butterfly has been worked, continue with 6 rows of mesh st.
Now work 11 mesh stitches and begin the next butterfly on the 12th. The 3rd butterfly is then worked, keeping it symmetrically in balance with the second by counting 10

Black shawl in filet crochet

Materials: 14½ oz (400 grams) 3-ply wool in black. Aluminum crochet hook size D.
Stitches used: mesh stitch (see page 22), with blocks and spaces.
To make: Ch 3 and then, working in mesh st, increase 1 st on each side as follows: on first and last dc of each row work 2 dc, ch 1 and 1 dc.
Begin to work the first butterfly in the center of Row 14, following the diagram (1 cross = 3 dc).

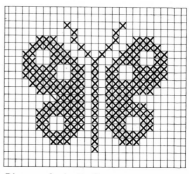

Diagram for butterfly

Poncho

mesh sts back from the end of the row. When these 2 butterflies have been worked, continue with 6 more rows of mesh st.

On next row work another 2 butterflies each side and another in the middle. The 4th should start on the 12th mesh st and the 6th on the 11th st from end of row (turning ch makes the 12th bar).

The 5th butterfly should be lined up with the first central one. When these 3 butterflies have been worked, continue with 6 more rows of mesh st.

On the next row work another 2 butterflies each side, as before, and 2 in between, lined up with the 2nd and 3rd butterflies.

There will now be 10 butterflies in all.

Work 13 rows in mesh st.

Work one row of sc and one row of reverse sc on the long side. On the 2 equal sides make a 12 in (30 cm) fringe (see page 169).

Poncho

Materials: 25 oz (700 grams) knitting worsted in equal amounts of various colors. Aluminum crochet hook size F.

Stitches used: half double crochet, double crochet.

Ch 80 and join with a sl st into first ch to form a circle.

For 1 round work: * 1 hdc, ch 1, skip 1 st *

Continue for another 9 rounds, working the dc into the ch loops of previous round. At the same time, increase gradually until there are 60 hdc with 1 ch between each.

Change color.

Round 1: * (2 dc, ch 2, 2 dc) into same st. (1 corner made), (skip 2 sts, ch 1, 2 dc into next st) 9 times, ch 1, skip 2 sts *.

Round 2: * 1 corner, (2 dc into ch loop, ch 1) 10 times *.

Continue in this way, changing color every 2 rounds, until the desired

length is reached.
Complete by working 1 row of sc around entire outside edge and by making a fringe about 2 in (5 cm) long.

Lady's coat

Materials: 54 oz (1500 grams) knitting worsted, 3 buttons.
Aluminum crochet hook size H.
Stitches used: shell stitch (see page 44), single crochet, reverse sc.
Back: Make a ch 19½ in (50 cm) long and work in shell st for 43½ in (110 cm).
Half front: make a ch 12 in (30 cm) long and work in shell st for 37½ in (95 cm). Now begin to decrease gradually until shoulder edge measures 7 in (18 cm). Work another half front in the same way but in reverse.
Sleeve: Make a ch 15½ in (40 cm) long and work in shell st for 20½ in (52 cm). Make second sleeve to match. Sew the sides together, sew shoulder and sleeve seams. Insert sleeves.
Collar: On 20 in (50 cm) around neck edge, work 6 in (15 cm) of shell st.
Work 1 row of sc and 1 row of reverse sc all around the collar, cuffs, both fronts and lower edge.
Sew buttons on left side, evenly spaced, and turn cuffs back.

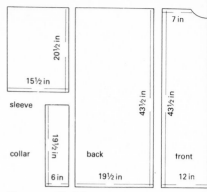

Diagram of lady's coat

Lady's jacket

Materials: 22 oz (600 grams) knitting worsted in white, a few grams each in red and black. Aluminum crochet hook size H.
Back: With white ch 50 and work in dc for 30 rows. Fasten off.
Right front: (this is worked sideways, the base chain constituting the long front edge). With white wool ch 50 and work in dc changing the colors as follows:
2 rows white, 1 row red, 3 rows white, 1 row black, 3 rows white, 1 row red, 2 rows white. Fasten off.
Work the left side in the same way.
Sleeve: with white wool ch 22 and work in dc for 24 rows, increasing evenly so that there are 28 sts by Row 24.
Work a further 9 rows with white wool, gradually decreasing until 6 sts are left on Row 9. Fasten off. Make second sleeve to match.
Sew side, shoulder and sleeve seams. Set sleeves in.
Collar: work 9 rows around neck edge in dc. Fasten off.

Lady's coat

174

Complete jacket by working a row of shrimp st in black (or red) wool all round edge of jacket, including the collar, and round the edge of the sleeves which can be turned back to form cuffs.

Belt: make 2 ch loops 1 in (2.5 cm) long and sew them to each side of jacket to carry the belt. To make the belt, plait several long strands of all 3 colors, finishing ends by knotting and fraying out the cut strands to form tassels.

Diagram of mauve sweater

Mauve sweater

Materials: 11 oz (300 grams) knitting worsted in mauve, 4 oz (30 grams) in white. Aluminum crochet hook size H.

Stitches used: ridge stitch, dc, sc.

Ribbing: Ch 14 and work 47 rows in ridge st (work into *back* loop only instead of through both loops).

Back and half sleeves: crocheting first row directly on to ribbing, work 20 rows in dc. Now ch 24 on each side of work and continue on all sts in dc for 10 rows. Work 1 row in white wool, 1 row in mauve, 1 row in white.

Make the front and half sleeves in the same way, including the ribbing. Sew the 2 pieces together. Finish the sleeves off with a border of 10 rounds in sc, working alternate rounds of mauve and white. If you wish the edge to be mauve, start with a round in white.

Hat

Materials: 4 oz (100 grams) sport yarn in shaded or mixture colors. Aluminum crochet hook size D.

Stitches used: ridged hdc (work into *back* loop only instead of through both loops), hdc, reverse sc, sc. (The hat is worked from the wrong side.)

Ch 3 and join with sl st to form a ring. Work in rounds of hdc, increasing regularly, until there is a flat disc 4 in (10 cm) in diameter. Continue for another 10 rounds. In the next round, increase 1 st every 2 sts. Continue for another 4 rounds, increasing regularly to ensure that the shaping is correct. Complete with 1 round of reverse sc.

Decorate the hat with a flower made as follows: ch 4 and join with sl st into first ch to form a ring.

Round 1: work 10 hdc into ring.

Rounds 2, 3 & 4: *3 hdc into hdc, skip 2 sts*. Continue from * to * for all 3 rounds, without fastening off at end of Round 4.

Make one or more leaves as follows: continuing from last st worked, ch 7 and work 1 sc into each ch, fasten off.

Lady's jacket

Mauve sweater

Hat

White and gold skirt

Materials: 18 oz (500 grams) knitting worsted in white, 9 oz (250 grams) gold Lurex, 1 round button base. Aluminum crochet hook size G.
Stitches used: dc, sc, reverse sc.
The skirt is worked with the two threads (1 wool, 1 Lurex) together and is made up of 4 equal pieces sewn together.
Instructions: Ch 45 and work for 25½ in (65 cm) in dc, gradually and regularly decreasing on each side until there are 27 sts left.
Make another 3 pieces in the same way. Sew all seams, leaving 6 in (15 cm) open on one side for fastening.
Around waist edge, work 8 rows in sc and 1 row in reverse sc. On Row 4 make a horizontal buttonhole (page 30), of 3 sts near corner of opening at side front.
Cover the button by working a small disc in the same yarns as the skirt and gathering it in underneath the base. Sew in position near corner of opening at side back.

White and gold sleeveless slipover

Materials: 7½ oz (200 grams) knitting worsted in white. 4 oz (100 grams) gold Lurex. Aluminum crochet hook size G.
Stitches used: openwork stitch no 11 (see page 87), sc, reverse sc.
Back: Make a ch 15½ in (40 cm) in length and work in openwork st no 11 for 11 in (27 cm), decreasing 1 st on each side when work measures ¾ in (2 cm) and again when it measures 2½ in (6 cm).
When work measures 9 in (23 cm), increase 1 st on each side and again when it measures 10½ in (26 cm).
Shape armhole by decreasing 2 sts in the first row and another st in the second (increases and decreases to be worked always on the dc row).
Continue for 3½ in (9 cm) then shape the neckline by decreasing 12 sts at center of work. Work straight on right side for 5½ in (14 cm) and fasten off.
Return to left side and work to match.
Front: as for Back.
Sew the 2 pieces together and complete by working 1 row in sc and 1 row in reverse sc around the edge of both armholes, the neck edge and the lower edge of slipover.

White and gold skirt with sleeveless slipover and lurex cap

Diagram of slipover and skirt

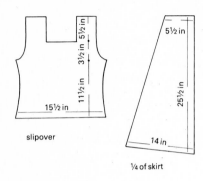

slipover

¼ of skirt

Lurex cap

Materials: 6 reels of Lurex, all 6 strands of which are worked together. Aluminum crochet hook size H.

Ch 4 and join with a sl st into first ch to form a ring.

Round 1: work 10 sc into ring.

Round 2: 20 dc worked in between sc of previous row.

Continue for another 6 rounds, always working between sts of previous row and increasing regularly on each round until there are 60 sts on 8th round.

Continue without increasing for a further 9 rounds, closing the final round with 1 sl st.

Cut the strands, fasten off and neaten the ends by weaving them invisibly into the work.

Silver evening top

Materials: 7½ oz (200 grams) silver Lurex worked 6 strands at a time. Aluminum crochet hook size H.

Stitches used: four-leaved clover stitch (see page 68), dc, tr, reverse sc.

Lower part: Ch 100 and work 22 rows in four-leaved clover stitch. Fasten off but leave a long end of Lurex to sew seam. Make sure that this seam comes at center back.

Upper part: to make one cup, ch 15 and work in dc, with 1 dc, ch 1 and 1 dc into the end ch. Work back in dc along the unworked side of base ch.

Work another 4 rows on both sides, with 1 dc, ch 1 and 1 dc into the ch of previous row.

Work the last row as follows: 2 dc into 1 st, skip next st. Make another cup to match and sew them to the front of the lower part of garment, slightly overlapping the cups at center front.

At the top of each cup work on 5 sts in dc for 24 in (60 cm). Work 1 row in sc and 1 row in reverse sc around the lower edge and the top edge, excluding the halter ties.

Bikini swimsuit

Materials: 7½ oz (200 grams) crochet cotton No 5 in yellow and brown. Aluminum crochet hook size 2.

Bra: Ch 19 in yellow cotton.

Row 1: 18 sc.

Row 2: 17 sc.

Row 3: 3 sc into end sc and then work 17 sc along unworked side of base ch.

Row 4: (brown cotton) 19 dc, 3 dc on center sc, 19 dc on second side.

Row 5: work in sc with 3 sc on center dc at turning point.

Rows 6 & 7: (yellow cotton) as Rows 4 and 5, working 3 sts into center st each time.

Rows 8 & 9: (brown cotton) as Rows 4 and 5.

Rows 10 & 11: (yellow cotton) as Rows 4 and 5.

Bikini swimsuit

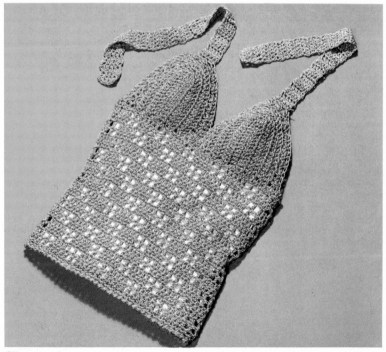

Silver evening top

181

Row 12: (brown cotton) *1 dc, ch 2, skip 1 st, 3 dc on next st*.

Row 13: Work in sc, with 2 sc into each ch-2 loop and 5 sc on the 3 center dc.

Row 14: work in dc, with 3 dc on center sc.

Row 15: (yellow cotton) work in sc.

Row 16: as Row 11.

Row 17: as Row 12.

Row 18: *1 sc, ch 5, skip 3 sts*.

Row 19: (brown cotton) *1 sc into same st as sc in Row 18 was worked, 4 dc into next ch-5 loop *. Fasten off.

Work second cup in the same way.

Complete bra by working, in yellow cotton, on lower edge of one cup, as follows: *1 sc on each st, 4 sc on dc, ch 3*. Rep from * to * and continue along lower edge of second cup. The two cups are now joined. Do not break yarn. Ch 120 and work 1 row of sc.

Rejoin yarn to the first st worked and ch 120. Work 1 sc into each ch.

Join yellow cotton at top of one cup and ch 120. Work 1 sc into each ch. Fasten off. Make a similar strap on the other cup.

Complete the bra in brown cotton with 1 row of reverse sc.

Pants: starting from the back, ch 86 in yellow cotton. Working one row in dc and one row in sc, change the color every 2 rows. Work 12 rows in this way. Continue for a further 28 rows, alternating the colors, but decreasing regularly on each side until 20 sts are left for the crotch. Work in sc for 32 rows.

On next row, still working in sc, increase 2 sts at each side (4 sts) and continue to increase 4 sts in each row for another 11 rows.

Continue in sc and dc for a further 12 rows, without increasing.

Fasten off. Make 2 insertions in brown cotton for the sides as follows: ch 12, work 16 rows in sc.

Waistcoat

Sew insertions to side edges of back and front of pants and complete by working 1 row of sc and 1 row of reverse sc around edge of leg openings and top edge.

Waistcoat

Materials: 18 oz (500 grams) knitting worsted in gray, 5 buttons. Aluminum crochet hook size J.

Stitches used: alternating stitch no 1 (see page 38), single crochet.

Back: make a ch 16¾ in (42 cm) in length.

Work in alternating st no 1 for 16¾ in (42 cm). Now decrease 4 sts at each side for armholes and continue in alternating st no 1 for another 8¾ in (22 cm).

Half Front: make a ch 8 in (20 cm) in length.

Work in alternating st no 1 for 4¾ in (12 cm). Now decrease 1 st at beg of each alternate row for V-neck. When 16¾ in (42 cm) have been worked

182

from the beginning, decrease 4 sts for armhole on the side opposite the front shaping and continue for another 8¾ in (22 cm) in alternating st no 1.

Work the second Half Front to match, with shaping on opposite sides.

Sew up the side and shoulder seams.

Complete the armholes, V-neck, front edgings and lower edge by working 3 rows of sc. On one front, make 5 evenly spaced vertical buttonholes.

Sew buttons on other side to correspond with buttonholes.

Diagram of man's jacket

Man's jacket

Materials: 54 ozs (1500 grams) knitting worsted. 6 buttons. Aluminum crochet hook size I.

Stitches used: basket-weave stitch (see page 39), single crochet.

To make the jacket a little lighter, the basket-weave stitch has been modified as follows: Row 1: dc. Row 2: * 2 raised dc (yo, insert hook from front to back of vertical bar of first dc, bring forward between second and third dc, yo and complete as for normal dc), 2 reverse raised dc (worked in same way except that hook is inserted from back to front and brought to the back of work between second and third dc *. On following rows, alternate the pattern every 2 rows so that ordinary raised dc are worked over reverse raised dc.

Back: Ch 54 and work in basket-weave st for 19½ in (50 cm). Decrease on both sides for armholes: 3 dec on one row, 2 dec on next row, 1 dec on next row. Continue in basket-weave for another 9 in (23 cm). Fasten off.

Half Front: Ch 20 and work in basket-weave for 19½ in (50 cm). Decrease on one side only for armhole as on Back. Continue as for Back. Work the second Half Front, reversing the dec for armhole.

Sleeve: Ch 30 and work in basket-weave for 15½ in (40 cm) increasing 1 st on each side every 10 rows.

Now follow dec instructions for Back and continue decreasing regularly for 8 in (20 cm) until 3 sts remain.

Work second sleeve in same way.

Sew up side, shoulder and sleeve seams. Set sleeves in.

Collar: Make a ch the same length as the 2 Fronts and back neck edge. Work in sc for 4¾ in (12 cm). When 1¼ in (3 cm) have been worked of left border, make the first 3 buttonholes, equally spaced from each other. After a further 2½ in (6 cm) have been worked, make 3 more buttonholes to correspond with the first three. Sew border to both front edges and back neck edge.

Complete sleeves with a 2¾ in (7 cm) border of sc, worked separately. Join seam, set in line with sleeve seam and sew on to *right* side of work. Turn cuffs back. Sew buttons on Right Front to correspond with buttonholes.

Man's jacket

Blue matinée coat

Materials: 3½ oz (100 grams) sport yarn in blue. A small quantity in white. A length of narrow baby ribbon (optional). Aluminum crochet hook size D.

Stitches used: openwork st no. 5 (see page 83), dc, sc, reverse sc.

Back & Front up to armholes: Ch 130 and work in openwork st no. 5 for 6½ in (16 cm). Remove hook from working loop but do not fasten off.

Sleeves: (both the same) Ch 40 and work in openwork st no. 5 for 6 in (15 cm). Remove hook from working loop but do not fasten off.

Yoke: Pick up working loop on Front and work in white wool in openwork st no. 5 across half Front, top of one Sleeve, Back, top of second Sleeve and second half Front for 4 rows. Now work 5 rows in sc in blue wool, 2 rows in white, 6 rows in blue, decreasing regularly until 54 sts remain on completion of yoke. Sew up side and sleeve seams.

Around neck and wrist edges work *

1 dc, ch 1, skip 1 st * for insertion of cords.

Finish off neck, wrist, front and lower edges with 1 row of sc and 1 row of reverse sc.

If not using ribbon, make a fairly long ch and work 1 row sc for neck tie and 2 shorter ones for wrists. Thread through ribbon (or cord) insertion holes.

White matinée coat

Materials: 4 oz (100 grams) sport yarn in white. A length of narrow baby ribbon (optional). Aluminum crochet hook size D.

Stitches used: arabesque stitch (see page 75), single crochet, double crochet, reverse sc.

Back: Ch 54 and work in arabesque

Blue matinée coat

White matinée coat

st for 6 in (15 cm) ending with Row 1 (1 dc, 1 ch, 1 dc). Now work 1 row in sc, working only into each ch st of previous row, thus gathering the work for beg of yoke. Remove hook from working loop but do not fasten off.

Half Front: Ch 27 and work to yoke as for Back. Remove hook from working loop but do not fasten off.

Make second Front to match.

Sleeves: (both alike) ch 35 and work in arabesque st for 5½ in (14 cm), ending with Row 1 and a row of sc worked into each ch st of previous row. Remove hook.

Join Back to 2 Fronts by sewing side and sleeve seams together.

Yoke: start by picking up working st with white wool on Right Side and work *1 row in dc and 1 row in sc *, 3 times. Now change to blue wool and rep from * to *. Change to white wool and rep from * to *. Dec evenly over these 10 rows so that 51 sts remain.

Finish off neck opening, with blue wool, by working a ribbon insertion row (1 dc, ch 1, skip 1 st). Work a similar row on each sleeve edge.

With blue wool work 1 row of sc and 1 row of reverse sc around wrist edges of both sleeves, down edges of both fronts and along lower edge. Make 3 cords, as described in previous pattern, and thread through insertion holes. If preferred, ribbon can be used instead of crocheted cords.

Baby's coat-bag

Materials: 7½ oz (200 grams) angora in white (worked double). 4 oz (100 grams) angora in red (worked double). 12/13 in (32 cm) heavyweight zip fastener. Aluminum crochet hook size F.

Stitches used: Crazy single crochet (see page 42), single crochet.

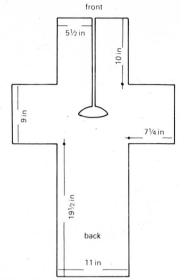

Diagram of baby's coat-bag

Ch 44 and work in crazy single crochet for 19½ in (50 cm), alternating the colors: 7 rows in white, 4 rows in red, 12 rows in white, 4 rows in red, 7 rows in white. Now ch 30 in red wool on both sides of work and work 5 rows in red and 5 rows in white.

Stop work at center 3 motifs and work 7 rows in white on each side separately. Now work 1 row in red and ch 6 on inside edge for front neck-opening. Work 4 rows, still in red. On only 6 center motifs, work 7 rows in white, 4 rows in red, 12 rows in white.

Return to center back and work another Half Front to match. Work 30 sts in white wool round neck edge in dc. Now work 7 more rows in sc, increasing 2 sts at beg of every row.

Finish off collar with 2 rows in sc (1 white and 1 red), working right around the collar to center front. With red wool, work 2 rows in sc

Baby's coat-bag

around wrists and down edges of both center Fronts. Sew zip fastener into center opening. Sew up sleeve and side seams, folding the first 11 rows (7 white and 4 red) up to meet lower edges of both fronts. Stitch top of flap to both lower edges of 2 Front halves.

Child's pink dress

Materials: 9 oz (250 grams) sport yarn in pink. Small quantity of contrasting color (brown is suggested). 1 small button. Aluminum crochet hooks sizes D and F.
Stitches used: simple shell stitch (see page 64), single crochet, reverse sc.

Front: with size D hook starting from waist, ch 110 and work in simple shell st for 15 rows. Dec 2 shells on each side for armholes and work another 15 rows. Stop work at center 11 shells and work 1 row on each shoulder separately. Fasten off.
Back: work as for Front until 3 rows have been worked after armhole dec. Now divide for back opening, working each half separately.
Join side seams and turn work right side out. On ch at waist, with size F hook, work the skirt in the round for 18 rounds in simple shell st. Fasten off.
Finish off neck edge, back opening and armholes by working 2 rows in sc and 1 row in reverse sc.

Child's pink dress

Make a cord in brown wool and thread through holes at waist.
Sew button to left side of neck opening.

Child's jacket

Materials: 11 oz (300 grams) knitting worsted. A few grams in blue, green and yellow. Aluminum crochet hook size G.

Stitches used: double, single crochet, elongated single crochet (ordinary sc worked in row *before* previous row, i.e. 2 rows back).

Back: Ch 28 and work 6 rows in dc. Continue working as follows:
Row 1: * 3 dc in blue, 3 dc in white *, ending with 4 dc in blue.
Row 2: * 3 dc in white, 3 dc in yellow *, ending with 4 dc in white.
Row 3: dc in green.
Row 4: * 3 dc in yellow, 3 dc in white *, ending with 4 dc in yellow.
Row 5: * 3 dc in white, 3 dc in blue *, ending with 4 dc in white.
Continue for another 5 rows in white.
Decrease 2 sts at each side for armholes and work a further 6 rows.
Stop work at center 7 sts and work 1 row on each shoulder separately.
Half Front: Ch 21 and work 18 dc for the same number of rows and with the same color changes as on Back. After armhole dec has been worked, increase 5 sts on opposite side over next 7 rows. Then work 3 rows on 5 sts of collar.
Make second Half Front to match, with shapings on opposite sides.
Sleeve: Ch 21 and work 18 dc for 16 rows, repeating the same sequence of color as for Back. Continue for a further 8 rows, gradually decreasing to 7 sts.
Make a second sleeve to match.
Pocket: Ch 6 in white wool and work in dc for 3 rows.
Make another pocket to match.
Join side, shoulder, sleeve and center back collar.
Finish off with 1 row in white in sc and 1 row in yellow as follows: * 1 sc, 1 elongated sc *, repeat from * to * for entire row. This border is worked around wrists, all around the jacket and along one edge of each pocket.
Sew pockets to each half front, ensuring that they are straight. Make two loops for belt by making 2 pieces of ch about 1 in (3 cm) long and sew to each side seam at waist level.
Belt: With white wool, make a chain 46 in (120 cm) long and work 2 rows in dc. Finish belt off with 1 row in yellow: * 1 sc, 1 elongated sc *, repeat from * to * all around belt. Thread through belt loops at each side.

2-color sweater

Materials: 5½ oz (150 grams) knitting worsted in beige. 7½ oz (200 grams) knitting worsted in rust. Aluminum crochet hook size F.

Stitches used: hdc, broken check in 2 colors (see page 55).

Back: Make a ch 10½ in (26 cm) in length and work 3 rows of hdc in rust wool. Continue for 9½ in (24 cm) in broken check in both colors. Now dec 3 sts on each side for armholes. Continue for a further 6¾ in (17 cm) in 2-color st. Stop at center 8 sts and work 1 row on each shoulder separately.

Front: work as for Back, stopping work 2 rows earlier for neck division and work 3 rows on each shoulder.

Sleeve: Make a ch 6 in (15 cm) in length and work 3 rows of hdc in

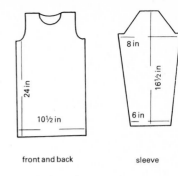

front and back   sleeve

Diagram of 2-color sweater

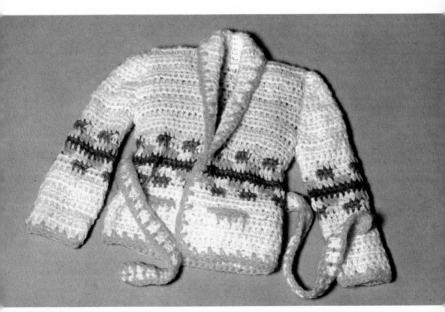

Child's jacket

rust. Continue for 9¾ in (25 cm) in broken check in both colors, increasing gradually on each side to a width of 8½ in (22 cm). Now decrease 3 sts on each side and continue for a further 6¾ in (17 cm) in 2-color stitch, decreasing regularly and gradually until 4 sts remain.

Work another sleeve to match.

Join side, shoulder and sleeve seams. Set sleeves in.

Work 2 rounds of hdc with rust color wool on neck edge.

Girl's robe

Materials: 12½ oz (350 grams) sport yarn in red. Aluminum crochet hook size D.

Stitches used: simple shell st (see page 64), dc, sc, reverse sc.

Back: Ch 68 and starting in the 3rd ch from hook, work * 1 shell, skip 1 st *, ending with a dc. Work follow-

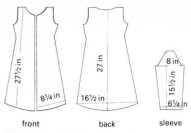

Diagram of girl's robe

ing row: 3 turning ch, 1 shell into ch between the 2 dc of previous row, ending with 1 dc. Continue in this way for approximately 11¾ in (30 cm), then decrease 1 st regularly on each side until 4 shells have been lost at each side.

Armhole: Row 1 – dec 2 shells on each side.

Row 2 – dec 1 shell on each side.

Rows 3–9 – work straight until back measures 27 in (69 cm).

2-color sweater

Girl's robe

Stop work at 7 center shells (back neck edge) and work each shoulder separately: 1 row of sc across all shells and 1 row across 3 shells only. Fasten off.

Right Front: Ch 38 and work as for back, shaping on one side only.

Left Front: as Right Front, with shaping on one side only.

Sleeves (both alike): Ch 28 and work 12 in (30 cm) increasing gradually until 1 extra shell has been completed on each side. Decrease 2 shells in Row 1 of armhole and 1 shell gradually on following rows until 5 shells remain.

Collar: Ch 40 and work 5 rows of shells.

Finishing off: Join side, sleeve and shoulder seams. Set sleeves in. Sew collar into position (from right side of work). Work 1 row of sc and 1 row of reverse sc around all edges. Make a cord in the same yarn and thread it through holes in pattern at waist level.

PLACEMATS TABLECLOTHS AND BEDSPREADS

The fascination of tradition

The patterns described in this section undoubtedly come within the most demanding area of this fascinating craft and as a result they represent the greatest challenge to the skill of the expert crocheter.

Perhaps the nostalgia conjured up by these designs for an age when it was the prerogative of rich and noble families to own such delicate and elegant work is part of the reason for its fascination. Or it may be that the meticulous workmanship, close attention to detail and patience involved are sufficient satisfaction in themselves, with the knowledge that the results will be imaginatively creative designs emerging from the simplest of basic materials – a fine thread and a small hook.

Placemats, tablecloths, runners and bedspreads worked in either lacy patterns or in filet, with simple and complex stitches blended together, represent the most traditional, classical aspect of crochet. They remind us of elegant town and country houses of the past where gracious bedrooms would have been adorned by such lovely bed coverings as the 19th century double bedspread, instructions for which we offer you in the following pages, which originally came from one of the great homes belonging to the House of Savoy. Of course, such a masterpiece represents many months of work and it is not simple. But the satisfaction of producing such a beautiful thing is sufficient reward for the patience and time expended.

However, the type of intricate work described here fits in just as well in modern settings as it did in times past. And with modern methods for laundering and conditioning fabric, combined with the beautiful crochet cottons available now, there is no reason why the old and the new should not live in harmony together, for the one is complementary to the other.

One suggestion to ease the laundering problem is to place crocheted mats, tray-cloths, runners, etc under glass.

Centerpiece no 1

Note: The following patterns on pages 192-226 are recommended for experienced crocheters only.

Centerpiece No 1

Materials: Crochet Cotton No 20, steel crochet hook size 10.
Ch 8 and join with a slip st into first ch to form a ring. (Replace first dc with 3 ch or first tr with ch 4, whichever is appropriate, at beg of each round. End each round with 1 sl st into 3rd or 4th starting ch of previous round.)
Round 1: Into base ch work 1 dc, ch 3.
Round 2: (3 dc, ch 5) into each ch-3 loop.
Round 3: Sl st to 5th ch, (1 sc, ch 9, 1 sc) into same ch as 5th sl st, ch 5. Continue to end of round, working motif in brackets into 3rd of each ch-5 loop followed by 5 ch.
Round 4: (9 dc, ch 3, 9 dc) into ch-9 loop.
Round 5: Sl st to 5th dc, *1 dc, ch 5 into same dc as 5th ch, (1 sc, ch 3, 1 sc) into ch-3 loop between dc, ch 5*. Rep from * to * to end of round.
Round 6: Into each ch-5 loop of previous round work 4 tr, separating each group of tr with ch 1, and in each ch-3 loop work 1 tr, ch 2, 1 tr.
Round 7: 1 sc into each ch separating the tr groups of previous round, ch 7.
Round 8: Sl st to 4th ch and work 1

Centerpiece no. 2

sc, ch 7. Continue to work 1 sc, ch 7 in 4th ch of each ch-7 loop to end of round.

Round 9: as Round 8.

Round 10: *(8 tr, ch 3, 8 tr) into ch-7 loop, 1 sc into next loop*. Rep from * to * to end of round.

Round 11: Sl st to 4th tr, *1 dc, ch 5, (1 sc, ch 3, 1 sc) into ch-3 loop, ch 5, 1 dc into 4th tr, ch 5*. Rep from * to

* to end of round.

Round 12: as Round 6.

Round 13: as Round 7.

Rounds 14, 15 & 16: as Round 8.

Round 17: *8 tr separated by 1 picot (picot = ch 3, 1 sc on tr) into first loop, 1 sc into next loop*. Rep from * to * to end of round.

Fasten off.

Centerpiece No 2

Materials: Crochet Cotton No 20, steel crochet hook size 11.

Ch 10 and join with a sl st into first ch to form a ring. (Replace first dc with ch 3 at beg of each round. End each round with 1 sl st into 3rd starting ch, except while working ch lace when each round ends with ch 2, 1 dc into first sc of same round.)

Round 1: Work 28 dc into ring.

Round 2: 46 dc.

Round 3: 64 dc.

Round 4: *1 dc, ch 2, skip 1 st*. Rep from * to * to end of round.

Round 5: *1 sc, ch 5*. Rep from * to * into each ch-2 loop.

Rounds 6, 7 & 8: *Ch 5, 1 sc into each loop of previous row*. Rep from * to * to end of round.

Round 9: *Ch 6, 1 sc*. Rep from * to * to end of round.

Round 10: Ch 6, 5 dc into 3rd of 6 ch just worked, *1 dc into ch-6 loop of previous row, ch 3, 5 dc into dc just worked*. Rep from * to * to end of row, ending with 1 sl st into 3rd of 6 turning ch.

Round 11: Sl st to 3rd ch, *ch 5, 1 sc into 3rd ch of next dc group, ch 7, 1 sc into next 3rd ch*. Rep from * to * to end of round.

Round 12: *(1 sc, 1 hdc, 4 dc, 1 hdc, 1 sc) into ch-5 loop, (1 sc, 2 hdc, 3 dc) into ch-7 loop, ch 4, (2 unfinished tr, yo, draw yarn through all 3 loops on hook) into back loop of second of 3 dc just worked, ch 4, 1 sc into same second dc of 3 dc, (3 dc, 2 hdc, 1 sc) into same ch-7 loop*. Rep from * to * to end of round, finishing with 1 sl st on first sc.

Round 13: Sl st to first dc, *(1 dc, ch 3, 1 dc) into 3rd dc of previous round, ch 5, (1 dc, ch 3, 1 dc) into closing st of 2 tr cluster of previous row, ch 5*. Rep from * to * to end of round, finishing with 1 sl st on first dc.

Round 14: *1 sc into first ch-3 loop, **(2 hdc, 2 dc, 2 tr, 2 dc, 1 hdc, 1 sc) into next ch-5 loop** (1 sc, ch 3, 5 tr, ch 3, 1 sc) into next ch-3 loop, rep from ** to ** once*. Rep from * to * to end of row, finishing with 1 sl st on first sc.

Round 15: Sl st to first tr, *1 tr, ch 7, 1 sc into 3rd ch of tr group of previous row, ch 5, 1 sc into last tr of same group, ch 7, 1 tr between first and second tr of next group*. Rep from * to * to end.

Round 16: (1 sc, 1 hdc, 5 dc, 1 hdc, 1 sc) into each loop of previous row.

Round 17: Sl st to 3rd dc of 5 dc group in previous row, *1 sc on 3rd dc, ch 7, 1 sc on first dc in next group, ch 7, 1 sc into 4th dc in same group, ch 7, 1 sc into 3rd dc of next dc group, ch 7*. Rep from * to * to end of row, finishing with ch 4, 1 dc on first sc.

Rounds 18 & 19: *Ch 7, 1 sc into each loop of previous row*. Rep from * to * to end of row.

Round 20: 2 dc, ch 5 into each ch-7 loop of previous row.

Round 21: *2 dc on 2 dc, ch 3, 1 sc into ch-5 loop, ch 3*. Rep from * to * to end of round.

Round 22: *2 dc on 2 dc, ch 5*. Rep from * to * to end of round.

Round 23: as Round 21.

Round 24: as Round 22.

Round 25: as Round 21.

Round 26: *2 dc on 2 dc, ch 7*. Rep from * to * to end of round.

Round 27: *2 dc on 2 dc, ch 4, 1 sc into ch-7 loop, ch 4*. Rep from * to * to end of round.

Round 28: as Round 26.

Round 29: as Round 27.

Round 30: as Round 26.

Round 31: as Round 27.

Round 32: as Round 26.

Round 33: *9 dc into ch-7 loop, ch 4, 3 sc into next ch-7 loop, ch 4*. Rep from * to * to end of round.

Round 34: *On 9 dc of previous row work (1 dc, ch 1) 8 times and 1 dc, ch

3, 2 sc on 3 sc, ch 3*. Rep from * to * to end of round.

Round 35: *(2 dc, 1 picot = ch 3, 1 sc on second dc just worked, ch 1) into each ch separating the 9 dc (8 times in all), ch 2, 1 sc on 2 sc, ch 2*. Rep from * to * to end of round.

Fasten off.

Centerpiece No 3

Materials: Crochet Cotton No 20, steel crochet hook size 11.

Ch 10 and join with a sl st into first ch to form a ring.

Round 1: Ch 1 (= 1 sc), ch 7, work *1 sc, ch 7* into ring. Rep from * to * 11 times, ending with 1 sl st into starting ch.

(From now on, the first sc of each row will be replaced by ch 1 and a dc by ch 3. Instead of the full 'ending with 1 sl st into starting ch,' at the conclusion of each round, the words 'close round' will be used.)

Round 2: 3 sl st to central stitch of first loop. *1 sc into loop, ch 3*. Rep from * to * 12 times and close round.

Round 3: *1 sc into first loop, ch 7, 1 sc into same loop, ch 3*. Rep from * to * 12 times and close round.

Round 4: 3 sl st to central point of first loop, *1 sc into ch-7 loop, ch 7*. Rep from * to * 12 times and close round.

Round 5: *1 sc on sc, ch 5, 1 sc into next loop, ch 5*. Rep from * to * and close round.

Round 6: *(1 dc, ch 2, 1 dc) into first loop (corner), (1 sc into next loop, ch 5) 5 times*. Rep from * to * 4 times and close round.

Rounds 7 to 12: *1 corner into ch-2 corner loop, (1 sc, ch 5) into every following ch-5 loop*. Rep from * to * 3 times and close round.

Round 13: *1 corner into corner loop, ch 1, (5 dc, ch 1 into next loop) along one side*. Rep from * to * 3

times more and close round.

Round 14: *3 sc into corner loop, 1 sc into next ch-1 loop (ch 5, 1 sc into next loop) along one side*. Rep from * to * 3 times more and close round.

Round 15: Sl st to 4th sc, *1 sc on sc, ch 20, skip 3 ch-5 loops, 1 sc on next sc, (5 sc into next loop, ch 1) 5 times, 1 sc on next sc, ch 20, skip 3 ch-5 loops, 1 sc on next sc, ch 6, skip 3 sc at corner*. Rep from * to * 3 times more and close round.

Round 16: *24 sc into ch-20 loop, (5 sc on 5 sc, ch 3) 5 times, 24 sc into next ch-20 loop, 10 sc into ch-6 loop*. Rep from * to * 3 times more.

Round 17: *23 sc, ch 3, (1 sc into next ch-3 loop, ch 5) 4 times, ch 3, skip 1 sc, 23 sc on next 23 sc, skip 1 sc, 8 sc on 8 sc, skip 1 sc*. Rep from * to * 3 times more and close round.

Round 18: *22 sc, ch 4, (1 sc into next loop, ch 5) 3 times, 1 sc into next loop, ch 4, skip 1 sc, 30 sc*. Rep from * to * 3 times more.

Round 19: *1 sc, ch 12, skip 10 sc, 1 sc, ch 12, skip 10 sc, 1 sc, ch 12, skip 2 loops, 1 sc into next loop, ch 12, skip 2 loops, 1 sc, ch 12, skip 10 sc, 1 sc, ch 12, miss 10 sc, 1 sc, ch 5, skip 3 sc, 1 sc, ch 5, skip 3 sc*. Rep from * to * 3 times more and close round.

Round 20: *(1 sc on 1 sc, 14 sc into ch-12 loop) 6 times, 2 sc on sc, 8 sc into ch-6 loop, 2 sc on next sc, 8 sc into next loop, 2 sc into next sc*. Rep from * to * 3 times more and close round.

Rounds 21 & 22: 1 sc on every sc of previous round, working 2 sc into same st on each side of corner loops.

Round 23: *4 sc, ch 9*. Rep from * to * 119 times more and close round.

Round 24: 4 sl st to central point of ch-9 loop, *1 sc into ch-9 loop, ch 4*. Rep from * to * to end and close round.

Round 25: *1 sc into ch-4 loop, ch

Centerpiece no. 3

5*. Rep from * to * to end and close round.

Round 26: as Round 24.

Rounds 27 to 31: *1 sc into ch-4 loop, ch 6*. Rep from * to * to end and close round.

Round 32: *8 sc into each ch-6 loop*. Rep from * to * to end, close round. Fasten off.

Centerpiece No 4

Materials: Crochet Cotton No 20, steel crochet hook size 11.

This centerpiece is made up of 7 flower motifs worked separately.

1st flower motif: Ch 8 and join with a sl st into first chain to form a loop. (Replace first dc with ch-3 or first tr with ch-4 and close each round with 1 sl st into 3rd or 4th starting ch.)

Round 1: work 24 dc into ring.

Round 2: *1 dc, ch 2, skip 1 st*. Rep from * to * 12 times altogether.

Round 3: 6 tr into each of the 12 ch-2 loops.

Round 4: *1 dc into first tr, 5 unfinished dc, on each of next 5 dc, yo, draw yarn through all 6 loops on hook, ch 8*. Rep from * to * 12 times altogether.

Round 5: 7 sc into each ch-8 loop, 1 picot (= ch 3, 1 sl st into 7th sc just worked), 7 sc. Fasten off.

In working the rest of the flower motifs, make 2 joining loops in last round as follows: 7 sc, 1 sc (by inserting hook into picot of previous flower motif), 7 sc.

Centerpiece no. 4

Centerpiece no. 4

Centerpiece No 5

Materials: Crochet Cotton No 20, steel crochet hook size 11.

Ch 6 and join with a sl st into first ch to form a ring.

Round 1: 12 sc worked into ring.

Round 2: *1 dtr on sc of previous row, ch 5*.

Round 3: Sl st to 3rd st of ch-5 of previous row, *(1 dtr, ch 5, 1 dtr) into same 3rd ch*. Rep from * to *, working on 3rd ch of each ch-5 loop, to end of row and close round.

Round 4: (1 sc, 1 hdc, 2 dc, 5 tr, 2 dc, 1 hdc, 1 sc) into ch-5 loop between dtr of previous row.

Round 5: sl st to center of first scallop, *1 dtr, ch 5, 1 dtr, ch 7*. Rep from * to *.

Round 6: *(3 unfinished dtr, yo, draw yarn through all 4 loops on hook, ch 3) 3 times into ch-5 loop, 3 unfinished dtr, yo, draw yarn through all 4 loops on hook (4 petals); ch 4, 1 sc into 4th ch of ch-7 loop in previous row, ch 4*.

Round 7: Sl st to end of 2nd of 4 petals of previous row; * into ch-3 loop between 2nd and 3rd petals work 4 petals as shown in Round 6, ch 4, 1 unfinished tr into next loop, 1 unfinished tr into next loop, yo, draw yarn through all 3 loops on hook, ch 4*. Rep from * to *.

Rounds 8 & 9: as Round 7 but, on Round 9, work 5 ch into each loop before and after the 2 dc cluster.

Round 10: sl st to ch loop between 2nd and 3rd petals of previous row, *12 tr into ch-3 loop, ch 6, 1 unfinished tr into first ch loop, 1 unfinished tr into second ch loop, yo, draw yarn through all 3 loops on hook, ch 6*.

Round 11: *(1 tr, ch 1) 11 times on 11 tr of previous rnd, 1 tr, ch 4, 1 unfinished tr into first ch loop, 1 unfinished tr into second ch loop, yo, draw yarn through all 3 loops on hook, ch 4*.

Round 12: *(1 tr, ch 2) 11 times on 11 tr of previous rnd, 1 tr, ch 1, 1 tr on 2-tr cluster, ch 1*.

Round 13: 1 sc into ch loop preceding 12 tr of previous rnd, 1 sc between first and second of 12 tr, (ch 4, 1 sc between next 2 tr) 3 times, ch 4, (1 dc, ch 4, 1 dc) 4 times between 6th and 7th tr, ch 4, skip 6th and 7th tr, (1 sc between next 2 tr, ch 4) 3 times, 1 sc between last 2 tr, 1 sc into next ch*. Fasten off.

Centerpiece No 6

Materials: Crochet Cotton No 20, steel crochet hook size 11.

Ch 8 and join with a sl st into first ch to form a circle.

Round 1: work (1 dc, ch 1) 12 times into ring.

Round 2: 2 sc into each ch of previous rnd.

Centerpiece no. 5

Round 3: *1 dtr, ch 7, skip 1 st*. Rep from * to * to end of rnd.

Round 4: *1 dc on dtr, (ch 1, skip 1 st, 1 dc) 3 times, ch 1*. Rep from * to * (48 dc in all).

Round 5: 2 sc into each ch of previous row.

Round 6: *1 tr tr (triple treble = yo 4 times, insert hook into next st or loop, as instructed, yo, draw yarn through, [yo and draw through 2 loops on hook] 5 times), ch 5, 1 tr between 2nd and 3rd oblique loops of tr tr, skip 3 sts* (24 groups)

Round 7: Sl st to center of first group, *2 tr into center of group, ch 7, 1 sc into center of next group, ch 7*.

Round 8: *2 tr on each of 2 tr of previous row, ch 7, yo twice, insert hook into next ch loop, yo, draw yarn through, yo, draw yarn through 2 loops on hook, yo, insert hook into next ch loop, yo, draw yarn through, yo, draw yarn through 2 loops on hook, (yo, draw yarn through 2 loops on hook) 3 times (1 group formed), ch 7*.

Round 9: *2 tr on first 2 of the 4 tr of previous row, 1 tr on each of next 2 sts, 2 tr on 4th st, ch 7, work 1 group inserting hook into next 2 loops, ch 7*.

Round 10: *2 tr on first 2 of the 6 tr

Centerpiece no. 6

of previous row, 4 tr, 2 tr on 6th tr, ch 7, work 1 group inserting hook into each of following ch loops, ch 7*.

Round 11: *Skip first tr, 6 tr, (ch 7, 1 sc into next ch loop) twice, ch 7*.

Round 12: *Skip first tr, 4 tr, (ch 7, 1 sc into ch loop) 3 times, ch 7*.

Round 13: *Skip first tr, 2 tr, (ch 7, 1 sc into ch loop) 4 times, ch 7*.

Round 14: sl st to center of ch loop following 2 tr of previous row, *1 sc into ch loop, ch 7, 1 sc into next ch loop, 12 dc into next ch loop, 1 sc into next ch loop, ch 7, 7 sc into ch loop preceding 2 tr of previous row, ch 7*.

Round 15: sl st to first ch loop, *1 sc into ch loop, on next 12 dc of previous row work (1 dc, ch 1) 11 times, 1 dc, 1 sc into next ch loop, ch 7, 1 sc into next ch loop, ch 7*.

Round 16: Sl st to first ch loop, *1 sc into ch loop, ch 2, (1 dc between 2 dc of previous row, ch 2) 9 times, 1 dc between last 2 dc of previous row, ch 2, 1 sc into next ch loop, ch 7*.

Round 17: *1 sc into first ch-2 loop, (1 sc between the 2 dc, ch 4) twice, 1 sc between next 2 dc, ch 5, 1 dc between 5th and 6th dc, ch 4, 1 dc, ch 5, 1 sc between 7th and 8th dc, ch 4, 1 sc between 9th and 10th dc, 1 sc into next ch-2 loop, (2 sc, ch 3, 2 sc) into next ch-7 loop*. Fasten off.

Centerpiece no. 6

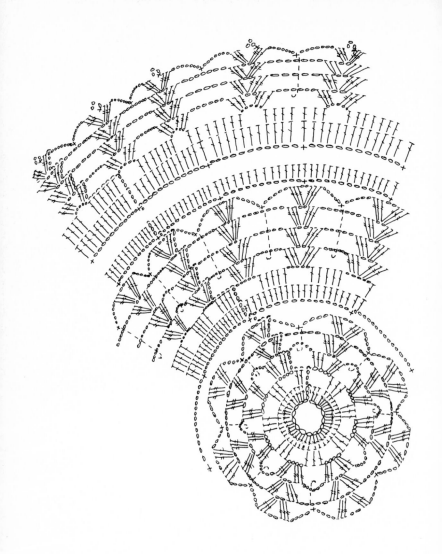

Section of Decoratively pointed centerpiece

Decoratively pointed centerpiece

Decoratively-pointed centerpiece

Materials: Crochet Cotton No 8, aluminum crochet hook size 2.

Ch 15 and join with a sl st into first ch to form a ring. (Replace the first dc of each row with ch 3, the first tr with ch 4 and the first sc with ch 1. Instead of 'ending with 1 sl st into starting ch' at the conclusion of each round, the words 'close round' will be used.)

Round 1: work 40 dc into ring and close round.

Round 2: *3 dc, ch 4, skip 2 sts*. Rep from * to * another 7 times and close round.

Round 3: *3 tr, ch 2, 3 tr, ch 6, into each ch-4 loop*. Rep from * to * to end and close round.

Round 4: 2 sl st to ch-2 loop (and in following rows), *(3 tr, ch 2, 3 tr), ch 5 into loop*. Rep from * to * another 7 times and close round.

Round 5: *(3 tr, ch 2, 3 tr) into ch-2 loop, ch 4, 1 sc into ch-6 and ch-5 loops of Rounds 3 and 4, ch 4*. Rep from * to * another 7 times and close round. (There will now be a star with 8 points.)

Fir-tree centerpiece

Round 6: *1 sc into ch-2 loop, ch 14*. Rep from * to * another 7 times and close round.

Round 7: *1 dc on sc, 18 dc into ch-14 loop*. Rep from * to * and close round.

Round 8: *5 dc, ch 5, skip 3 sts*. Rep from * to * and close round.

Round 9: *(3 tr, ch 2, 2 tr) into each ch-5 loop, ch 6 *. Rep from * to * and close round.

Round 10: *(3 tr, ch 2, 3 tr) into each ch-2 loop, ch 5 *. Rep from * to * and close round.

Round 11: *(3 tr, ch 2, 3 tr) into each ch-2 loop, ch 7 *. Rep from * to * and close round.

Round 12: *(3 tr, ch 2, 3 tr) into each ch-2 loop; ch 5, 1 sc into ch loops of Rounds 9, 10 and 11, ch 5*. Rep from * to * and close round. (19 pointed motifs).

Round 13: *1 sc into ch-2 loop, ch 11*. Rep from * to * and close round.

Round 14: *1 dc on sc, 12 dc into next ch loop, 1 dc on sc, 13 dc into next ch loop*. Rep from * to * and close round.

Round 15: *6 dc on 6 dc, ch 5, skip 2 sts*. Rep from * to * and close round.

Round 16: as Round 9.
Round 17: as Round 10.
Round 18: as Round 11.
Round 19: *(3 tr, ch 2, 3 tr) into each ch-2 loop, ch 6, 1 sc into ch loops of Rounds 16, 17 and 18, ch 6*. Rep from * to * and close round. (32 points).
Round 20: as Round 13.
Round 21: *1 dc on sc, 11 dc into next ch loop, 1 dc on next sc, 12 dc into next ch-2 loops*. Rep from * to * and close round.
Round 22: *7 dc on 7 dc, ch 5, skip 2 sts*. Rep from * to * and close round.
Round 23: as Round 9.
Round 24: as Round 10.
Round 25: as Round 11.
Round 26: *(3 tr, ch 3, 1 sc) on last of the 3 tr just worked (= 1 picot), 3 tr into each ch-2 loop, ch 6, 1 sc into ch loops of Rounds 22, 23 and 24, ch 6*. Rep from * to * and close round. (45 pointed motifs).
Fasten off.

Fir-tree centerpiece

Materials: Crochet Cotton No 20 in écru, steel crochet hook size 10.
Ch 12 and join with a sl st into first ch to form a ring. (Replace first st of each round as follows: sc with ch 1, dc with ch 3, tr with ch 4. Close each round with 1 sl st into ch 1, 3rd or 4th starting ch.)
Round 1: work 22 dc into ring.
Round 2: 22 dc (1 dc on each dc).
Round 3: 44 tr (2 tr on each dc).
Round 4: *4 unfinished tr, yo, draw yarn through all 5 loops on hook, ch 5*. Rep from * to * ending with ch 5 and 1 sl st into 4th starting ch.
Round 5: 9 sc into each ch-5 loop.
Round 6: sl st to 5th sc of first loop, *1 sc, ch 9*. Working on 5th sc of each of following loops, rep from * to *.

Round 7: 13 sc into each ch-9 loop.
Round 8: Sl st to 7th sc of first loop, *1 sc, ch 13*. Working on 7th sc of following loops, rep from * to *.
Round 9: 17 sc into each ch-13 loop.
Round 10: Sl st to 9th sc of first loop, *(3 tr, ch 2, 3 tr) on same 9th sc, ch 11*. Working on 9th sc of following loops, rep from * to *.
Rounds 11 & 12: Sl st to ch-2 loop of previous row, *(3 tr, ch 2, 3 tr) into same ch-2 loop, ch 5, 1 sc into 6th ch of ch-11 loop of previous row, ch 5*. Starting in next ch-2 loop, rep from * to *.
Round 13: As Round 12, working 5 ch instead of 2 ch between the 3 tr.
Round 14: Sl st to ch-5 loop, *11 tr, ch 5, (1 dc, ch 2, 1 dc) into sc of previous round, ch 5*. Rep from * to *.
Round 15: *(1 tr, ch 1) on each of 10 tr of previous row, 1 tr on 11th tr, ch 4, 1 sc into ch-2 loop between 2 dc of previous row, ch 4*. Rep from * to *.
Round 16: *(1 tr, ch 2) 10 times, 1 tr, ch 3*. Rep from * to *.
Round 17: as Round 16.
Round 18: *Ch 7, 1 sc into next loop, skip 1 loop*. Rep from * to *.
Rounds 19 to 26: *Ch 7, 1 sc into next loop*. Rep from * to *.
Round 27: *3 dc into ch-7 loop, ch 3*. Rep from * to *.
Round 28: *1 dc on second of 3 dc of previous row, ch 1, (1 dc, ch 1, 1 dc) into ch-3 loop, ch 1*. Rep from * to *.
Round 29: *(2 dc, ch 3, 2 dc) into first loop, ch 3, skip 1 loop, 20 sc (1 sc on each dc and 1 sc into ch loop), skip 1 loop, ch 3*. Rep from * to * (14 groups of 20 sc).
Round 30: Sl st to ch-3 loop between 4 dc *([2 dc, ch 2] 3 times, 2 dc) into same ch-3 loop, ch 3, 18 sc on 2nd–19th sc of previous row, ch 3*. Working from next ch-3 loop, rep from * to *.
Round 31: Sl st to first ch-2 loop, *1 group (= 2 dc, ch 2, 2 dc) into same

ch-2 loop, ch 3, 1 group into next loop, ch 3, 1 group into 3rd loop, ch 3, 17 sc on sc, ch 3*. Working from next ch-2 loop, rep from * to *.

Round 32: Sl st to first ch-2 loop, *1 group into same ch-2 loop, ch 3, (1 group, ch 2, 1 group) into second loop, ch 3, 1 group into 3rd group, ch 3, 15 sc, ch 3*. Working from next ch-2 loop, rep from * to *.

Round 33: Sl st to first ch-2 loop, *1 group into same ch-2 loop, ch 3, 3 groups separated by ch-2 into next 3 loops, ch 3, 1 group into 5th loop, ch 3, 12 sc, ch 3*. Working from next ch-2 loop, rep from * to *.

Round 34: Sl st to first ch-2 loop, *1 group into same ch-2 loop, ch 3, 1 group into second loop, ch 2, 2 groups separate by ch-2 into 3rd loop, ch 2, 1 group into 4th loop, ch 3, 1 group into 5th loop, ch 4, 9 sc, ch 4*. Working from next ch-2 loop, rep from * to *.

Round 35: Sl st to first ch-2 loop, *1 group into same ch-2 loop, ch 3, 5 groups separated by ch-2 into next 5 loops, ch 3, 1 group into 7th loop, ch 5, 7 sc, ch 5*. Working from next ch-2 loop, rep from * to *.

Round 36: Sl st to first ch-2 loop, *1 group into same ch-2 loop, ch 3, 2 groups separated by ch-2 into next 2 loops, ch 2, 2 groups separated by ch-2 in 4th loop, ch 2, 2 groups separated by ch-2 into 5th and 6th loops, ch 3, 1 group into 7th loop, ch 4, 5 sc, ch 4*. Working from next ch-2 loop, rep from * to *.

Round 37: Sl st to first ch-2 loop, *1 group into same ch-2 loop, ch 3, 7 groups separated by ch-2 into next 7 loops, ch 3, 1 group into 9th loop, ch 4, 2 sc, ch 4*. Working from next ch-2 loop, rep from * to *.

Round 38: Sl st to first ch-2 loop, * **1 group with picot (= 2 dc, ch 3, 1 sc into second dc, 2 dc) into same ch-2 loop, ch 3**. Working from next ch-2 loop, work from ** to ** into remaining 8 ch-2 loops, 1 sc into next ch-4 loop before sc, 1 sc into ch-4 loop after sc*. Rep from * to *.
Fasten off.

Lacy motif

Materials: Crochet Cotton No 20, steel crochet hook size 11.
Ch 5 and join with a sl st into first ch to form a ring.
Round 1: Work 9 sc into ring and close with a sl st into first st of round.
Round 2: 2 sc into each st, working *only* into the back loop of the sts (ridged sc). 18 sts in all.
Rounds 3, 4 & 5: Increasing 6 sts evenly in each round, work in ridged sc.

Lacy motif

Rectangular mat

Round 6: *1 sc, ch 5, skip 2 sts*. Rep from * to * 11 times more.
Round 7: Sl st to 3rd ch in ch-5 loop, *1 sc into same 3rd ch, ch 1, **1 picot (= ch 3, 1 sl st into first ch), ch 1, 1 picot**, ch 3, rep from ** to **, ch 1, 1 sc into same ch, ch 4*. Rep from * to * 11 times more.
Round 8: Sl st to second st in ch-3 loop, *1 sc into same second ch, ch 1, **1 picot, ch 1**, rep from ** to ** twice more*. Rep from * to * 11 times more.
Fasten off.

Rectangular mat

Materials: Crochet Cotton No 5, aluminum crochet hook size B.
This mat consits of 96 identical motifs joined together in 8 rows of 12 motifs each.
1st motif: Ch 8 and join with a sl st into first ch to form a ring.
(Replace the first dc of every row with ch 3 and end with 1 sl st into 3rd starting ch.)
Round 1: work 16 dc into ring.
Round 2: *1 dc, ch 3, skip 1 st*. Rep

Border in filet crochet for rectangular
cloth and diagram

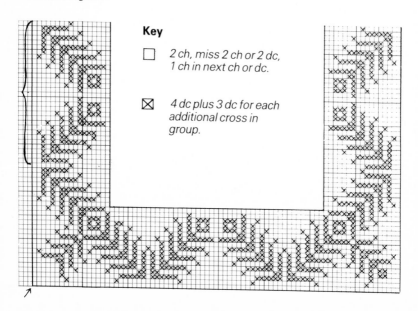

Key

☐   2 ch, miss 2 ch or 2 dc,
1 ch in next ch or dc.

⊠   4 dc plus 3 dc for each
additional cross in
group.

from * to * 8 times altogether.
Round 3: *4 tr into first ch-3 loop, (replace first tr with ch 4), ch 9, 4 tr into 2nd ch-3 loop, ch 2*. Rep from * to * 4 times altogether, ending with 1 sl st into 4 starting ch.
Fasten off.
Work the other 95 motifs in the same way but join each one, when working Round 3, to those already completed as follows:
Round 3 (joining round): *4 tr, ch 4, 1 sc into 5th ch of ch-9 loop of motif already completed, ch 4, 4 tr.
Round 3: *4 tr into first ch-3 loop, 1 sc into 5th ch of ch-9 loop of completed motif, ch 4, 4 tr into 2nd ch-3 loop, ch 1, 1 sc into ch-2 loop of completed motif, ch 1*. Rep from * to * to end of round, close round and fasten off.
When all 96 motifs have been worked and the rectangle completed, work border as follows:
Round 1: on each side work: 4 tr and ch-3 into each loop, and into each corner loop work: 4 tr, ch 6 and 4 tr.
Round 2: *([1 tr, ch 1] 3 times, 1 tr) into first loop, ch 4, 1 sc into next loop, ch 4*. Rep from * to * along each side, working (1 tr, ch 1) 7 times into each ch-6 corner loop.
Round 3: *3 sc into ch-4 loop after sc of previous row, (1 sc, 1 picot, 1 sc) into ch between each tr, 3 sc into next ch-4 loop*. Rep from * to * along each side, working (1 sc, 1 picot, 1 sc) 6 times into each corner.
Fasten off.

Border in filet crochet for rectangular cloth

Materials: Crochet Cotton No 20, steel crochet hook size 10.
Stitches used: mesh stitch with blocks and spaces (see page 22).
Start at short edge of border and make 248 ch.

Row 1: 1 dc in 8th ch from hook (= 1 square), * miss 2 ch, 1 dc *. Rep from * to * (= 81 squares).
Continue in patt from chart (reading even rows from left to right and odd rows from right to left) until Row 17 has been completed.
Row 18: (Wrong side), patt across 17 squares, miss 47 squares, join in a 2nd ball of yarn and patt across remaining 17 squares.
Continue in patt, working each side separately, until Row 56 has been completed.
Rep Rows 27-56 (For a longer border these rows may be repeated once again).
To complete patt sequence on sides, rep Rows 27-33.
Row 34: (Wrong side), patt across 17 squares, make 140 ch, then taking care to keep chain untwisted, patt across remaining 17 squares, breaking off 2nd ball of yarn.
Continue in patt across all sts, working from Row 17 back to Row 1.
Fasten off.
Lay finished border over fabric and stitch firmly together. Neaten edges of fabric.

Square tablecloth

Materials: 61 oz (1700 grams) (approx) crochet cotton No 5 in écru, aluminum crochet hook size B.
Specifications: 66 × 66 in approx (170 × 170 cm).
324 large motifs worked separately and joined together, according to directions given after instructions for first motif, to form 18 strips of 18 large motifs. 255 small motifs are also worked to fill the spaces between the large ones.
Large motif
Ch 5 and join with a sl st into first ch to form a ring. (Replace the first dc in each round with ch 3 or the first tr

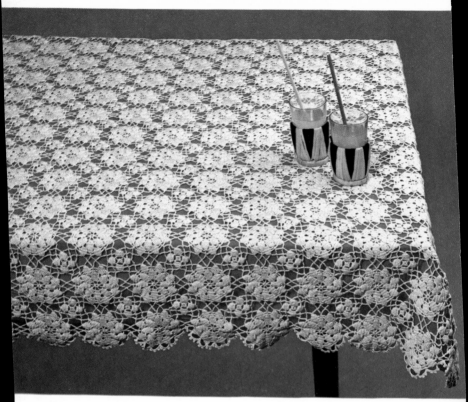

Square tablecloth

with ch 4. Close each round with 1 sl st into the 3rd or 4th starting chain of the same round.)

Round 1: work (1 tr, ch 3) 8 times into ring.

Round 2: (5 dc, ch 2) into each ch-3 loop. (8 times)

Round 3: *5 dc on 5 dc, 1 dc into ch-2 loop, ch 5*. Rep from * to * 8 times altogether.

Round 4: *6 unfinished tr, yo, draw yarn through all 7 loops on hook (1 cluster), ch 3, 5 dc into ch-5 loop of previous row, ch 3*. Rep from * to * 8 times altogether, ending round with 1 sl st on closing st of first tr cluster.

Round 5: *1 dc on cluster, ch 3, 5 dc on 5 dc, 1 dc into ch-3 loop*. Rep from * to * 8 times altogether.

Round 6: *Ch 11, skip 1 dc, 5 unfinished tr on next 5 dc, yo, draw yarn through all 6 loops on hook, ch 11, 1 sc on dc*. Rep from * to * 8 times altogether. Fasten off.

The 18 motifs which are made into strips are joined together as Round 6 is being worked as follows:

Round 6 (joining round): ch 11, skip 1 dc, 5 unfinished tr on next 5 dc, yo, draw yarn through all 6 loops on hook, 1 sc into corresponding loop of motif to be joined, ch 5, 1 sc on dc of previous round, ch 5, 1 sc into next loop of motif to be joined, ch 5; continue as for Round 6 of first motif. As the strips are made, the motifs will be joined to those each side of them as well as to those above and below but 2 loops will remain free between one join and the next. The spaces thus formed

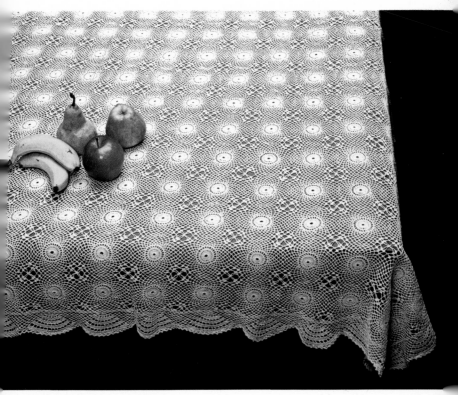

White rectangular tablecloth

will be filled with the small motifs, which are worked as follows:

Small motif

Ch 4 and join with a sl st into first ch to form a ring. (Close each round with a sl st into starting ch of same round.)

Round 1: work 8 sc into ring.

Round 2: *1 dc, ch 5, skip 1 st*. Repeat from * to * 4 times altogether.

Round 3: (7 dc, ch 5) into each of the 4 ch-5 loops.

Round 4 (joining round): *7 unfinished tr, yo, draw yarn through all 8 loops on hook into 7 dc of previous row, 1 sc into a free loop in large motif to be joined, ch 5, 1 sc into ch-5 loop of Round 3, ch 5, 1 sc into next free loop in large motif, ch 5*. Rep from * to * 4 times in all, thus joining the free ch loops of the large motifs. Fasten off. Complete the tablecloth by working the following edging on all 4 sides as follows:

Into each ch-11 loop (3 sc, 1 picot) 3 times, 3 sc.

Into each ch-5 loop (3 sc, 1 picot, 3 sc).

Fasten off and weave all loose ends of yarn into back of tablecloth.

White rectangular tablecloth

Materials: 18 oz (500 grams) Crochet Cotton No 40, steel crochet hook size 12.

Specifications: Approx 60 × 80 in (150 × 200 cm). 280 circular motifs joined to form 20 strips of 14.

First motif: Ch 15 and join with a sl st into first ch to form a ring.

(Replace first dc in each round with ch 3 and first tr with ch 4. Close with 1 sl st into 3rd or 4th starting ch).

Round 1: work 24 dc into ring.

Round 2: (1 dc, ch 1) 24 times.

Round 3: 2 sc into each ch.

Round 4: *1 dc, ch 2, skip 1 st*. Rep from * to * to end of round.

Round 5: 3 sc into each ch-2 loop.

Round 6: *1 sc, ch 5, skip 2 sts, 1 sc, ch 5, skip 1 st*. Rep from * to * (28 loops) and continue with 1 sc into first loop without closing the round.

Rounds 7 & 8: *1 sc into each loop, ch 5*.

Rounds 9 & 10: *1 sc into each loop, ch 6*.

Round 11: *3 dc, ch 5, 3 dc (corner) into first loop, (ch 6, 1 sc into next loop) 6 times, ch 6*. Rep from * to * 4 times altogether.

Round 12: *3 dc into ch loop before corner, (ch 6, 3 dc, ch 11, 3 dc) into ch-5 corner loop between 6 dc of previous row, ch 6, 3 dc into next loop (ch 6, 1 sc into next loop) 5 times*. Rep from * to * 4 times altogether. Fasten off. Work the rest of the motifs in the same way, joining them to each other on Round 12 as follows:

Round 12 (joining round): *3 dc into ch loop before corner, ch 3, 1 sc into corresponding loop of first motif, ch 3, 3 dc, ch 6, 1 sc into 6th of ch-11 of motif or motifs to be joined, ch 6, 3 dc, ch 3, 1 sc into corresponding loop, ch 3, 3 dc, (ch 3, 1 sc into corresponding loop to be joined, ch 3, 1 sc into loop of previous row) 5 times altogether, ch 3, 1 sc into corresponding loop, ch 3*. Rep from * to * on each side of the motifs to be joined. On the 4 motifs which form the 4 corners of the tablecloth, replace the ch-11 between the dc with ch-3.

When the strips have been completed, to make up the main part of the tablecloth work the following border starting from one of the corners.

Round 1: *(3 dc, ch 3, 3 dc) into ch-3 corner loop, ch 6, 1 sc into each loop across*. Rep from * to * on each remaining corner and 3 sides.

Round 2: *(3 dc, ch 3, 3 dc) into ch-3 corner loop, 4 dc into each ch loop*.

Round 3: *(3 dc, ch 3, 3 dc) into ch-3 corner loop, ch 6, 1 sc into first of next 4 dc*.

Round 4: *8 tr separated by ch-2 into corner loop, ch 2, (1 sc into next loop, ch 6) 10 times, 1 sc, ch 2, 4 tr separated by ch 2 into next loop, ch 2*.

Round 5: 9 groups of 3 tr clusters (= 3 unfinished tr, yo, draw yarn through all loops on hook) separated by ch 2 into ch loops between tr in previous row, *ch 2, (1 sc, ch 6) 9 times, 1 sc, ch 2, 5 groups of 3 tr clusters separated by ch 2, ch 2*. Rep from * to * along remaining sides and work 9 groups of 3 tr clusters separated by ch 2 at each remaining corner.

Round 6: 10 groups of 4 tr into each ch-2 corner loop, *(1 sc, ch 6) 8 times, 1 sc, 6 groups of 4 tr into each of the following ch-2 loops*. Rep from * to * along remaining sides and work 10 groups of 4 tr into each ch-2 corner loop.

Round 7: (1 tr on first corner tr, ch 3, skip 2 sts) 13 times, *1 sc, (ch 6, 1 sc) 7 times, (ch 3, 1 tr, skip 2 sts) 7 times, ch 3. Rep from * to * along remaining sides and work (1 tr, ch 3, skip 2 sts) 13 times into remaining 3 corners.

Round 8: 13 groups of 4 tr into each ch-3 corner loop, *(1 sc, ch 6) 6 times, 1 sc, 8 groups of 4 tr into each of following ch-3 loops*. Rep from * to * along remaining sides and work 13 groups of 4 tr into each ch-3 corner loop of remaining 3 corners.

Round 9: (1 tr on first corner tr, ch 3, skip 2 sts) 18 times on each corner. *1 sc, (ch 6, 1 sc) 5 times, (ch 3, 1 tr, skip 2 sts) 9 times, ch 3*. Rep from * to * along remaining sides.

Round 10: 17 groups of 4 tr into each ch-3 corner loop, on each corner. *(1 sc, ch 6) 4 times, 1 sc, 10 groups of 4 tr into each of the following ch-3 loops. Rep from * to * along remaining sides.

Round 11: (1 tr on first corner tr, ch 3, skip 1 st) 22 times, on each corner, *1 sc, (ch 6, 1 sc) 3 times, (ch 3, 1 tr, skip 2 sts) 12 times, ch 3*. Rep from * to * along remaining sides.

Round 12: 22 groups of 4 tr into each ch-3 corner loop, on each corner. *(1 sc, ch 6) twice, 1 sc, 13 groups of 4 tr into each of following ch-3 loops*. Rep from * to * along remaining sides.

Round 13: *1 sc, ch 6, skip 3 sts*. Rep from * to * for entire round.

Round 14: *1 sc into each ch loop, ch 6*.

Round 15: *(3 sc, 1 picot, 3 sc) into each ch loop*.

Fasten off and weave all loose ends of yarn into back of tablecloth.

Double-bed coverlet

Materials: 72 oz (2,000 grams) Crochet Cotton No 20 in white, steel crochet hook size 11.

Specifications: 739 hexagons joined in strips of 25½ motifs. (In rows starting with a tr, replace stitch with ch 4. Close each round with 1 sl st into top of starting ch.)

Hexagon

Ch 8 and join with a sl st into first ch to form a ring.

Row 1: work 24 tr into ring.

Row 2: *(1 tr, ch 4, 1 tr) into first st, skip 1 st, ch 4, 1 dtr, ch 4, skip 1 st*. Continuing into next tr of previous row, rep from * to * 5 times more (12 loops in all).

Round 3: *(1 tr, ch 4, 1 tr) into ch-4 loop, ch 4, 1 sc into ch, 1 sc on dtr, 1

Overleaf, double-bed coverlet

sc into next ch, ch 4*. Rep from * to * to end of round.

Round 4: *(1 tr, ch 4, 1 tr) into ch-4 loop between 2 tr, ch 4, 1 tr into ch, 3 tr on 3 sc, 1 tr into next ch, ch 4*. Rep from * to * to end of round.

Round 5: *(1 tr, ch 4, 1 tr) into ch-4 loop between 2 tr, ch 4, 4 tr into ch-4, 5 tr on 5 tr, 4 tr into next ch-4, ch 4*. Rep from * to * to end of round.

Work the rest of the hexagons in the same way, joining them to each other on Round 5 as follows:

Round 5 (joining round): *(1 tr, ch 2, 1 sc into corresponding loop of first hexagon, ch 2, 1 tr) into ch-4 loop between 2 tr, ch 4, 1 sc into first tr of first hexagon, 7 tr, 1 sc into 7th tr of first hexagon, 6 tr, 1 sc into 13th tr of first hexagon, ch 4*. Rep from * to * on all sides to be joined.

When the coverlet is complete, fill in the empty spaces on the sides with quarter hexagons worked in the same way.

Complete by working 1 row of tr around the entire coverlet.

Fasten off and weave all loose ends into back of work.

Double-bed coverlet in filet crochet

Materials: 65 oz (1,800 grams) Crochet Cotton No 40, steel crochet hook size 12.

Specifications: approx 102 × 110 in (260 × 280 cm) made up of a central square approx 40 × 40 in (100 × 100 cm) consisting of 40 strips of 40 motifs each, a wide border in filet crochet and an edging in openwork crochet.

(Replace first dc in each round with ch 3 and close with 1 sl st into 3rd starting ch.)

First motif

Ch 8 and join with a sl st into first chain to form a ring.

Round 1: work (1 dc, ch 2) 8 times into ring.

Round 2: *4 dc into first ch-2 loop, ch 5, 4 dc into next loop, ch 1*. Rep from * to * 4 times altogether. Fasten off.

Work the next motif, joining it to one side of the first motif while working Round 2 as follows:

Round 2 (joining round): 4 dc, ch 2, 1 sc into 3rd ch in ch-5 loop of first motif, ch 2, 4 dc into next loop, 1 sc into next ch of first motif, 4 dc into next loop, ch 2, 1 sc into 3rd ch in ch-5 loop of first motif, ch 2.

Continue until there are 40 motifs in the first strip.

Continue making the rest of the strips in the same way, joining the motifs on two sides until the square is completed.

Work right around the square, starting from one corner, as follows:

Round 1: (1 dc, ch 5, 1 dc) into 3rd ch of ch-5 corner loop, ch 3, 1 dc on first dc of first group, ch 3, 1 dc on next sc, ch 3, 1 dc on 4th dc of second group, ch 3, 1 dc on sc joining motifs, ch 3*. Rep from * to * on all 4 sides of square.

Round 2: 3 dc into corner ch on all 4 corners, 1 dc on every dc and 1 dc into each ch on all 4 sides.

Continue working in filet crochet design, following the diagrams on pages 224-5 and 222-3.

Openwork border for outer edge:

Round 1: starting from one corner, *2 dc, ch 2, 2 dc, ch 2, 2 dc, ch 2, 2 dc into corner*. Rep from * to * on remaining 3 corners. *Ch 7, 1 sc into 3rd dc, ch 7, skip next 2 sts, (3 dc, ch 2, 3dc) into next dc*. Rep from * to * on all 4 sides.

Round 2: *(2 dc, ch 2, 2 sc) into each ch-2 corner loop*. Rep from * to * on remaining 3 corners. *Ch 5, 1 sc into first ch-7 loop, ch 5, 1 sc into next ch-7 loop, ch 5, (3 dc, ch 2, 3 dc) into ch-2 loop between 6 dc*. Rep from * to * on all 4 sides.

Round 3: *(2 dc, ch 2, 2 dc) into each ch-2 loop between corner dc (3 times altogether)*. Rep from * to *

on remaining 3 corners. *Ch 7, 1 sc into ch-5 loop between sc, ch 7, (3 dc, ch 2, 3 dc) into ch-2 loop between dc*. Rep from * to * on all 4 sides.

Round 4: *(2 dc, ch 2, 2 dc) into each ch-2 loop between corner dc (5 times altogether)*. Rep from * to *

Diagram of borders for double-bed coverlet in filet crochet, illustrated overleaf, (enlarged detail on pages 222-3)

223

Detail of diagram for internal border in filet crochet

on remaining 3 corners. Rep from * to * as for Round 2 on all 4 sides.

Round 5: On all 4 corners, work as for corners in Round 3, repeating sequence 5 times instead of 3. On all 4 sides, rep from * to * as for Round 3.

Round 6: On all 4 corners, work as for corners in Round 5. On all 4 sides, rep from * to * as for Round 2.

Round 7: *(2 dc, ch 2, 2 dc) into each ch-2 loop between corner dc, ch 2, (1 sc into next loop, ch 2) 5 times*. Rep from * to * on remaining 3 corners. On all 4 sides, rep from * to * as for Round 3.

Round 8: *(2 dc, ch 2, 2 dc) into each ch-2 loop between corner dc, ch 2, (1 sc into next loop, ch 2, 1 sc into next loop, ch 2) 5 times*. Rep from * to * on remaining 3 corners. On all 4 sides, rep from * to * as for Round 2.

Round 9: *(2 dc, ch 2, 2 dc) into each ch-2 loop between corner dc, ch 5, (1 sc into ch-2 loop between 2 sc, ch 5) 5 times*. Rep from * to * on remaining 3 corners. On all 4 sides, rep from * to * as for Round 3.

Round 10: *(2 dc, ch 2, 2 dc) into each ch-2 loop between corner dc, ch 5, (1 sc into next loop, ch 5, 1 sc into next loop, ch 5) 5 times*. Rep from * to * on remaining 3 corners.

On all 4 sides rep from * to * as for Round 2.

Round 11: as for Round 9.

Round 12: as for Round 10.

Round 13: (2 dc, ch 2, 2 dc) into ch-2 loop between corner dc, ch 7, 1 sc into loop between 2 sc, **(ch 7, 2 dc, ch 2, 2 dc) into next loop between 2 dc, ch 7, (2 dc, ch 2, 2 dc) into next loop between 2 sc**. Rep from ** to ** twice, ch 7, 1 sc into next loop

Yellow cot-blanket

between sc, ch 7, (2 dc, ch 2, 2 dc) into ch-2 loop. Rep from beg of round on each corner. On all 4 sides rep from * to * as for Round 3.

Round 14: As for Round 10 on each corner, repeating sequence 7 times instead of 5. On all 4 sides, as for Round 2.

Round 16: as for Round 14.

Round 17: as for Round 15.

Fasten off and weave all loose ends into back of coverlet.

Yellow cot-blanket

Materials: 14½ oz (400 grams) baby yarn in yellow, aluminum crochet hook size B.

Stitches used: raised shell stitch (see page 92), double and single crochet.

Make a chain 30 in (80 cm) in length and work in raised shell st for approx 36 in (90 cm).

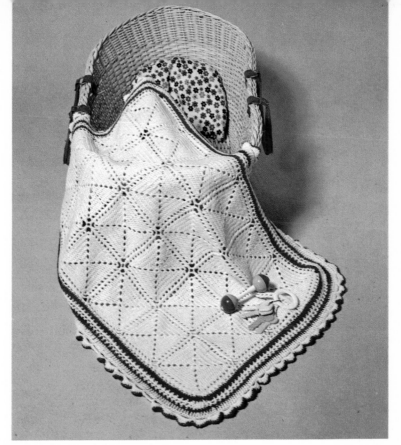

White carriage blanket with red border

Complete blanket with the following border:

Round 1: Ch 1, 1 sc into each st, close round with a sl st into first ch.

Round 2: (replace first dc in each round with ch 3) *3 dc into same st on corner, **ch 5, skip 3 sts, 4 sc into next 4 sts, skip 3 sts, ch 5, 2 dc on next 2 sts**,*. Rep from ** to ** to next corner and from * to * to end of round.

Round 3: *7 dc into 3 corner dc, **ch 5, 2 sc on 2 sc, ch 5, 2 dc on 2 dc**,*. Rep from ** to ** to next corner and from * to * to end of round.

Round 4: *(replace first sc in each round with ch 1) (6 sc, ch 5, 6 sc) into 7 corner dc, **ch 5, 1 sc on 2 sc of previous round, ch 5, 4 sc, ch 5, 4 sc on 5 dc**,*. Rep from ** to ** to next corner and from * to * to end of round.

Fasten off.

White cot-blanket

White and red carriage blanket

Materials: 11 oz (300 grams) baby yarn in white, small amount of baby yarn in red (or other contrasting color), aluminum hook size 2.

This rug consists of 24 squares, worked separately, and sewn together invisibly.

Square: With white wool ch 8 and join with a sl st into first ch to form a ring.

Round 1: Into ring, work ch 3, 2 dc, *ch 3, 3 dc*. Rep from * to * 3 times and close round with 1 sl st into 3rd starting ch.

Round 2: Ch 3, 2 dc on 2 dc of previous row, *(2 dc, ch 3, 2 dc) into ch-3 to form corner loops, 3 dc*. Rep from * to * to end of round, closing with 1 sl st into 3rd starting ch.

Rounds 3, 4 & 5: as for Round 2, working dc on dc and the corners into ch-3 corner loops.

Round 6: *Ch 5 on corner (1 dc, ch 1, skip 1 st) along the side*. Rep from * to * to end of row, closing with 1 sl st. Fasten off.

Work another 23 identical squares. Join them together to form a rectangle of 6 × 4 squares with small, neat stitches which do not interfere with the design.

Complete rug with the following border:

Round 1: (white wool) work in sc, with ch 3 into each corner.

Round 2: (white wool) *1 dc, ch 1, skip 1 st; on the corners skip 2 ch and work 3 dc*.

Round 3: (red wool) *1 dc on dc, 1 dc into ch; 4 dc into each corner*.

Rounds 4 & 5: (white wool) as Round 2, working 7 dc into corners.

Round 6: (red wool) as previous round.

Round 7: (white wool) *1 tr on each st*.

Round 8: (white wool) *1 sc, ch 6, skip 5 sts*.

Round 9: (white wool) *(1 hdc, 7 dc, 1 hdc) into each ch loop*.

Round 10: (red wool) reverse sc for entire round.

Fasten off.

White cot blanket

Materials: 11 oz (300 grams) sport yarn in white. Aluminum crochet hook size D.

Stitches used: large star stitch (see page 92), hdc, reverse sc.

Make a ch 25½ in (65 cm) in length and work in large star st for 45 in (115 cm).

Complete the blanket with 8 rows of hdc, working 3 sts into same st on each corner. Put the finishing touch with 1 row of reverse sc. Fasten off.

Cushion no. 1

Materials: Knitting worsted in red and a small quantity in black. Aluminum crochet hook size H.

Make a chain to the length desired,

(Left) Cushion no. 1 (Right) Cushion no. 2

in multiples of 4 sts.

Round 1: starting on 4th ch from hook, work in dc to end.

Round 2: * 4 front post dc (see page 38), (insert hook between first and second vertical bar of st and bring it forward between 2nd and 3rd vertical bar), 4 back raised dc (worked in same way as previous 4 except that hook is inserted from back to front and then brought out towards the back) *. Rep from * to * to end of row.

Repeat for 4 rows altogether and then reverse the order (4 back and 4 forward, etc.).

Continue in this way until the desired sized is reached.

For the back of cushion, make the same number of ch and work in dc until back is the same size as front.

Join front to back on 3 sides, insert cushion pad and sew 4th side. Complete with 1 row of sc and 1 row of reverse sc in contrasting color.

Cushion no. 2

Materials: Medium weight household string in blue, red and white. Aluminum hook size D.

With red cotton, ch 5 and join with a sl st into first ch to form a ring.

Round 1: Work 10 sc into ring.

Round 2: * 2 sc on each sc of previous round *. Rep from * to * to end of round, closing with 1 sl st.

Round 3: (blue cotton) * 1 hazelnut (= 3 unfinished dc, yo, drawn yarn through all loops on hook) on each st of previous round, ch 1 *. Rep from * to *, closing with 1 sl st.

Round 4: Sl st to first ch, * 1 hazelnut (= 4 unfinished dc, yo, draw yarn through all loops on hook) into ch, ch

2 *. Rep from * to * to end of round.

Round 5: as Round 4 but working 3 ch between hazelnuts.

Round 6: For this and next 2 rounds carry the white cotton through the work even when the red parts are being worked and vice versa. To change color, work the last stitch of the first color without finishing it completely; now take the second color and finish the stitch with it. * (Red cotton) 7 tr into ch-3 loop of previous round (finish the 7th tr with white cotton); with white cotton, work 1 group of 3 dc into each of the next 4 spaces (finish the last dc of the 4th group with red cotton) *. Rep from * to * to end of round.

Round 7: * (red cotton) (2 dc between 2 tr of previous row) 6 times (12 dc now worked in red cotton), with white cotton work 1 group of 3 dc into each of next 5 spaces *. Rep from * to * to end of round.

Round 8: * (red cotton) (1 dc, ch 1, 1 dc) between 3rd and 4th of 12 red dc of previous row, (1 dc, 1 ch, 1 dc) between 5th and 6th dc, (1 dc, ch 1, 1 dc) between 7th and 8th dc, (1 dc, ch 1, 1 dc) between 9th and 10th dc. Change to white cotton – 3 dc between 11th and 12th red dc, 1 group of 3 dc into each of next 4 spaces, 1 group of 3 dc between first and second of next 12 dc. * Rep from * to * to end of round.

Round 9: (white cotton) starting from a corner, * 3 dc between 3rd and 4th red dc of previous row, ch 2, 1 group of 3 dc between 5th and 6th red dc, 1 group of 3 dc between 7th and 8th red dc, 1 group of 3 dc into each of next 5 spaces, 1 group of 3 dc between first and second red dc *. Rep from * to * to end of round.

Round 10: Sl st to ch-2 corner loop, * (1 group of 3 dc, ch 2, 1 group of 3 dc) into same ch-2 corner loop; 1 group of 3 dc into each of next 7 spaces. * Rep from * to * to end of round.

Round 11: Sl st to ch-2 corner loop * (1 group of 3 dc, ch 2, 1 group of 3 dc) into same ch-2 corner loop; 1 group of 3 dc into each of next 8 spaces *. Rep from * to * to end of round.

Round 12: Sl st to ch-2 corner loop, * (1 group of 3 dc, ch 2, 1 group of 3 dc) into same ch-2 corner loop; 1 group of 3 dc into each of next 9 spaces *. Rep from * to * to end of round.

Continue working in the same way until required size is reached or slightly smaller to allow for following 3 rounds of border.

Round 1: (blue cotton) * (2 dc, ch 2, 2 dc,) into ch-2 corner loop; 1 dc into each st along side *. Rep from * to * to end of round.

Round 2: (red cotton) * (2 dc, ch 2, 2 dc) into ch-2 corner loop; 1 dc into each st along side *. Rep from * to * to end of round.

Round 3: (white cotton) * (2 dc, ch 2, 2 dc) into ch-2 corner loop; 1 dc into each st along side *. Rep from * to * to end of round.

Make another square, the same size, in dc and join it to the front on 3 sides. Insert cushion pad and sew up the 4th side.

Table runner in filet crochet

Materials: Crochet Cotton No. 20. Steel crochet hook size 10.
Stitches used: blocks and spaces in mesh st (see page 22).

Table runner in filet crochet (diagram overleaf)

Ch 180 and work the first row in mesh st then continue as shown in diagram until desired length is reached. (1 cross corresponds to 3 dc).

Border in filet crochet for towel

Materials: Crochet Cotton No. 20. Steel crochet hook size 11.
Stitches used: mesh stitch (1 dc, ch 3, skip 3 sts, 1 dc), blocks and spaces in mesh stitch (see page 22).
Ch 56 and work according to diagram until desired length has been reached (1 cross on the diagram corresponds to 4 dc).

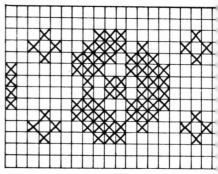

Diagram of flower motif for towel

Sew border to edge of towel and make a fringe (see page 169) 6 in (15 cm) in depth, knotting it 3 times.

Diagram for table runner in filet crochet

Towel with border in filet crochet

GIFTS AND THINGS TO MAKE

Easy-to-make patterns and practical ideas

So many useful and attractive things can be made with a crochet hook, some yarn and the simplest of stitches. The daily routine can be very much enlivened if unusual, colorful objects – made by our own hands or by the hands of a friend – help us in the monotony of domestic chores. For instance, bright pot-holders and oven-gloves, shopping bags, little baskets or mats can give an air of originality to every room in the home. The ideas covered in this section should be regarded only as suggestions – your own imagination will be able to conjure up so many more original schemes.

For the children, too, there are toys reminiscent of the rag dolls of our grandparents' day. Crocheted toys can be as bright and full of color as rainbows and a child appreciates the individuality of hand-made dolls – no other child ever has one exactly the same. It is usually the hand-made toy that becomes the favorite and inseparable bedtime companion.

Unusual materials can be used, too, to make a gift that is quite out of the ordinary. Such things as cord, strips of leather or fabric, twine, string, etc., are only a few suggestions. It is up to you to develop the ideas we give you here and to make something that reflects your personal taste, to create for the sheer joy of creating something which is truly yours, made with your own hands.

Yellow belt

Materials: Yellow twine (or string). 1 belt buckle. Aluminum crochet hook size B.
Ch 8 and work in sc for about 38 inches (approx 1 meter).
Work 1 row in sc and 1 row in reverse sc right around the strip. Fasten off.
Make a loop by working in sc on 4 ch until strip is slightly longer than width of belt. Fasten off and stitch to wrong side of belt. Slip the buckle over the end of belt nearest to loop and stitch down on wrong side.

White belt in afghan stitch

Materials: 2 oz (50 grams) dishcloth type cotton. 1 belt buckle. Afghan hook size D.
Ch 7 and work in afghan st for 38 inches (approx 1 meter).
Fasten off.
For loop, ch 3 and work in afghan st for 4 in (10 cm).
Fasten off.
Work 1 row of sc around the strip.
Sew loop in position and slip buckle over end of belt and stitch down firmly. Press the belt under a damp cloth.

Yellow belt and white belt in afghan stitch

Red slippers

Materials: 4 oz (100 grams) knitting worsted. Aluminum crochet hook size D.

Stitches used: sc, sl st, dc, hdc. Ch 23 and work up and down each side, without reversing the work or closing a round, as follows:

Round 1: 3 sc into second ch from hook, 1 sc into each ch as far as the st before center of ch (13 sts worked on 11 ch so far). 1 hdc into each of following 5 ch, 1 dc into each of next 5 ch, 5 dc into last ch and mark 3rd dc as point of toe. Work back along other side of ch, keeping the stitches corresponding to the stitches first worked. End with 1 sc into same st into which 3 sc were worked at beg of round.

Round 2: 2 sc into each of next 2 sts, 1 sc into each st up to the 5 dc for toe. Work 2 sc into each of these 5 dc, marking the 2 central sts. Work symmetrically back along other side.

Round 3: 2 sc into first st, 1 sc into next st (center back), 1 sc into each following st up to the 5 groups of 2 sts at toe. * 1 sc into 1 group, 2 sc into next group, * and rep from * to * 5 times altogether.

Work along other side symmetrically.

Round 4: * 1 sc into next st, 2 sc into following st * twice; 1 sc on each st up to 5 toe sts; * 1 sc on next st, 2 sc on following st * 5 times altogether; 1 st on each st.

Round 5: 1 sc into each of next 2 sts, 2 sc into following sts, 1 st into next sts, 2 sts into following sts, 1 st into

each st up to a point opposite the center of ch, 1 hdc into each of next 3 sts, 1 dc into each st up to the 5 groups at toe; * 2 dc into following sts, 1 dc into next st * 5 times.
Work symmetrically, in same way, along other side.
Round 6: 1 sc on each st, working into front loop only, until first st is reached.
Rounds 7, 8, 9 & 10: 1 sc on each st, working into both loops, for entire round.
Round 11: 2 sc into next 2 sts, * 1 sc into next 2 sts, (= 1 decrease), 1 sc into sc *. Rep from * to * up to the toe. * 1 sc into 2 sts, 1 sc into next st *. Rep from * to * 5 times. Work symmetrically, in same way, along other side.
Round 12: 1 sc into each st, 1 dec at center back, 5 sts at toe.
Round 13: 1 st into each st.
Round 14: 1 sl st into each st up to the 3 toe sts; ch 20 for lace, 1 sl st on second ch from hook and on each of the next 18 ch, sl st to same position on other side of slipper and work a second lace in the same way.
Make a second slipper to match.

Blue slippers

Materials: Knitting worsted (approx 4 oz (100 grams). Aluminum crochet hook size E.
Each slipper consists of 8 squares.
Square: Ch 4 and join with a sl st into first ch to form a ring.
(Replace first dc with ch 2 and first sc with ch 1, closing each round with 1 sl st into starting ch.)
Round 1: work * 3 dc, ch 2* 4 times into ring.
Round 2: * 3 dc on 3 dc (2 dc, ch 2, 2 dc) into ch-2 corner loop *. Rep from * to * to end of round. (7 dc on each side).
Round 3: * 6 dc along side (2 dc, ch 2, 2 dc) into ch-2 corner loop *. Rep from * to * to end of round (10 dc on each side).
Rounds 4 and 5 : 1 sc on each st, 3 dc into corner ch. Fasten off.
Work another 7 squares in the same way and sew them together as indicated in diagram.
Finish off the 4 turned-back edges as follows: *(1 sc, ch 2, 1 tr) into same st, skip 1 st *. Rep from * to * on all 4 edges and fasten off.
Make a second slipper to match.

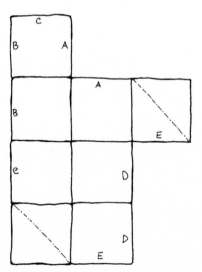

Diagram for blue slippers. Sew squares together as shown, then stitch sides marked with the same letter, folding back at dotted lines.

Red, blue and 3-color slippers

3-color slippers

Materials: Sport yarn worked double (i.e. 2 strands at a time), aluminum crochet hook size F.

Sole: (starting from heel). Ch 6, 5 sc into second ch from hook, continue working in sc, starting each row with ch 1 and increasing 1 st on both sides every 2 rows twice. Continue until work measures 3 in (8 cm), increasing 1 st on both sides every 2 rows twice. When 5½ in (14 cm) have been worked from beg, shape toe by decreasing 1 st on both sides every 2 rows three times. When work measures approx 6¼ in (16 cm), fasten off.

Upper: Ch 8 and work in hdc (starting from second ch from hook – 7 hdc in all), increasing 1 st at both sides on every row 4 times. Continue to increase 1 st at both sides every 3 rows twice (19 hdc). When work measures approx 3 in (8 cm) from beg, fasten off.

Return to last 5 sts of front just finished and work back of upper in hdc for 4 in (10 cm). Fasten off. Work the other half of back of upper in the same way, on first 5 sts of front. Make up by joining the 2 back halves with a flat seam at center back. Now join the upper to the sole.

Finish off with 1 row of sc over all stitched seams.

Make a second slipper in the same way.

Pot-holders in the shape of a tomato and a vase

Tomato-shaped pot-holder

Materials: Crochet Cotton No 5, aluminum crochet hook size B.
With red cotton, ch 4 and join with a sl st into first ch to form a ring.
Round 1: Work 10 sc into ring.
Round 2: Working only on 5 sts, work 6 sc, turn.
Round 3: 10 sc, turn.
Round 4: 14 sc, turn.
Round 5: 22 sc, turn.
Round 6: 24 sc and, without turning, work 7 sc over sts of first round left unworked, turn.
Continue working complete rounds, increasing a few stitches on each round for a further 14 rounds and turning work at end of every round.
Round 21: reverse sc.
With green cotton, work 2 leaves as follows: Ch 7 and work 1 row in sc increasing 2 sts at the sides and 2 sts in the middle for 3 rounds.
Make another leaf in the same way.
Make a stem: ch 22 work 1 row of sc. Join leaves at 2 points, and sew stem into position.

Stitch the leaves and stem on to the pot-holder. Make a ring of 10 ch worked in sc and stitch it to the top where leaves join.

Vase-shaped pot-holder

Materials: Crochet Cotton No 5 in light and dark green, aluminum crochet hook size B.
With light green cotton ch 8 and join with a sl st into first ch to form a ring. (Close each round with a sl st into first starting st.)
Round 1: Work 12 sc into ring.
Round 2: 18 sc.
Round 3: 24 sc.
Round 4: 30 sc.
Round 5: * Ch 1, 1 group (= 4 dc worked into same st in Round 3, leaving threads fairly loose to avoid pulling, remove hook from working loop and insert it in the ch st worked at beg of sequence; pick up working loop again and close it tightly with 1 ch), 2 sc *. Rep from * to * to end of

Acorn-shaped pot-holder and a square pot-holder

round (9 groups separated by 2 sc).
Round 6: 44 sc.
Rounds 7, 8 and 9: as Round 6.
Round 10: as Round 5 (22 groups separated by 2 sc).
Rounds 11, 12, 13 and 14: sc.
Rounds 15, 16, 17 and 18: Work 20 sc only; turning after each 20 sts, have been worked in each row.
Row 19: With dark green cotton, * 1 sc, 1 sc made by inserting hook 1 row back, 1 sc made by inserting hook 2 rows back, 1 sc made by inserting hook 1 row back *. Rep 4 times more.
Rows 20 and 21: 20 sc.
Make 2 loops on each side to form handles: Ch 15, work 20 sc. Sew them into position on pot-holder.

Acorn-shaped pot-holder

Materials: Crochet Cotton No 5 in brown and yellow, worked double, aluminum crochet hook size D.
With 2 strands of brown yarn ch 12.

Round 1: 12 sc on one side of ch and 12 sc on opposite side.
Round 2: as Round 1 inc 32 sts at each end.
Round 3: Elongated sc (see page 37), covering previous first 2 rows of sc, inc 5 sts at each end.
Rounds 4 and 5: sc.
Round 6: Covering Rounds 4 and 5, work in elongated sc, inc 3 sts at one end and 5 sts at the other.
Rep Rounds 4, 5 and 6, 3 times more, increasing the elongated sc to 5, 7 and 9 sts respectively at one end to 7, 9 and 11 at the other.
Work 1 round in reverse sc and fasten off.
With yellow cotton (2 strands) work 2 leaves as follows: ch 12 and work 2 sc, 2 hdc, 2 dc, 4 tr, 1 dc, 2 hdc, 2 sc; turn work around and work along opposite side of ch, 2 sc, 2 hdc, 1 dc, 4 tr, 2 dc, 2 hdc, 2 sc.
Work another leaf in the same way.
Sew the leaves to the widest part of the pot-holder. Between the 2 leaves, work a ring of 10 ch with 2 strands of yellow cotton.

Little chef pot-holder and white and green pot-holder

Square pot-holder

Materials: Medium-weight household string, aluminum crochet hook size D.

Ch 12 and join with a sl st into first ch to form a ring.

Round 1: Work 18 sc into ring. This forms the hanging ring and is the only round as the rest of the potholder is worked back and forth, as follows:

Row 2: (right side) ch 1, 4 sc; 3 sc into 1 st (corner), 4 sc, turn.

Row 3: (wrong side) ch 1, 5 sc, 3 sc into center corner st, 5 sc, turn.

Row 4: Ch 1, 6 sc worked into back loops only of each st (ridged sc), 3 ridged sc into center corner st, 6 ridged sc.

Rep Rows 3 and 4, working 3 sts into center corner st on each row, until work measures 8 in (20 cm) from side to side. Fasten off.

2-color Catherine wheel pot-holder

2-color Catherine wheel pot-holder

Materials: Crochet cotton No 5 in white and green, aluminum crochet hook size B.
With white cotton, ch 8 and join with a sl st into first ch to form a ring.
Round 1: Work 14 sc into ring.
Round 2: 28 sc.
Round 3: * With green cotton work 4 sc on 4 sc, ch 2, skip 1 st; with white cotton work 4 sc, ch 2, skip 1 st *. Rep from * to * 3 times altogether (the strand not in use is carried under the sts).
Round 4: * With green cotton skip 1 st, 3 sc on 3 sc of previous row, 2 sc into next 2 ch, ch 2; with white cotton skip 1 st, 3 sc on sc, 2 sc into 2 ch, ch 2 *. Rep from * to * 3 times altogether.
Continue in this way, increasing 1 st on each whorl in every round until there are 114 sts (19 sts to each whorl).
Make 12 ch and join with sl st into sc. Work 18 sc into ring and fasten off. Sew loop to main fabric making sure that join is neat and strong.

Little chef pot-holder

Materials: Crochet cotton No 5 in white and red, small quantity of black, aluminum crochet hook size B.
With red cotton ch 11.
Row 1: Starting in second ch from hook, work 10 sc.
Continue in sc, increasing 1 st at beg and end of each row until there are 32 sts. Work 10 rows straight.
With white cotton, work another 17 rows straight.
Inc 5 sts on each side and work in sc for 7 rows.

Fasten off.
With white cotton ch 12, join into a ring and work 18 sc into it. Attach to top center edge of white crochet.
With black crochet cotton, embroider the main features of the face.

White and green pot-holder

Materials: Crochet Cotton No 20 used double, aluminum crochet hook size B.
With white cotton ch 4 and join with a sl st into first ch to form a ring.
(Close the following rounds with a sl st.)
Round 1: Work 8 sc into ring.
Round 2: 12 sc.
Round 3: 16 sc.
Continue until Round 12 has been worked, increasing a few sts on each round to ensure that the disc remains flat.
Round 13: With green cotton, * sc, insert hook into work 2 rounds back and work 3 sc (keeping yarn loose), skip 1 st *. Rep from * to * to end of round.
Round 14: Sc.
Rounds 15 & 16: With white cotton, sc.
Rounds 17, 18 & 19: With green cotton, sc.
Round 20: With white cotton, as Round 13.
Round 21: Sc, ending with ch 15 formed into a ring for hanging. Work 20 sts into it. Fasten off.

Square lettuce-shaker or shopper

Materials: Crochet Cotton No 5, aluminum crochet hook size B.
Ch 180.
Row 1: Ch 5 (= 1 dc and ch 2), skip 2 sts, 1 dc into 3rd, *ch 2, skip 2 ch, 1

dc *. Rep from * to *.

Row 2: Ch 5, * 1 dc on dc, ch 2 *. Rep from * to *, ending with 1 dc into second of 5 starting ch of previous row. Rep Row 2 until a complete square is obtained.

Work 2 rounds of sc along all 4 sides of square, with (2 sc, ch 1, 2 sc) into each corner space.

Finish off with the following scallops: * 1 sc, 2 hdc, 2 dc, 2 hdc, 1 sc *. Rep from * to * right around the square.

Fasten off.

Join the 4 corners with 2 lengths of ch st, worked in sc.

Vegetable or shopping bag

Materials: Crochet Cotton No 5, aluminum crochet hook size B.

Ch 6 and join with a sl st into first ch to form a ring.

Round 1: Ch 5 (= 1 dc and ch 2), * 1 dc, ch 2 *. Rep from * to * 9 times more and close with 1 sl st into 3rd of 5 starting ch.

Round 2: Ch 5, 1 dc into first space, ch 2, * 1 dc into next sp, ch 2 *. Rep from * to * to end of round, increasing 1 sp in round as follows: (1 dc, ch 2, 1 dc) into 1 sp where inc is to be worked. Close round with 1 sl st into 3rd starting ch.

Rounds 3 & 4: As Round 2, inc 7 spaces in each round.

Round 5: As Round 2, inc 5 spaces.

Round 6: As Round 2, inc 4 spaces.

Round 7 & 8: As Round 2, inc 4 spaces.

Round 9: As Round 5.

Round 10: As Round 6.

Rounds 11 & 12: As Round 5.

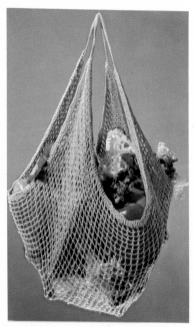

Square lettuce-shaker or shopper

Vegetable or shopping bag

Decorative basket no 1

Continue for a further 25 rounds, working as for Round 2 but without increasing.

Work 1 rnd in hdc (1 hdc into each sp and 1 hdc on each dc).

Complete bag by working 3 rounds of hdc, decreasing 14 sts over the 3 rounds. Fasten off.

Ch 30 and work 5 rows of hdc. Fasten off. (1 handle.)

Make another handle to match. Sew both handles to top of bag, evenly spaced, and finish off all edges with 1 row of reverse sc.

Decorative basket no 1

Materials: Crochet Cotton No 5 worked double (2 strands), aluminum crochet hook size D.

First of all, select a bowl whose shape you like, as this will be the 'mold' on which the basket will be based.

Make a circle, in sc, the same size as the base of the bowl.

Fasten off.

Make a length of ch in multiples of 12 plus 9 plus 2 (for selvedges), equal to the circumference of the disc already worked.

Row 1: 1 sc (selvedge), *9 sc, ch 8, miss 3 ch*, ending with 1 sc.

Row 2: 8 sc, * ch 5, 1 sc on 4th ch of ch-8 loop, ch 5, skip 1 sc of previous row, 7 sc, skip 1 sc*, ending with 1 sc and 1 sc for selvedge.

Row 3: 1 sc, ch 2, *skip first sc of previous row, 5 sc, ch 5, 3 sc (= 1 sc to right of next sc of previous row, 1 sc into st itself, 1 sc to left of same st), ch 5*, ending with 5 sc, ch 2 and 1 sc for selvedge.

Row 4: 1 sc, ch 3, * 3 sc (skipping first and last sc of previous row), ch 5, 5 sc (= 1 sc to right of 3 sc of previous row, 3 sc on 3 sc, 1 sc to left of same 3 sc), ch 5*, ending with 3 sc, ch 3, 1 sc for selvedge.

Row 5: 1 sc, ch 5, * 1 sc on center of 3 sc of previous row, ch 5, 7 sc, worked as above, on 5 sc of previous row, ch 5*, ending with 1 sc on center of 3 sc of previous row, ch 4, 1 sc for selvedge.

Rounds 6, 7 and 8: in sc.

Fasten off.

Press both pieces of basket under a damp cloth. Sew the strip to base with invisible sts and join the two selvedges together. Complete the basket by working 1 round of reverse sc around top edge.

To keep the basket firm, immerse in

Decorative basket no 2

a strong solution of sugar dissolved in water. For this make a thick sugar syrup by boiling some sugar in 2 cups of water (bring to boil slowly, stirring until sugar is dissolved). To avoid crystallization while boiling, add a small quantity of glucose or a pinch of cream of tartar. When syrup is clear, leave until completely cold. Now immerse the basket, making sure the syrup penetrates right into the fabric. Mold it around your chosen bowl and leave to dry (ideally upside down, with bowl supported on top of a saucepan stand or something similar).

Basket no 2

Materials: Crochet Cotton No 5, worked double, aluminum crochet hook size D.

Follow directions for Basket no 1 until base disc has been worked.

Side strip: Ch 8 and join with a sl st into first ch to form a ring.

Work 18 dc into ring, turn. Work 1 sc into each dc, * turn, ch 8, join up with semi-circle just made by working 1 sl st into 4th sc, turn, 18 dc into ch ring just made and link up with 1 sl st into corresponding st of previous semi-circle, turn, 18 sc into dc, 1 sl st into corresponding st of previous semi-circle *. Rep from * to * until length corresponds to circumference of base disc. Fasten off.

Press both pieces carefully under a damp cloth and sew the strip to base with invisible stitches. Sew a flat seam where strip abuts. Finish off the top edge with 1 row of reverse sc.

Stiffening: see last paragraph of directions for Basket no 1.

Broomhead cover in loop stitch

Materials: 5½ oz (150 grams approx) knitting worsted, small quantity in contrasting color, aluminum crochet hook size H.

Stitches used: loop stitch (see page 62), dc.

Ch 54 and work in loop st for 6 in (15 cm).

Now work in *rounds*, 1 dc on each st for 10 rounds.

This will produce a bag which will cover a broomhead.

In a contrasting color, make a ch about 38 in (1 metre) long and thread it through a row of dc. Place over broomhead, draw tie up fairly tight and knot into a bow.

Oven glove

Materials: Colored ribbon, tape or strips of cotton fabric, small quantity in second color, aluminum crochet hook size J.

With main color ch 25 and join with a sl st into first ch to form a ring.

Work 1 round into ring, in sc.

Continue with a round of sc in second color and then 9 rounds in main color, without increasing at all.

Leaving 8 sts unworked, continue on remaining sts, inc 2 sts on next round. Work 8 more rounds straight and another 3 rounds, decreasing on these so that all sts have been worked off at end of 3rd round. Fasten off.

Return to the 8 unworked sts for thumb. Working in rounds, continue for 5 rounds. In last round, hold work so that front and back of thumb are together and work a sl st through front and back sts. Fasten off.

Finish off with 1 row of reverse sc around wrist edge.

Pot-holder and saucepan mat

Materials: Colored ribbon, tape or strips of cotton fabric, small quantity of second color, aluminum crochet hook size J.

Ch 3 and work in sc for 3 rounds, increasing from time to time to keep work flat.

*Work 1 round in second color. Return to main color and work 1 round in reverse sc, making a hang-

Broomhead cover in loop stitch

Oven glove, pot-holder and saucepan mat in colored ribbons or tape

Oval bedside or bathroom mat

ing loop before fastening off.* (Pot-holder completed.)

For saucepan mat, work 9 rounds in main color, increasing to keep work flat. Continue from * to *.

Oval bedside or bathroom mat

Materials: Colored ribbon, tape or strips of cotton fabric, small quantity in second color, aluminum crochet hook size J.

Ch 45. Work in sc (1 sc, ch 1, 1 sc) into last ch, work sc along opposite side of ch, ending with (1 sc, ch 1, 1 sc) into last ch.

Continue for another 12 rounds, increasing from time to time on the sides to maintain oval shape (for the increases, instead of working 2 sts on the same, work 1 st and ch 1).

Work 1 round in second color.

Work another 6 rounds and finish off with 1 row in reverse sc.

White and blue bag

Materials: Ribbon, tape or strips of cotton fabric, aluminum crochet hook size J.

Ch 15. Work in sc (1 sc, ch 1, 1 sc) into last st, work in sc along opposite side of ch, ending with (1 sc, ch 1, 1 sc) into last st. (The increases in the following rows are made by working 1 st and ch 1 instead of working 2 sts into the same st.)

Work another 4 rounds in sc, increasing 3 sts from time to time on the sides to maintain oval shape.

Now work 1 round, without increasing, in ridged sc (= work into back loop only).

Continue straight in sc for another 16 rounds.

Work 1 round in second color.

Work another 5 rounds in main color.

Finish off the bag with 1 round of reverse sc.

Make 2 handles in second color: ch 40, 1 sc into each ch.

Stitch them invisibly, evenly spaced, at right-angles to the line in 2nd color.

Hammock

Materials: Colored string, tape or strips of cotton fabric, 2 holed wooden cross-pieces, with 16 evenly spaced holes, synthetic cord or rope and strong synthetic string, 2 steel rings, aluminum crochet hook size J.

Hammock

Ch 100 and work:
Row 1: * Ch 5, 1 tr, skip 5 ch *.
Row 2 and following rows: *1 tr on tr, ch 5, skip 5 sts*.
The hammock should be a rectangle of 20 spaces by 50 spaces. *Now weave a strong cord around all loops on one long outside edge. Continue along short edge, taking it through holes in wooden cross-pieces as shown in illustration *. Rep from * to *. Insert one end of a strong piece of cord through first hole in one of the cross-pieces. Knot end firmly. * Now weave around all loops along 1 short end of hammock, carrying cord through holes in cross-piece to anchor crochet to cross-piece.
Continue to weave cord down one long side of hammock *. Rep from * to *, ensuring that end of cord is firmly lashed to cross-piece.
Where the cord emerges on outside of cross-pieces, thread the string through these large stitches into a large steel ring. Ensure that the knots securing these strings are firmly fastened.

Funny bunnies

Materials: 5½ oz (150 grams) sport yarn in pink or beige, a few grams (or left-over pieces) in several colors, material for stuffing, aluminum crochet hook size D.
Head: This is formed from 2 circles of crochet worked as follows: Ch 5 and join with a sl st into first ch to form a ring.

White and blue bag

Working first round in sc into ring, continue in sc, increasing regularly to keep work flat, until circle measures 6 in (15 cm) in diameter. Sew circles together, leaving a small space for stuffing at neck edge.

Body: Starting from seat, make a flat circle in sc 4¾ in (12 cm) in diameter. Continue for another 14 rounds, decreasing regularly until 30 sts remain.

Arms: (Work 2): Ch 5, join with a sl st into first ch to form a ring and work 8 sc into ring.

Increase 6 sts while working second round, then continue working straight for another 12 rounds.

Legs (work 2): Ch 8, work 7 sc, 3 sc into last ch, and then work 7 sc into opposite side of ch, ending with 3 sc into last st. Work 2 rounds without increasing then decrease on next 3 rounds at the front until 14 sts remain. Work another 11 rows straight.

Ears (work 4): Ch 18, work 15 dc, 5 dc into last ch and then work 15 dc back on opposite side of ch. Turn and work 1 row in sc all around

When second piece has been made, join it to the first by working 1 row of sc (in contrasting color) all around, working through edge sts of both pieces together. Leave lower end open.

Stuff the head, body, arms and legs and sew together. Stitch ears to top of head.

For the girl bunny, make a dress as follows: Ch 30, join to first ch with a sl st. Work 1 dc into each ch and continue straight for 5 rounds, changing colors on each round. Work 1 row in sc. Make 2 short lengths of ch and work in sc for 1 row for shoulder straps. Sew these to the skirt and slip bunny into dress. (You may find it simpler to slip skirt over bunny's tummy before stitching shoulder straps to it.)

Clowns in colorful discs

Materials: 4 oz (100 grams) of odds and ends of knitting worsted in 6 colors (suggested here – yellow, orange, red, pink, blue and green), some fine string, a number of round beads with a hole through the center (wooden, if possible) and 2 or 3 little bells, aluminum crochet hook size D. The clown is made up of 15 yellow circles, 12 orange, 12 red, 12 pink, 12 blue and 12 green.

To make a circle: Ch 6 and join with a sl st into first ch to form a ring. Work 7 rounds in sc, increasing regularly to keep circle flat.

Thread string through first bead and then, using it double, through center of circles, alternating 3 circles in one color with a bead, for the arms and legs, ending with 1 yellow disc at ends of both arms and legs. Thread string from both legs (4 strands) through remaining 11 yellow circles for body and tie securely with ends of arm string. Make two circles for neck frill by working as above in sc for 10 rounds and then working 2 sc in every st for 2 rounds. Thread all strings through both circles and fasten securely through a bead or button.

Work a ball or 2 circles for head in sc. Stuff head and sew into top bead or button.

Make a hat, using all the colors, starting from center top and increasing until hat slips comfortably over head. Continue straight until a few rounds of each color have been worked.

Turn edge up to form a brim, stitch invisibly onto head and decorate, for example, with 2 or 3 bells.

Embroider face with black wool or small pieces of felt.

The smaller clown is made in the same way, except that the crocheted circles are sewn together

Funny bunnies

Clowns in colorful discs

without being spaced out with beads.

Heat-resistant mat in cord

Materials: Fine picture cord or ordinary string, aluminum crochet hook size D.
The mat is made up of 6 leaves, worked separately.
For each leaf, ch 11.
Row 1: Starting in second ch from hook work 9 sc, 5 sc into last ch, 9 sc on opposite side of ch (wrong side of work), turn.
Row 2: (Right side) Ch 3, skip first st, 9 ridged sc (= work into back loop of st only. Only ridged sc is used in each row and is abbreviated to rsc), 5 rsc into 3rd of 5 sc of previous row, 9 rsc along second side, turn.
Row 3: Ch 3, 10 rsc, 5 rsc into 3rd of 5 rsc of previous row, 10 rsc along second side, turn.
Rows 4 to 8: as Row 3, increasing 1 st on each side and always working 5 rsc into central st at point of previous row. In Row 8 there will be 15 sts on each side and 5 on center st.
Fasten off.
Work 6 more leaves in the same way and stitch them together to form a six-pointed star.

Carnation key-ring

Materials: Crochet Cotton No 5 in green and red, aluminum crochet hook size C.
With green cotton ch 4 and join with a sl st into first ch to form a ring.
Round 1: Work 10 sc into ring, closing with a sl st.
Round 2: In dc, increase 6 times (16 sc).
Continue until Round 12 has been worked (no increases).
Rounds 13, 14 and 15: With red cotton, work 3 sc into each sc of previous row.
Round 16: * 3 sc, 1 picot (ch 3, 1 sc into last sc worked) *. Rep from * to *. Fasten off.
With green cotton ch 40, work 1 row in sc. Thread stem through key and stitch both ends to green part of carnation.

Heat-resistant mat in cord

Carnation key-ring

INDEX

Index